For Captain Jake Branam, Kelley Branam,
Scott Gamble, and Sammy Kairy

And
for Caroline and Jerry, always

MURDER
ON THE
HIGH SEAS

The True Story of the
Joe Cool's Tragic Final Voyage

CAROL SORET COPE

BERKLEY BOOKS, NEW YORK

THE BERKLEY PUBLISHING GROUP
Published by the Penguin Group
Penguin Group (USA) Inc.
375 Hudson Street, New York, New York 10014, USA
Penguin Group (Canada), 90 Eglinton Avenue East, Suite 700, Toronto, Ontario M4P 2Y3, Canada
(a division of Pearson Penguin Canada Inc.)
Penguin Books Ltd., 80 Strand, London WC2R 0RL, England
Penguin Group Ireland, 25 St. Stephen's Green, Dublin 2, Ireland (a division of Penguin Books Ltd.)
Penguin Group (Australia), 250 Camberwell Road, Camberwell, Victoria 3124, Australia
(a division of Pearson Australia Group Pty. Ltd.)
Penguin Books India Pvt. Ltd., 11 Community Centre, Panchsheel Park, New Delhi—110 017, India
Penguin Group (NZ), 67 Apollo Drive, Rosedale, North Shore 0632, New Zealand
(a division of Pearson New Zealand Ltd.)
Penguin Books (South Africa) (Pty.) Ltd., 24 Sturdee Avenue, Rosebank, Johannesburg 2196,
South Africa

Penguin Books Ltd., Registered Offices: 80 Strand, London WC2R 0RL, England

The publisher does not have any control over and does not assume any responsibility for author or third-party websites or their content.

MURDER ON THE HIGH SEAS

A Berkley Book / published by arrangement with the author

PRINTING HISTORY
Berkley mass-market edition / March 2011

Copyright © 2011 by Carol Cope.
Cover photos: *Fishing Boat* © Peter McBride/Getty; *Buoy* © Minifilm/Shutterstock.
Cover design by Annette Fiore Defex.

ISBN: 978-0-425-23977-3

BERKLEY®
Berkley Books are published by The Berkley Publishing Group,
a division of Penguin Group (USA) Inc.,
375 Hudson Street, New York, New York 10014.
BERKLEY® is a registered trademark of Penguin Group (USA) Inc.
The "B" design is a trademark of Penguin Group (USA) Inc.

PRINTED IN THE UNITED STATES OF AMERICA

10 9 8 7 6 5 4 3 2 1

Most Berkley Books are available at special quantity discounts for bulk purchases for sales, promotions, premiums, fund-raising, or educational use. Special books, or book excerpts, can also be created to fit specific needs.

For details, write: Special Markets, The Berkley Publishing Group, 375 Hudson Street, New York, New York 10014.

PROLOGUE

"We launched at first light," reported Lieutenant Andrew Baines, pilot and search-and-rescue commander of the United States Coast Guard Air Station in Miami, Florida. At dawn on September 24, 2007, he lifted off in a bright orange HH-65 Dolphin helicopter with the Coast Guard insignia. The helicopter launched from the deck of the *Confidence*, a 210-foot Reliance class Coast Guard cutter that had sailed all night from Key West to get in position in the Florida Straits. The mission: to search for survivors of an "over-due," a fishing boat that had failed to return to Miami Beach the previous day after a charter to Bimini in the Bahamas. Six Americans, including the captain of the boat and his wife, were missing.

The Atlantic Ocean was dimpled with small waves, the sky pearly on the eastern horizon, throwing pale light across the dark water. Later, the day would become overcast, turning the sea rough and the wind blustery. But now, at seven o'clock on this Monday morning east of the Florida Keys, conditions were close to ideal for the search.

The cutter *Confidence* quickly receded below the helicopter, which climbed and banked to begin tracking the search grid. With a crew of four—pilot, copilot, and two flight mechanics—to run the rescue basket and a full load of equipment, the chopper's interior was cramped. The engine whine and rotor chop created a deafening roar inside the small cabin. Conversation was impossible without mikes and headsets.

The chopper continued its search track across the Florida Straits just north of the Cuban coast. The strengthening light illuminated the ocean beneath them, tracing the outline of the broad, shallow, sandy Cay Sal Banks in palest aqua, shading off into deeper azure water. The most remote of the Bahamas island chain, the Banks are famous among divers for a large formation of mysterious "blue holes," vertical caves that plummet hundreds of feet into the ocean depths. This was also a well-known navigation point in the Florida Straits and a visual warning that the Cuban coast was very close—only about thirty miles to the south. Tensions always ran high in this area of the straits bordering Florida, Cuba, and the Bahamas, where desperate refugees from Cuba or Haiti tried to get to Florida in homemade rafts, on stolen boats, or in smugglers' leaky, dangerously overloaded wooden scows. And there was a long history of piracy in the area, most recently by drug smugglers who ambushed and seized boats, killing and dumping the occupants.

From the chopper, the Cay Sal Banks atoll was a beautiful sight, so shallow that parts of it were above sea level, fringed with palms and even a few small buildings. On the northern rim of the atoll was Elbow Cay, an abandoned lighthouse where recreational boaters occasionally stopped. The southwestern tip, known as Anguilla Cay, was another popular spot to anchor for a swim and picnic.

After forty minutes in the air, one of the flight mechanics

saw what appeared to be a bright orange marker in the water. Lieutenant Baines banked away from the search track to investigate. As the helicopter drew closer, they could see it was an orange life raft, its light blue canopy shielding the interior. Lieutenant Baines orbited the chopper around the raft, using the rotor wash to blow the canopy back. Inside were two men, fully dressed and obviously alive. As the pilot maneuvered the chopper into a hold over the raft, flight mechanic Christopher Janisko leaned out the open door and signaled the men in the raft to jump into the ocean and swim to the rescue basket being lowered to the water. The first to jump was the smaller, apparently older man. He swam over to the basket, climbed in, and was hauled inside the hovering chopper.

Once the survivor was aboard, Janisko shouted a question at him, but the noise in the cabin was deafening. The man pointed to his ear, indicating he couldn't hear. Janisko ripped a page from the "fly-away book" the crew always took aboard and wrote on it: "4 hours west of Bimini." The man took the pen and wrote back: "Hijacking 4 killed we were abandoned w/ the boat. The girl was still alive but wounded, but that was 2 days ago."

Janisko wrote, "Vessel Name *Joe Cool*." But the survivor responded, "Baby Sissy??" Janisko was confused about the name of the missing boat, but he didn't pursue it. He passed the note to Lieutenant Baines.

Next aboard was the taller, younger man from the raft. Neither seemed injured. Both looked exhausted.

Obviously there were no more survivors to rescue in the surrounding waters.

The helicopter banked and returned to the cutter *Confidence*.

CHAPTER ONE

Star

Star Island Drive is one of the most exclusive addresses in South Florida. The road circles tiny Star Island, one of three residential islands just north of the MacArthur Causeway, which carries six crowded lanes of traffic back and forth between the city of Miami and South Beach, the southern tip of Miami Beach. The causeway runs along the northern edge of Government Cut, a deep channel lined on its southern edge with cruise ships bound for exotic Caribbean destinations. When the cruise ships move out into Government Cut heading out to sea, the sight is stunning, especially at night, as if magical, floating cities are gliding away on a path of silver. The Port of Miami is a very busy place, yet just across the MacArthur Causeway the small residential islands offer peace, privacy, and luxury.

Star, as it is known by those fortunate enough to live there, was the first man-made island in Biscayne Bay, and it had a glamorous aura from the beginning. Just after World War I, wealthy entrepreneur Carl Fisher—who'd fallen in love with

South Florida in general and Biscayne Bay in particular—
built Star using material dredged up from the shallow bay,
which was then bolstered, banked, and compacted until the
island was a foundation for development just above sea level.
It was tiny—only one thousand feet by twenty-six hundred
feet—but it had a lovely oval shape that seemed to hover just
above the clear waters of Biscayne Bay. The bay water was
so clear then that Fisher would take a boat out, hold a looking glass down into the water, and see straight to the bottom,
a paradise filled with colorful tropical fish. Development
would change all that, but Biscayne Bay is still delightfully
blue and reasonably clear, with a clean, sandy bottom that
reflects sunlight upward.

Carl Fisher was a visionary as well as a developer, and he
built a yacht club and a casino on Star Island; long gone
now, but the island retained its allure of privilege and ex-
clusivity. Soon, two other residential islands were created,
Hibiscus and Palm, and the two of them were eventually
linked together by a small bridge. Once the Government Cut
deepwater channel and the Port of Miami were dredged in
the 1920s, a rudimentary, rickety wooden bridge was built
between Miami and Miami Beach. This eventually became
MacArthur Causeway, and soon a small bridge was built
to connect Palm and Hibiscus islands to the causeway. Before these bridges were built, the three islands could only be
reached by water. These lush residential islands seemed to
float like a mirage in the azure waters of Biscayne Bay during the day and like soft pearls of light strung across the
glowing necklace of the causeway at night. Star had its
own separate bridge from the causeway, a picturesque arch
lighted by antique lampposts and watched over by a tropical-
white-uniformed guard who welcomed residents home and
recorded license tag numbers from visitors. All thirty estates
on the island were waterfront, and almost all hosted yachts
at their private backyard docks on Biscayne Bay.

Star Island has been home to the notorious and the celebrated, such as NBA star Shaquille O'Neal; actress/comic Rosie O'Donnell; music stars Gloria and Emilio Estefan; the entertainer currently known as Diddy; and Donald Pliner, the couture shoe designer who occasionally customized court shoes for basketball stars. In the notorious-to-bizarre category was the Ethiopian Zion Coptic Church, part of the Jamaican Rastafari movement, which maintained a large religious compound on the island where cannabis was used freely as a sacrament. A member of the church had inherited the house and grounds, and the Coptics, as they were known, moved in during the late 1970s. A lengthy legal battle ensued, and outraged neighbors testified in court that marijuana smoke routinely polluted their glamorous island and that the "sacrament" was being distributed as ganja spliffs to adults and even children who were clearly not part of any congregation. Neighbors were relieved when the Florida Supreme Court finally ruled that Star's restrictive zoning code prohibited a church on the island. The Coptics and their giant charismatic leader, the six-foot-seven Brother Louv, were also convicted in a federal court of smuggling several tons of their illegal sacrament into the country. The Coptics decamped. Neighbors were jubilant. Rosie O'Donnell later purchased the house.

The ambience on Star returned to serene and luxurious, an idyll of wealth and privilege with lavish estates, guesthouses, cottages, and staff quarters invisible from Star Island Drive and reached only by long, winding driveways secluded by lush plantings reminiscent of British colonial days in the Caribbean. The noise of traffic and the hustle and random street crime of the cities was far away. Most residents couldn't even see their next-door neighbors' homes. Even when a nude love scene between two beautiful young actresses, Denise Richards and Neve Campbell, was being filmed for the movie *Wild Things* in a swimming pool behind a resident's house on Star, most of the neighbors were unaware that anything unusual was going on—indeed, the presence of the film crew may have been the most unusual aspect of the scene.

One resident, however, noticed what was happening and walked over to offer his assistance. He was Harry Branam, known as "Pop" to his extended family, and he lived nearby in a large family compound with his wife, Jeannette, sons Joe and Jeff, and later their assorted wives, girlfriends, children, stepchildren and grandchildren, who came and went. The film crew politely refused his help and asked him to leave, but Harry took no offense. It was a story he repeated with relish for years. Although rich enough to own a compound on Star, Harry Branam and his family were definitely not part of the celebrity scene. They lived modestly, at least by Star Island standards, and appreciated their safe, quiet neighborhood where the kids and their friends could play outdoors and do the usual childhood things without too much supervision. Harry was the creative genius behind Lyn-Rand Metal Fabrications, Inc., a metal fabrication plant in the Miami working-class suburb of Opa Locka. He had a particular talent for envisioning new and better ways to create engineering components for urban necessities like traffic switch boxes and light-rail connections, and his engineering and business acumen added up to an extremely lucrative business that employed his family and kept them in comfort on Star.

The Branams had bought into Star in 1976, when, during one of South Florida's cyclical real estate slumps, they paid a bargain $250,000 for a waterfront estate on Star Island Drive. The main house was a two-story, eight-bedroom white house fronted by columns, and there were assorted outbuildings, plenty of landscaped lawn, and several docks along the seawall on Biscayne Bay. The big white house was visible from MacArthur Causeway and became something of a landmark. Once, when Rosie O'Donnell was asked where she lived in Miami, she replied, "On Star." Where, exactly, on Star? "Next to the big white house," she answered. Everyone who lived on the island, and even those just passing by on the causeway, recognized the big white house with the columns.

Jeannette Branam had found the house and was determined to move the family to this beautiful island, away from the middle-class neighborhood where they then lived, in the Miami suburb of Hialeah near Harry's plant in Opa Locka. By that time, Jeannette and Harry had three grown children: Boneta Lynn Branam, twenty-four; Joe Harry Jr., twenty-two; and Jeffrey, twenty. Their daughter, Boneta, had married young and moved away, but Joe and Jeff came to live with their parents. Star became the center of family life for the proudly Irish Branam clan, a fractious bunch that grew to include children, grandchildren, and even great-grandchildren.

Male friends of the Branam boys were always welcome for a meal or a place to stay indefinitely. They were treated like family by Harry and Jeannette, but the same didn't apply to the Branam wives and girlfriends. Harry did his best to remain neutral and congenial with everyone, and all his children's friends called him "Pop." But none of the women ever seemed good enough for Jeannette's boys, and wives and girlfriends came and went. A small, mercurial woman, Jeannette had wild, curly dark hair streaked with white. Family members said that she ruled the compound with an iron will. According to relatives, she meddled in her sons' marriages, and not surprisingly, the Branam boys wound up divorced. Everyone except Harry seemed cowed by Jeannette's intense, unpredictable moods, which created insecurity, shifting alliances, and crosscurrents within the family. But even as grown men, "the boys" stayed on Star. The glamorous island exerted an irresistible, magnetic, almost magical force field on their lives.

Joe and Jeff went to work for Harry in the family business, and they all came home at night to Star, where they spent their free time boating, fishing, and swimming in the clear, warm blue waters off South Florida, with Biscayne Bay as their backyard and playground. Joe's then ten-year-old son, Jake, got up early every morning and stayed out past dark to sail, fish, hang around the nearby charter docks at the Miami Beach Marina, and conduct experiments on the water. His grandfather Harry once found Jake and some pals trying to construct a diving bell off the end of the dock with a hose, a bucket, some weights, and a face mask. Jake became good friends with the Estefans' son, Najib, and for a time both attended Gulliver, a private prep school in Miami. As a teenager, Jake learned to navigate and fish so well that professional charter fishing boats would take him along to help out. He knew the ocean, could read the weather, always kept track of the boat's position in the water, and seemed to have an uncanny ability to locate the best fishing spots. To the charter fishing crowd, Jake seemed reliable, careful, and safety-conscious beyond his years. He was also good company for the sportfishing charter passengers and crew, and the pros treated him as an equal on the boats.

As he gained more experience, Jake became an expert seaman. As a teenager, he kept a marine radio in his bedroom tuned to the emergency channel, listening to traffic about vessels in trouble calling for help. He made a contest of arriving at the scene in his own boat even before the professional salvage companies could get there—a contest he often won. After a hurricane tore through South Florida, he salvaged a forty-seven-foot sailboat named *Son of a Sailor*. Following a dispute over salvage and storage charges, the owner abandoned the boat and it became Branam property. Jake, his father, and his half brother Scott Gamble raced *Son of a Sailor* for years in the Biscayne Bay regatta circuit.

Jake taught sailing and managed the racing team at the Coconut Grove Sailing Club, one of three yacht clubs on the Biscayne Bay waterfront in the charming Miami suburb of Coconut Grove. He supervised the team's trips around the United States and to international destinations for regattas. For a time, Jake became well known in the racing circuit in Newport, Rhode Island, where he once crewed on an America's Cup contender.

But while Jake Branam loved sailing and yacht racing, his favorite water sport was fishing. The charter fishing docks at Miami Beach Marina are within hiking distance of Star, and Jake hung out there as much as possible. On the docks, he met Samuel Kairy, someone who loved the ocean and fishing at least as much as he did. Sammy and Jake became best friends, bound by common interests and a love of life, fun, and good times—and, especially, anything and everything to do with the ocean. Sammy had been fishing since he was three years old, when his father, Albert, would take him out to Haulover Marina to throw a line off the dock or on afternoon trips on one of the party boats that took tourists and locals out for a day of fishing in the clear, blue waters off the coast of Miami. Sammy and his dad would catch all the good eating fish so plentiful in those days, such as red snapper and grouper and yellowtail; they caught so many fish they couldn't use them all, even with two younger brothers, Ilan and Kassin, and their mother, Marian, at home. After a fishing expedition, Albert would call all the neighbors to his house to pick up fresh fish for their dinner.

Sammy's family was "very structured," as he once wrote in a school essay, with parents who kept close watch on their three sons and worked hard to influence them to get a good education and choose professional careers. His mother, Marian, was from Paraguay, and his father, Albert, was a religious Jew of Egyptian descent. Even as young adults, the Kairy boys continued to live at home with their parents in North Miami. Their family bonds were strong, they enjoyed each other's company, and the boys saw no reason to leave home, except for their college studies. After high school graduation, Sammy went off to the University of Tennessee, but it didn't last long. Too far from the ocean, he told his

parents. This place isn't for me. He came back home and
enrolled at Florida International University in Miami, ma-
joring in marine biology. He was very bright, an excellent
student, but he longed to be out on the ocean every day, not
just studying about it in school.

The Branam family, by contrast, could be described as
rather complicated and unconventional. Jake's grandparents
Harry and Jeannette both came from working-class families.
Harry's parents divorced in Mississippi when he was thirteen, and he moved with his mother and sisters to Washington, D.C., where he eventually met Jeannette Kruse. Harry
had worked hard in school and excelled at math, algebra,
geometry, mechanical drawing, and architectural drafting.
When he was sixteen, he went to work to help support his
mother at a metal fabrication plant after school and on weekends. This proved to be an ideal environment for his talents
and ambitions and led to his lifelong, extremely successful
professional career. Harry also developed a strong commitment to providing a good life for his family and a generous
helping hand. Jeannette Kruse grew up to be a stunningly
beautiful young woman who aspired to escape the hardships
of her bitter childhood. When Harry and Jeannette met in
school as teenagers, the attraction was instant. They married
soon thereafter, when she was eighteen and he was barely
twenty. And they eventually moved to South Florida, where
their three children were born.

Jake's parents also had their own dramas: Joe had married
Jake's mother, Shirley Gamble, a pretty blond divorcée who
brought four young children of her own to the marriage—
sons Shawn and Scott and daughters Michelle and Amie,
who was only two years old—before having their son Jake
together in 1980. At first the family lived in the suburb of
Miami Lakes, where the children went to school. Joe and
Shirley enjoyed the South Florida boating scene, especially
the sailing regattas. One of their best friends was well-known
Miami sailor and sailmaker Charlie Fowler, a large, round-

bellied, congenial man who attended the couple's frequent regatta parties at their Miami Lakes home after races.

But when Jake was about nine, Joe and Shirley divorced. It was a very bad divorce, even by Branam family standards, with allegations of tapped telephones, surveillance by private investigators, and many ugly accusations. Joe returned to Star Island to live with his parents and his brother, Jeff. The five children stayed with Shirley in Miami Lakes, but soon Jake was asking to move to Star Island to live with his father and the rest of the Branam clan. Shirley was reluctant, but she knew that her son's whole life was the ocean, fishing, and boating. Harry Branam personally promised Shirley that he would take good care of Jake and that she could see her son whenever she wanted. Finally, Shirley agreed and allowed Jake to move to Star Island. Harry kept his promises to Shirley. He adored his grandson Jake and made sure that the boy had every advantage that he could provide.

After high school, Jake Branam attended Miami-Dade Community College, where he earned his associate's degree. More important, he earned his captain's license, the Licensed Master 100-Ton Open Waters certification, with an endorsement for towing and sailing, and he was also certified as a sailing instructor and dive master. He went to work as lead operator for H2O Salvage and Rescue, supervising a six-man crew on rescue and salvage operations, and then as a charter captain for SeaCross Sports Fishing. But his dream was to make his living with his own sportfishing charter company. He wanted to buy a luxury sportfisher and form a partnership with his dad, Joe, that he could operate with his cousin Jon, and his best friend, Sammy Kairy.

But then came Jeannette and Harry Branam's own disastrous divorce.

In a Miami divorce court, ugly allegations flew between the two stubborn, strong-willed people, and when the final decree was entered in September 1998, Harry was off the island for good and even barred from running his own business, Lyn-Rand Metal Fabrications, Inc., which then had ninety-three employees and was grossing over $8 million per year, according to Harry. Jeannette kept everything, the business and the Star Island compound. Sons Joe and Jeff continued to reside there, as did grandsons Jake, Jon, and, eventually, Jake's half brother Scott Gamble. Despite their love for Harry, none of them wanted to leave Star. Who could blame them? It was home, the tropical island paradise they had known and loved. Joe and Jake kept in close touch with their father, but they stayed firmly in place in the family compound.

On his own, Harry started from scratch, building an engineering consulting firm, and was soon earning a good living again. After he left Star, he lived for a time at the Marriott Biscayne Bay Marina on his fifty-six-foot Azimut, a large Italian-built yacht originally named *The Jeannette* years earlier. Even though strong boating tradition and superstition forbade renaming a boat, Harry eventually had Jeannette's name painted over during a renovation. By then, everyone referred to the boat simply as "the Az." Across the marina dock, he met Maria Gagliardo, a woman ten years his junior, who loved the sea as much as he did and was living aboard her own yacht, a forty-five-foot Downeaster named *Rebel Clipper*, which she captained. The day Joe and Jake helped Harry move his boat into the slip across from the *Rebel Clipper*, they met Maria, liked her, and asked her to "keep an eye on the old man." With so much in common, Maria and Harry soon grew close, and they eventually moved in together into a luxury waterfront condominium on Belle Isle, one of Miami Beach's Venetian Isles. Maria was bright, good company, fun, and always happy to host the boys whenever they stopped by to see Harry. All the Branams seemed fond of her.

Sons Joe and Jeff continued to run Harry's metal fabrication plant, which they renamed Alliance Industries, and things seemed to settle down. But life in the Branam compound on Star Island had changed in a very fundamental way now that Harry was no longer there to run the business. Although Joe, Jeff, and even Jeannette worked hard to manage the plant, without Harry, innovation, productivity, and—worst of all—profits declined. All those years—despite family conflicts, disruptions, and tensions—Harry had never wavered in his commitment to provide handsomely for his entire extended family. The private schools, fine homes, sports cars, clubs, boats, and expensive toys were all the result of Harry's talent, commitment, and generosity.

But now Harry was gone for good. Those living in the Branam compound still had a roof over their heads, but it was beginning to leak. Jake and his father continued to plan for their sportfishing charter business, but the outlook was grim under these reduced financial circumstances. They decided they had to look for outside financing for their dream.

Throughout the years, Jake had remained close friends with his half brother, Scott Gamble. Where Jake was outgoing and gregarious, Scott was more reticent, especially with people he didn't know well. Once he was comfortable, Scott was funny and friendly, good company for his friends and family. Everyone always said Scott had a heart of pure gold, that he would give you the shirt off his back. In a South Beach bar with Jake one night, Scott fell in love with a young woman from Arizona. Because of his innate shyness, Scott hadn't had many love affairs, but this one really hit him. Soon, he decided to follow the woman home to Arizona to pursue the romance. Once there, he got a job with Sunbelt, a company that rented out large earthmoving and construction machines. Scott was a talented mechanic and he always enjoyed working on machines of any kind. Eventually, however, the romance soured and Scott was left at loose ends in Arizona. His sister Amie, by then a single mother raising a young son alone in the Miami suburb of Sunrise, called him constantly, begging him to come home to Florida. Scott and Amie had always enjoyed a special relationship. He was the big brother she idolized, and he adored his sister and nephew. He was very much a part of their lives. He missed them. Since he had reached a romantic impasse in Arizona, he decided to come back home to South Florida in 2006. Amie was overjoyed.

When he returned to Miami, Scott moved into the Branam Star Island compound, where there was plenty of room and he was welcomed as family. By then, the compound was also home to his stepfather, Joe; his half brother, Jake; Uncle Jeff Branam, who was divorced; and Jeff's own son, Jon. Scott and Amie Gamble formed a close bond with Jake and Jon, and life on Star seemed good.

Then tragedy struck, early in the summer of 2006, when Joe Branam died of a sudden, massive heart attack at the age of fifty-two. Jake was inconsolable, and the Branam clan was stunned by this untimely death. Family antagonisms were set aside—at least briefly—and Harry gave a touching eulogy at his son's funeral. Jake was sliding into a depression, and no one seemed able to help him recover from this devastating loss. Eventually, however, Jeff, Jon, and Jake decided they should try to move forward with the charter sportfishing plan. It was always Jake's dream, and if they could somehow make it happen, this might help him recover and move on with his life.

Jake resumed his search for the right boat for the project, and he finally found the *Joe Cool*.

CHAPTER TWO

The *Joe Cool*

After much research, Jake Branam found the perfect boat for his charter fishing business, a forty-seven-foot Buddy Davis–designed sportfisher available for purchase at a marina in South Carolina. It was a used boat but still a beauty. The name on the boat's stern was *Jeanne Marie*, but Jake wanted to call it *Joe Cool* after his dad, whom he had adored and missed desperately. Maybe, if he could find a way to make their dream of a charter fishing company come true, it might be a little bit like having his dad with him again. Jake recognized that the boat needed some work to make it the top-of-the-line charter fishing boat of his dreams. The fiberglass hull, brightwork, and teak needed refurbishing; the interior had to be spruced up; and Jake wanted to install expensive electronic upgrades for navigation and safety. He was eager to do most of the work himself, if he could find a way to get the boat. Jeff was willing, but money was becoming a problem in the Branam family compound.

Finally, Jeannette wrote to Jake's grandfather Harry to

ask for his help. She told him that she was struggling with Jake, since he was having a very difficult time dealing with the death of his father. Jeannette reminded Harry that before he died, Joe had been planning a charter business with Jake, which had been their dream. Jake couldn't pursue financing for the business alone, and Jeannette said she wasn't in a financial position to help. She asked Harry if he could find it in his heart to help Jake and make his dream come true.

Harry stepped up, as he always had for his family, and took out a loan for $220,000 in his own name to help purchase and refit the boat. Jake was ecstatic. He asked his pal Sammy Kairy to go with him to South Carolina to work on the boat. Sammy agreed to take a break from his studies at Florida International University and go with Jake. He wanted to be a part of the charter fishing enterprise; he already had his charter captain's license, and he was ready to go. However, his mother, Marian, disapproved. She thought Jake was unreliable, a bit of a troublemaker, always getting into scrapes and being bailed out by his grandfather. She warned her son that Jake was a bad influence who was going to get into trouble and take Sammy down with him. But Sammy laughed it off. He could take care of himself, he told his mother, and of course he would be careful.

JAKE Branam was twenty-six years old by then, ruggedly handsome and muscular, with the sun-bleached hair and perpetual tan of young men who spend their lives out on the water. He was also married and father to a young daughter who would be joined by a baby brother within the next year. His wife, Kelley, then twenty-nine, had grown up in landlocked Kalamazoo, Michigan. Kelley Van Laar was the second of four children, each with a different father; her pretty, blond mother Leanne Van Laar had struggled to raise daughters Genny, Kelley, and Megan, and son D. J. as a single parent until landing a good job as a flight attendant with TWA, which provided a living wage and health insurance benefits for her children. But the job required her to be away from home for several days at a time. Leanne patched together a series of nannies to care for the children while she was working, but her absences took a toll on her family, especially her oldest daughter, Genny, who felt abandoned by her mother and burdened by the responsibilities of being the eldest. But Kelley was a much easier, happier child. She was athletic, the first girl to play on the local high school football team, and a good Little League softball player. Kelley liked gymnastics more than the dancing classes Genny preferred, and she was a strong swimmer on the local swim team. She was more easygoing, less emotional than Genny. Leanne always thought of Kelley as "Scout," the tomboy daughter of lawyer Atticus Finch in one of her favorite movies, *To Kill a Mockingbird*. Like Scout, Kelley had large, dark brown eyes, straight brown hair, and those same bedrock values of a generous heart, kindness to animals and people, a sweet disposition, and a sunny nature.

After her high school graduation, Kelley tried studying at Kalamazoo Community College, but she grew bored in the small Michigan town. She knew someone who had moved to Miami, and she began to think of what her life might be like in such a place. On television and in the movies, she saw dazzling images of South Beach's glitzy celebrity ambience, so different from her quiet midwestern hometown, and she decided to make the move to Miami. Kelley settled in and began to work in bars and restaurants, waiting on tables and enjoying her new life. Miami and South Beach seemed like a tropical paradise, with their warm weather, nearly constant sunshine, and glamorous atmosphere of ostentatious displays of wealth unlike anything Kelley had ever seen back home in Kalamazoo. She was especially impressed with Star Island, which she passed frequently while driving along the MacArthur Causeway to and from Miami Beach, and a

particular house on the island caught her eye, an expansive
white mansion with columns. The house had a commanding
view of Biscayne Bay and Miami Beach and was very visible from the causeway.

By pure chance, Kelley Van Laar met Jake Branam one
night playing pool in a South Beach bar, and the attraction
was instant and mutual. Kelley was a slender, pretty young
woman, fun-loving, friendly, and down-to-earth, not snobby
like some of the South Beach beauties. She was astonished
and delighted to discover that the handsome young sea captain she had just met actually lived in the house of her
fantasies on Star. Their romance was fast, leading first to
Kelley's pregnancy, then marriage and life together in a
waterfront cottage in the Branam compound. But Kelley
never felt accepted on Star, no matter how hard she tried to
please the Branams. Unsurprisingly, Jake's grandmother
Jeannette disapproved of her. She thought Kelley wasn't
good enough for Jake. She tolerated their domestic arrangement, which soon included a tiny daughter who would be
joined by a son, but she didn't offer any help, even though
the children were Jeannette's own great-grandchildren.
Meanwhile, Jake's family and friends continued to drift in
and out of the compound and the cottage, and the young
family had little privacy.

In an effort to develop a career for herself, Kelley decided
to study nursing at Miami-Dade College, and her mother,
Leanne, by then married to Robert Uttmark and living in St.
Louis, agreed to pay for her tuition and books. Kelley did
well in her classes, and it began to look as though everything
would work out for her.

But when Leanne came to visit Kelley and her grandchildren on Star, she was dismayed by what she saw as the
casual, communal lifestyle in the Branam compound. It
seemed to her that even in this exclusive island compound, no one had any money, for one thing. Leanne bought
food, milk, diapers for the babies, clothes for her daughter

and grandchildren, and helped out as much as she could during her visits. She was there for the cesarean section births of both her grandchildren, but she was still unhappy at the way the Branam clan seemed to treat her daughter and the children. Leanne found Jeannette aloof, as if she thought that Kelley were "a country bumpkin." The others drifted in and out of the cottage, with no apparent concern about what Kelley or the babies might need. Kelley didn't have a car, and when Jake was out in his truck, she was stranded without a way to get to a store to buy food and diapers for the children.

Leanne liked Jake and thought he was an excellent sea captain—she always called him "Captain Jake"—but she didn't think he treated her daughter properly. His work kept him away from home much of the time, and she knew that Kelley suspected he was sometimes seeing other women on the sly. (For example, Sammy told his parents that Jake had a girlfriend when they were in South Carolina.) Jake was always a ladies' man, and there had never been a shortage of women in his life. Maybe he had married too young and had become a father before he was ready to settle down to family life. Leanne was living in St. Louis with her husband, Bob Uttmark, and still working as a flight attendant, so she couldn't stay long when she visited Kelley, although she came as often as she could manage. She often felt guilty when her visits ended. How could she leave her daughter so alone and isolated with two small babies on Star Island?

In fact, Kelley *was* mostly on her own as a new mother with no family support of her own nearby. Fortunately, however, Harry Branam and Maria Gagliardo welcomed her into their Belle Isle condo on Miami Beach, and they adored the children. They were a great source of companionship and comfort for Kelley, and she was grateful for their help with the kids.

Their marriage grew rocky, but Kelley and Jake continued to make a go of it. Jake's plans for the charter fishing company were taking shape. Kelley wasn't happy about the prospect of the *Joe Cool* and the sportfishing charter business, which, to her, meant that Jake would be out having fun on the boat all the time while she coped alone with her lonely life in the compound with two tiny children. She was also worried that something bad might happen to Jake so far out on the ocean. What would become of her and the kids then? Plus, even though she was an excellent swimmer, Kelley was afraid of the ocean, with its bottomless depths and complete isolation. She didn't feel comfortable on boats, and she had a particular fear of being far out on the ocean, having something bad happen, and not being rescued.

Regardless, Jake and Sammy spent months in South Carolina working on the boat and dreaming of the sportfishing charter business. One night, Sammy called his parents and told them that he had been picked up for speeding and his driver's license was suspended. Marian Kairy was upset but not really surprised. In her opinion, trouble seemed to follow Jake wherever he went—and when Sammy went with him, there was trouble for Sammy, too. But aside from that, the sportfishing charter business was making good progress. As soon as they could move the *Joe Cool*, Jake planned to dock it behind the Star Island compound and then look for a more visible berth to develop charter clients. He wanted to scout for steady corporate clients among the pricey hotels and resorts on Miami Beach, clients who could afford the luxury entertainment that a day on the *Joe Cool* would provide.

Finally, Jake and Sammy brought the *Joe Cool* home and docked the boat at Star to complete some final repairs. Then Jake and Jeff managed to buy an operating charter business, Sissy Baby Sport Fishing Charters, which owned a valuable lease on slip D-30 at the deluxe Miami Beach Marina adjacent to Monty's waterfront restaurant and bar. A Miami hot spot popular with locals and tourists, Monty's presided over spectacular views of Biscayne Bay and the Miami Beach

Marina. Its main dining area and the tiki bar on the outdoor deck were always packed with people having a good time and ready to spend some money. The D-30 slip was the best on the dock at the marina outside Monty's, right on the bulkhead and first in line on the broad walkway where casual lookers and serious charter prospects strolled. There, the *Joe Cool* got high visibility and great lighting. A large sign advertised SISSY BABY SPORT FISHING CHARTERS at the *Joe Cool*'s slip, and Jake and his friends made sure it was well lit at night.

The refurbished *Joe Cool* was the classiest charter boat on the dock, and Jake could hardly believe his good fortune in snagging this prime location. Almost as soon as they moved the boat into the slip, business began to pick up. Even though it was summer, the off-season for tourists in South Florida, the *Joe Cool* was soon booking half-day, three-quarter day, and sometimes full-day charters. They staffed the boat according to how many guests would be aboard and how long they would be out. Jake had plenty of experienced crew available. His cousin Jon was always around, his half brother Scott Gamble had moved back home from Arizona, and, of course, he counted on Sammy. The fishing was good. Relying on his instincts in finding the best spots, Jake and his crew and guests pulled in yellowtail, bonita, red snapper, grouper, tarpon, the occasional sailfish, and more than once, very large sharks. Sometimes he would call Harry's companion, Maria, from the boat and ask her what she wanted for supper, then fish to order for her.

The *Joe Cool* was now a first-class boat with all the extras, and it soon developed a reputation for good catches and a good time, especially with its expert and congenial captain and crew. The boat had two fuel tanks, one forward and one amidships, which could be used separately or in tandem depending upon the length of the charter. On the exterior hull, Jake added runners, fins that flared just below the waterline when the boat was at rest. At speed, the run-

ners helped lift the boat up to a fast plane, conserving fuel
and maintaining a comfortable, stable cruising ride. When
the engine was cut, the runners acted like a brake, bringing
the boat down to a quick stop. In the air-conditioned interior
were two marine toilets (or heads), a stateroom and bunks,
a tidy galley and salon with a table and seating for six, and
a chart table and navigation station. The boat was also fully
equipped with state-of-the-art electronics, communication,
and safety gear. There was a marine radio, an EPIRB (emergency position-indicating radio beacon), which activates
automatically when submerged in salt water, a self-inflating
life raft with flares and an emergency cache of food and
water, a new GPS (global positioning system) navigation
and tracking system, Coast Guard–approved life jackets for
crew and guests, and an electronic fish finder to hunt for fish
at depth.

Jake Branam had his charter captain's license, a wealth
of experience on the water, an abundance of reliable, skilled
crew among his friends and family, and a solid reputation
in the charter fishing community as an excellent seaman.
The emerging success of his charter business was beginning to dispel the gloom of his father's sudden death the
year before. His life's dream was finally coming to fruition,
and with the sad exception of the loss of his dad, he couldn't
have been happier.

SOMETIMES Sammy Kairy stayed aboard the *Joe Cool* at
the marina all night to recruit charter prospects who strolled
the dock looking at the boats. Since he had lost his driver's
license in the South Carolina incident, Sammy couldn't
drive, so his mother chauffeured him around. Marian didn't
mind driving Sammy, but she hated dropping him off on
Star Island or at the marina. She worried constantly that
something bad would happen, especially since he was now
working with Jake all the time on the *Joe Cool*. Marian

wanted her son to go back to school, finish his degree, and get a professional job in marine biology. Her family was well educated and she herself had been a dentist in her native Paraguay. But Sammy always laughed it off. "I'm just going to try this for now," he told her. "I need to be around the ocean."

"There are lots of crazy people around," she warned him. "Something could happen to you out on the ocean."

"That's where I want to be," Sammy said. "I want to be *in* the ocean. I want to be *part* of it. If I die, then that's where I want to be." Marian knew that her son was absolutely fearless and in fact had no fear of dying. But she feared for him every time he went out on the ocean with Jake Branam.

Once, Sammy and Jake were out on the boat together just off Key Biscayne when they saw another boat in trouble and sinking. Sammy was the first to jump overboard, with Jake right behind him, swimming out to save the others floundering about in the water. A news crew happened to record it, and Marian and Albert Kairy saw the tape on the TV news that night. They were proud of their son's bravery, his prowess in the water, and especially his readiness to help others. No doubt Sammy and Jake had saved the lives of those people in the water. But Marian couldn't stop worrying about Sammy going out on the ocean with Jake.

CHAPTER THREE

September 22, 2007

On Friday, September 21, 2007, Jake Branam and his crew moved the *Joe Cool* from the dock on Star Island to their slip at the Miami Beach Marina. They decided to catch a quick meal at Monty's before heading back to the island by car. Earlier in the day, Sammy Kairy had called his dad, Albert, to catch him before he went to synagogue for Yom Kippur. He loved his dad, and he just wanted to chat with him a little before he left for temple. Albert was always happy to hear from his son, but like Marian, he disapproved of Sammy's working with Jake. He especially disliked Sammy sleeping aboard the *Joe Cool*. Why do you sleep on the boat, he asked, when we have a beautiful home? Albert hoped Sammy would go back to school, but if he really wanted to be around the water all the time, maybe they could work out a small family business at the marina. He had brought this up with Sammy a week earlier, when he had stopped by the *Joe Cool* for a visit. Although he hardly ever used his video camera, that day Albert decided to film

Sammy, the boat, and the marina. Perhaps they could get space for a small shop on the dock to sell fishing tackle and boat supplies. Sammy smiled and said he'd think about it. But he stayed on the *Joe Cool*.

Sammy had also recently spoken with his brother, Kassin, about plans for the upcoming weekend. The brothers had always been very close, sharing a room with bunk beds when they were small. After high school, Kassin had gone on to study business and finance, a career path his parents considered more suitable—and safer—than Sammy's continuing love affair with the ocean. Kassin was living in Las Vegas and working for a company dealing in artwork, a branch of the same company his father worked for in Miami. Kassin also spent time with friends in San Diego, California. When he talked with Sammy, Kassin was getting ready to meet some of his pals for a weekend trip to Rosarito, Mexico, to hear an underground reggae band from San Diego called the Blood Fire Angels at a concert.

Kassin hadn't seen his brother since Thanksgiving 2006, so he urged him to come along to San Diego and then to Mexico. It would be fun, just a casual weekend trip. "Why don't you come with us?" Kassin asked Sammy. But Sammy declined, explaining that he was working on the *Joe Cool* and that they were hoping to have a charter that weekend. Kassin knew from long experience that Sammy was absolutely passionate about one thing: the ocean. As a young child, Sammy had been somewhat introverted, in Kassin's view, and the ocean and fishing were his outlets. He knew that Sammy could also be a bit stubborn, especially where the ocean was concerned. Whenever anyone suggested that Sammy's choice of fishing and the ocean might be a somewhat hazardous lifestyle, he would reply, "The way we're going, we're probably not going to live to see thirty. If I die, just go out and party with my friends. Party it up for me."

Kassin always shrugged off such talk. They were young and strong. Sammy was absolutely committed to his life on the ocean and fishing, and he wanted to live his life to the fullest, however long it might be. Kassin didn't necessarily agree with his brother's choices, but he knew it was futile to argue. He and Sammy were total opposites in some ways, but they completely understood and loved each other dearly. He knew that Sammy and his friend, Jake Branam, had spent many years together out on the water, and he believed that they could handle anything that might come their way. Kassin prepared for his weekend trip to Mexico with his friends. He never really expected Sammy to change his mind and join them. But Sammy told him, "I'll come to see you in Vegas as soon as our next charter is over."

That Friday evening, September 21, Sammy offered to stay aboard the boat at the Miami Beach Marina to prospect for charter passengers while the others returned to Star for the night. Later, he called Jake to say that two guys he met on the dock were definitely interested. They had introduced themselves as construction surveyors who had finished a job early, just gotten paid, and wanted to join their girlfriends in Bimini. They wanted to leave the following afternoon for a quick, one-way trip to Bimini, a straight shot from Miami Beach to the Bahamas, where they would hook up with their girlfriends on a boat already in Bimini Bay. They offered between $2,000 and $3,000 cash for the trip, which would take the *Joe Cool* only about two hours across the Gulf Stream to Bimini and then two hours back to Miami Beach. Why would they spend $3,000 for the boat trip, Jake wondered, when a flight from Miami to Bimini was quick and much less expensive—only about $150 each? Their girlfriends, now in Bimini, had mistakenly packed their passports, the guys told Sammy, so air travel was out. Jake asked his uncle Jeff what he thought. The *Joe Cool*'s business was charter sportfishing, not passenger transport. Fishing trips burned less fuel, earned good tips from successful clients, and enhanced the boat's reputation in the sportfishing community. Passenger transport consumed more fuel at high speed and didn't advance the *Joe Cool*'s core business. But Saturday afternoon was open on their schedule and Jake seemed excited about snagging the fledgling company's first Bahamas trip. Jeff was happy to see Jake beginning to come out of his depression over his dad's death. He said he didn't want to "rain on Jake's parade." After some further negotiation the following morning with Jeff, the charter passengers agreed to pay $4,000 cash for the one-way trip. Jeff gave the final okay. To conserve fuel and lighten the load on the boat, they decided to empty the forward fuel tank before taking off for Bimini. The midship tank would hold plenty of fuel for the round-trip and the ride would be smoother, anyway.

Surprisingly, Jake's wife, Kelley, suddenly decided to join them for the trip. She asked Harry and Maria if they would take care of their toddler daughter and four-month-old son, and the couple happily agreed. Having raised two sons herself, Maria was experienced at child care and greatly enjoyed it. Kelley was young, a new mother who knew little about taking care of babies and toddlers. Maria knew that Jake's business frequently kept him away from home and unavailable to help out. Kelley often felt overwhelmed by her solitary responsibilities, and Maria used her babysitting opportunities to teach Kelley the basics. Besides, Maria loved having the kids there. She and Harry doted on them and enjoyed every minute of their stays. Kelley told Maria that she didn't trust Jeannette to watch the children, and Jeannette never offered, anyway. Kelley took both young children to Harry and Maria's Belle Isle condo on Friday evening and looked forward to spending some time with her husband. Although a boat trip wouldn't have been her choice, she wasn't really worried. She knew that the *Joe Cool* was safe and well equipped. She knew that Jake was an expert captain and she trusted his skills. He loved the *Joe Cool* and she loved him. Ideal weather was predicted for the short trip. After dropping their passengers off in Bimini Bay, they would fish on the way home, relax, and enjoy themselves. It might even be fun.

Saturday, September 22, dawned clear and warm. Kelley packed the few things she would need on the boat and drove to the dock. Jake, his uncle Jeff, and cousin Jon were already there along with Sammy Kairy and Scott Gamble. The *Joe Cool* had just returned from a successful early-morning fishing charter and the crew was prepping the boat for the trip to Bimini. The forward fuel tank had been emptied and the middle tank filled. The crew was surprised to see Kelley arrive. Everyone knew she was afraid of the ocean and she had rarely set foot aboard the *Joe Cool*, but that day she seemed happy about the trip. It was just a short hop, and Sammy and Scott could easily handle the crewing chores. Jon usually went along on charters, but he didn't go out with them that day.

Soon their next charter passengers arrived on the dock. The shorter guy had sandy brown hair and looked to be in his thirties; the taller one was probably Cuban and much younger—maybe eighteen or nineteen. They were casually dressed in T-shirts and pants, and they carried six pieces of luggage, duffels, and backpacks, all black. One long bag looked big enough to hold a rifle or shotgun, but no one asked about it. They seemed friendly enough. The older guy did all the talking in a slight Southern drawl, while the younger one stood by. Jake and Jeff asked again why they wanted to go to Bimini by boat instead of a shorter, cheaper flight. The older guy repeated what he had told Sammy the night before: Their girlfriends had accidentally taken their passports to Bimini with them on a boat, and so they wouldn't be able to get through immigration at the Bimini airport. They had to go by water to meet the girls in Bimini Bay, and then they planned to spend some time at the Big Game Resort and Marina on Bimini. Jeff and Jake accepted the explanation, but it still seemed strange.

Sammy Kairy called his mother on his cell phone just

before they departed. He said, "Mom, this is the last time I'm going to work with Jake. Starting Monday, I'm going to work with Jon on the *Sissy Baby*." Jon now owned a new charter fishing boat named *Sissy Baby*, which was then docked in Fort Lauderdale. But Jon hadn't completed his charter captain's license requirements yet, so Sammy was going to captain for him. Marian was relieved that Sammy would soon be working with Jon instead of Jake. She considered Jon much more reliable and level-headed. Apparently, Sammy had finally reached the same conclusion, and she was pleased. She asked about the trip they were about to take. Sammy told her about the two charter passengers and their story of the girlfriends with their passports in Bimini Bay. Marian was instantly concerned about her son. "That's strange," she said. "That doesn't sound right. Do you know them?" Sammy answered that he had just met them once before. Now truly alarmed, Marian asked Sammy not to go on the trip, but he laughed it off. "Don't worry," he told his mother. "I'll be back. And this is the last time I'm working with Jake."

The older guy peeled hundred-dollar bills off a large wad and handed $4,000 to Jeff. The rest of the stash he put back in his pocket. The crew finished loading the boat with ice, drinks, and food for the trip, plus bait for fishing on the way back home. Jeff helped the passengers load their luggage aboard and settled them in the salon. No one asked for their identification or wrote down their names. No one examined their six black bags or asked to see the contents. No one questioned whether they were bringing weapons or drugs aboard. The *Joe Cool* was loaded, provisioned, and ready to shove off.

Jon reminded Jake that they had an important appointment the following day, Sunday, September 23. They planned to take the concierge of the luxury Loews Miami Beach Hotel and some friends out for an afternoon of fishing and fun. They were hoping for a steady arrangement to charter for the upscale hotel's corporate events and its well-heeled guests, and the outing would be a sales pitch for the business. The *Joe Cool* had to be back at the dock early on Sunday to be spruced up and provisioned for the important excursion. Jake promised they'd be back in plenty of time to load the champagne and expensive food they planned to impress their potential clients.

At the last minute, Jake called Maria on his cell. He said they were about to leave for Bimini and asked her what kind of fish she wanted them to catch for her on the way back. Maria told him that the kids were settled in just fine, as usual, and she asked a few casual questions about the trip. Then Jake said something strange. According to Maria, he suddenly had a bad feeling about the trip. She was alarmed and replied, "Then don't go. You don't need the money that badly. Don't take the boat out." But, she recalled, Jake said Jeff had already pocketed the passengers' money and he wasn't about to give it back, even if Jake changed his mind about the trip. It was an argument Jake knew he would lose, so he said nothing to his uncle about his misgivings. They were ready to shove off. He hung up. Maria called back, but no one picked up.

At 3:40 P.M., the *Joe Cool* loosened lines and shoved off into a postcard-perfect September Saturday afternoon. Jake and Kelley settled into the cockpit on the fly bridge, Jake at the controls, with the younger charter passenger sitting near Kelley on the starboard side, chatting and smiling in the sunshine. Sammy, Scott, and the other passenger were below, coiling lines and securing provisions in the galley. It was such a beautiful day that Jon decided to escort them out to the first orange buoy, riding his Jet Ski along the *Joe Cool*'s portside wake. "I saw my family and friends, and they were just laughing and having a good time like we always do. Every time we go out, we enjoy life. They were happy as can be," Jon later recalled. He waved good-bye as the boat picked up speed and headed east to Bimini. Then Jon turned his Jet Ski back to the dock where his dad Jeff was waiting for him.

It was the last day of summer. Neither Jon nor Jeff had any premonition that it was also the last time they would ever see the captain, his wife, or the crew of the *Joe Cool*.

CHAPTER FOUR

September 23–24, 2007

Sunday morning, September 23, promised another clear, sunny, warm day. Jon Branam was anxious to meet the *Joe Cool* at the dock at Monty's, clean it up, and fuel and prep it for their important afternoon cruise with the concierge and his friends from Loews Miami Beach Hotel. This could be the beginning of a steady, lucrative niche for the young company. They would no longer be dependent upon casual dock traffic for charter passengers. But when he checked the *Joe Cool*'s slip around 11:00 A.M., it was still empty. Despite repeated cell phone calls to everyone on the boat, there was no answer. Jon was annoyed. Where was the *Joe Cool*? He didn't want to rush preparations for the afternoon cruise or, worse, be late. Everything had to be on schedule and in top-notch shape to make the crucial first impression. Otherwise, the *Joe Cool* might not get a second chance.

By noon, Jon was puzzled. He had called around to friends and relatives, but no one had heard from the *Joe Cool*. Where could they be? Their planned afternoon cruise for the Loews group was now in serious jeopardy. If the boat didn't return almost immediately, Jon would have to call and delay—or even cancel—the sales trip.

By 3:00 P.M., Jon called Jeff about his growing concern. It was unlike Jake to be behind schedule and out of touch, especially today. He knew how important their afternoon plans were. The weather was still perfect. No sudden storms, no collisions at sea, no problems in the Gulf Stream had been reported. And still no word from the *Joe Cool*. Reluctantly, Jon canceled the Loews trip. And now the entire family was worried.

It was baffling. The Bimini charter was a short, straight shot from Miami Beach, across the Gulf Stream about forty-seven miles, and then into Bimini Bay, all in daylight in perfect weather. What could have gone wrong? The *Joe Cool* was in pristine condition and very well equipped. They had plenty of fuel for the round-trip. Jake was a skilled captain with very experienced crew. He knew his boat, and he knew those waters like the back of his hand from a lifetime of fishing and boating all around the area. Jake, Sammy, Scott, and Kelley were all young and healthy. So where were they?

By 4:00 P.M., Jeff Branam decided to notify the United States Coast Guard Station at Miami Beach that the charter fishing vessel *Joe Cool* was overdue—by several hours. The authorities in Bimini Bay had no record of the *Joe Cool*'s arrival there. Jeff gave the Coast Guard precise, detailed information about the boat's corporate owner, Sissy Baby Sport Fishing Charters, its registration, the time and place of departure, the float plan, the trip's destination, and the likely track the boat would have taken to Bimini. He identified the captain, his wife, and the crew.

There were also two charter passengers aboard, Jeff told the Coast Guard. But who were they? No one had checked any identification or taken down their names. A general physical description of two males, one older with a South-

ern accent and one much younger and taller, probably Hispanic, was the best he could do. It was obvious that not
even basic paperwork had been completed for the charter.
The payment had been all cash, so there would be no charge
receipts to use for identification, and there was no record of
the passengers' names, addresses, or next of kin.

By Sunday evening, the bad news had spread quickly in
the Miami Beach Marina and throughout Miami's close-knit
charter fishing community: The *Joe Cool* was long overdue
and out of communication. This was ominous, expecially
for such a reliable, experienced captain and crew and well-
equipped boat in fair weather. Everyone knew and liked the
Branams from long years on the water together as friendly
competitors and boating buddies. A few recalled the bad
old days in the 1980s when drug smugglers turned pirates
would ambush and seize a boat, killing everyone aboard
and tossing their bodies into the ocean. The hijacked vessel
would be used for a onetime load and then scuttled. What
could have happened to the *Joe Cool*? Could it be that some
kind of piracy was making a comeback in the waters off
South Florida?

The Coast Guard Station at Miami Beach was a busy one,
very experienced in handling overdue calls. Often, these
turned out to be mechanical breakdowns, miscalculations,
bad weather, or navigation or fuel problems on the boat. But
sometimes they were deadly. The Coast Guard took all overdue calls very seriously. A search-and-rescue operation was
dispatched immediately along the *Joe Cool*'s probable track
from Miami Beach to Bimini. The Branams waited anxiously for word, desperately hoping to hear that the boat had
had some minor problem and was being towed in to safety.

But Maria Gagliardo couldn't get Jake's final call to her
out of her mind. She obsessed over it, worried that Jake had
indeed had some sort of premonition of tragedy. Being
emotional by nature, Maria took such things very seriously.
As night fell, Jake and Kelley's young daughter began ask-

ing for her parents. She was expecting to go home to Star Island. "Mia" (as she called Maria), she'd ask, "when are Mommy and Daddy coming back?" Maria had no idea what to tell her.

MORE than 140 miles to the south of Miami Beach, the hundred-foot Coast Guard cutter *Pea Island* was on routine patrol just south of the shallow Cay Sal Banks at dusk on Sunday, September 23, very close to the coast of Cuba, on its mission to counter drugs and to conduct alien migrant interdiction operations. Executive Officer Ryan Henebery, second in command on the *Pea Island*, was in his stateroom when he felt the vibration of the ship's engines ramping up. He knew that likely meant that the ship was in pursuit of "a vessel of interest to law enforcement." Henebery immediately climbed to the bridge. He checked the surface search radar, which provided a 360-degree circumference, port to starboard, a search area of about ninety-six miles and about eight miles dead ahead. He noticed a "return," a small green blip about eight miles away, apparently drifting at about two knots, which the *Pea Island* was heading over to investigate. Daylight was fading as the object began to appear over the horizon. At first it looked like a sailboat, but as they drew closer, Henebery and the crew could see through binoculars that it was a white-hulled sportfisher. No one was visible on deck, and the boat seemed to be drifting along aimlessly on the current. The crew hailed the unknown vessel over the VHF radio, but there was no response. They sped closer still, and using binoculars, they saw the Florida registration insignia on the boat's hull. Yet no one was visible aboard the boat. The *Pea Island* used the ship's whistle and bullhorn and stationed crew on deck to wave and shout to attract the attention of anyone who might be belowdecks on the boat. Still nothing.

The Coast Guard would have to approach and likely

board the unidentified boat to investigate. The drifting boat was a dark, unmarked navigation hazard in a busy area of the Florida Straits, for one thing, and it was obviously a U.S.-registered vessel apparently abandoned. Something had to be wrong, and it was the Coast Guard's duty to find out the identity of the boat and its owners and occupants and take appropriate action. This area of the Florida Straits, bounded by the Cuban coast and the Florida Keys on the south and west, and by the Bahamas to the north and east, was a frequent zone of illegal immigration by water from Cuba or Haiti for desperate refugees willing to pay thousands of dollars and risk their very lives trying to reach the Florida coast. This stretch of water also had a long history of drug smuggling aboard boats, sometimes stolen, sometimes "fast boats" carrying a load from a "mother ship" in deeper water through this area to the Florida Keys.

Henebery decided to take a boarding team of three on a small orange outboard to the unidentified boat. With Henebery as boarding officer, the team approached the drifting boat and continued trying to make contact. As they drew alongside, they saw that the boat's stern gate, used for hauling fish aboard, was standing open, and obviously expensive fishing gear was lying around on the boat's fishing deck. The anchor line was out and dragging. The Gulf Stream was about six hundred feet deep at that point. The boat's salon door was also standing open, and Henebery and his boarding party could see gear strewn about inside the cabin as well. In the fading light, Henebery and the Coast Guard team boarded the boat.

Henebery and his party discovered the boat's stern speckled with what looked like spots of dried, brownish blood, and its interior in complete disarray. Cautiously, they investigated the entire boat, but they could find no one aboard. The interior cabin, galley, salon, stateroom, bunks, and heads were completely dark and empty. Henebery and his boarding crew inspected the abandoned boat's navigation control station and the fly bridge, and they determined that the engine was off, the fuel tanks were empty, the boat's batteries were dead, and the boat was dragging on anchor and drifting on the current. It was a mysterious "ghost ship."

The boat's marine radio, EPIRB, and GPS were intact, but nothing was working since there was no power on the boat, not even from the boat's batteries. Lieutenant Henebery sent for an electrician from the *Pea Island*, and he was able to rig enough power to check the boat's GPS track. The boarding party now identified the "ghost ship" as a sportfisher named *Joe Cool* out of Star Island, Florida. The *Pea Island* had not received word about the overdue boat, but clearly something was seriously wrong here. This was an expensive, well-equipped boat, and it wouldn't just disappear without someone looking for it. Using the power-rigged GPS tracking system, they determined that the boat had traveled from Miami Beach almost to Bimini in a straight line and then erratically veered off course, first to the northeast and then to almost due south on a wobbly track. The life raft seemed to be missing. In the darkened galley, the boarding crew found six marijuana cigarettes, a laptop, a cell phone, a camera, and a wallet with a Florida driver's license. The name on the driver's license was Guillermo Zarabozo, at an address listed as Hialeah, Florida.

Perhaps, Henebery thought, the *Joe Cool* had been anchored at nearby Anguilla Cay, a popular spot for a swim and a picnic, and the boat had simply drifted off anchor without anyone's notice. By now, it was full dark, and Henebery decided to conduct a shoreline search of the small island. The boarding crew walked its entire circumference in single file with flashlights, shouting to attract the attention of anyone who might be in the area. They found nothing and no one. They launched two parachute flares, lighting up the night sky to announce that the Coast Guard was there and searching. Still nothing. There was no response at all to their extensive search efforts. Lieutenant Henebery ordered the boarding crew to return to the cutter *Pea Island*.

IN the Miami suburb of Sunrise on Sunday night, September 23, Amie Gamble was waiting for her roommate, Jamie Hopkins, to return from a weekend trip to New York. Jamie's flight was scheduled for arrival at Miami International Airport at 11:00 P.M., and Amie's brother Scott Gamble had planned to pick her up. Amie had introduced Scott and Jamie, and they seemed to hit it off well. Finally, Scott seemed to have a girlfriend who was right for him. Shortly after the plane landed, however, Jamie called her roommate to say that Scott had not shown up, and she was still at the airport. She had called his cell phone but got no answer. As soon as Jamie had turned her cell phone back on after her flight, she found several messages to call the United States Coast Guard, but she hadn't taken the time to return the calls. What was going on? Amie had no idea. She had heard nothing from her brother or anyone else. Amie knew that Scott had gone along on the *Joe Cool* on a charter trip, but he had said he would be home in plenty of time to pick Jamie up at the airport. Amie's young son was sound asleep, so she couldn't leave to pick Jamie up herself. The two young women made arrangements for a friend to pick Jamie up and Amie anxiously awaited her return.

There was a knock at Amie's apartment door. She cautiously opened the door and was astonished to see a Sunrise Police Department cruiser outside. Two officers told her they were looking for Jamie. "That's my roommate," Amie replied. "She's on her way home from the airport. Is something wrong? I am Amie Gamble. Can you tell me what this is about?"

"Gamble?" the officer repeated. "Do you know a man named Scott Gamble?"

"That's my brother," she replied. "What's going on?"

The officers asked Amie if they could come inside to talk to her. They gently closed her front door, sat Amie down on her sofa, and told her, "I'm afraid we have bad news. The Coast Guard has notified us that the boat your brother was on has been found abandoned. There is no one aboard, and no sign of where your brother and the others might be."

Amie was stunned. She just couldn't take it in. "What happened?" she asked. But that was all the information the officers had for her. They stayed with her until Jamie arrived a short time later. By then, Jamie had called the Coast Guard, and she was told the same thing that Amie had just learned. Jamie asked the Coast Guard how they got her cell phone number. Apparently, Scott's cell phone had been found on the abandoned *Joe Cool*, and investigators had redialed the last number called from the phone, which happened to be Jamie's. The two young women were baffled and frightened. How could this be? They spent the rest of the night calling around to friends and relatives. Soon, everyone knew as much as they did—which wasn't much at all.

The information provided to the Branam family by the Coast Guard on Sunday night was sketchy. They were told that the *Joe Cool* had been located, abandoned and drifting, far south of its expected course to Bimini. There was no sign of the captain, his wife, the crew, or the passengers anywhere. The Coast Guard had searched a nearby island on foot. Nothing else could be done until morning. The current plan was for the *Pea Island* to take the boat in tow in daylight and transfer it to the Coast Guard's Miami Beach Station at a safe towing speed. The search for the missing people would be continued by others the following day.

At 4:30 A.M. on Monday, September 24, the phone rang in the Kairy household in North Miami, and Albert answered. The man on the other end of the line identified himself as Coast Guard. Still groggy from sleep, Albert thought, *This* can't be good. Someone calls at four thirty in the morning and it's the Coast Guard? What happened?

"Do you know Samuel Kairy?" the man asked.

"Yes," Albert replied. "That's my son. Is something wrong?"

"Sir, we believe your son is missing from a boat, the *Joe Cool*."

"What happened?" Albert asked in confusion. "You mean he fell off the boat?"

"No, sir," was the reply. "We found the *Joe Cool* floating empty. There was no one on board. Kelley Branam, Jake Branam, and Scott Gamble are also missing."

"Four people gone?" Albert asked. "What happened?"

But the man on the phone said he was sorry, that was all the information he had at that time. Someone would call again later. From that moment on, the Kairy family began to live their worst nightmare.

Albert called his sons, Ilan and Kassin. He reached Kassin in Rosarito, Mexico, at about 7 A.M. local time and alerted him to what he knew: Sammy was missing from the *Joe Cool*, along with Jake and Kelley Branam and Scott Gamble. Kassin was a bit tired and jet-lagged, as he and his friends had recently arrived from San Diego for their concert. Part of Kassin's childhood history with his brother had been constant pranks and jokes between them. Whenever Sammy said something, Kassin could never tell whether or not he was joking, so at first he assumed that this was another of Sammy and Jake's pranks. They might have gone off somewhere without telling anyone, maybe an island in the Bahamas. But he soon learned that his dad was dead serious and very upset. His mother, Marian, came on the line, and she was distraught, nearly hysterical. Kassin knew he had to go home at once to find out what was going on. He told his parents he would leave Mexico immediately, stop in San Diego and Las Vegas to pack up, and be home in Miami as soon as possible. But Kassin was still thinking—or at least hoping—this was some kind of foolish prank gone wrong.

Meanwhile, on Sunday evening, the Coast Guard cutter *Confidence* was on its routine patrol south of Key West, Florida, a distance of about one hundred miles from where the cutter *Pea Island* was on station with the *Joe Cool* drifting nearby. The cutter *Confidence* was in the process of transferring some undocumented migrants from their ship to another cutter when they were alerted to the developing situation in the Florida Straits regarding the abandoned sportfisher now identified as the *Joe Cool*. The *Confidence* immediately began traveling throughout the night to get into position in the Florida Straits to assist in the search for survivors of the abandoned boat at dawn the next day, Monday, September 24. The "overdue" alert had been communicated from the Coast Guard Station on Miami Beach, so the command staff of both the *Confidence* and the *Pea Island* knew that the *Joe Cool* had left Miami Beach on Saturday, September 22, with six Americans aboard, bound for Bimini Bay in the Bahamas. The boat never arrived in Bimini, and since it had been located and identified by Henebery and the boarding party, far off course, abandoned and drifting in the Florida Straits approximately thirty miles from the coast of Cuba, the Coast Guard's mission was now a coordinated search-and-rescue effort looking for survivors from the *Joe Cool* in the water or on the boat's missing life raft.

After traveling all night, the cutter *Confidence* reached its destination in the Florida Straits. At 7:00 A.M. on Monday, September 24, a helicopter was launched from the cutter's flight deck to begin tracking the search grid in the area near where the *Joe Cool* had been found abandoned the day before. Approximately forty minutes later, the chopper crew spotted a life raft with two men aboard. They could see several black bags and pieces of luggage inside the raft as well. On instructions from the crew, the men were hoisted from the water near the life raft to the helicopter one at a time in the helicopter's rescue basket. They both seemed to be in good physical condition, but they were strangely quiet. In the experience of the helicopter pilot and rescue crew, this was very unusual. People rescued from life-threatening peril on the open ocean were usually jubilant, grateful, and full of noisy thanks, hugs, and praise for those who had saved them. Maybe these two guys were in shock or something. Once the older man told the crew that there were no other survivors from the *Joe Cool* to search for, the chopper turned back to the cutter *Confidence* to transfer the survivors to the ship and await further instructions.

THE terrible news passed quickly among the Branam family and friends. What could have gone wrong? Jon Branam had not been aboard that day, but what if he had been with them on the boat as he usually was? Would Jon have been able to avert whatever had befallen the crew, or would he now be gone, too? And what about Kelley? It was her first real trip on the *Joe Cool*, a last-minute adventure for her. Whatever had happened, she must have been terrified. Everyone in the family knew that Kelley was afraid of the ocean and not at all comfortable on boats.

People began to gather at the Star Island compound, including Harry Branam. The looming tragedy overcame even Jeannette's strict rule that he was persona non grata there. It had been years since Harry had set foot in the compound on Star Island, and even his anguish over the missing crew couldn't disguise his dismay at the condition of his beloved home. When he and Jeannette had first bought the place in 1976, they had spent at least $1 million refurbishing, updating, and adding living space to their family home. The place must be worth at least $10 million by now, Harry thought, and there was no mortgage on the compound as far as he knew. Yet Harry could see that the house, outbuildings, and grounds were all deteriorating badly.

Amie Gamble, her roommate Jamie, Jon Branam, and other young friends clustered around the television in Scott Gamble's upstairs apartment in the beach house on Star Island. They kept running through the channels, searching for any news updates about the search for those missing from the *Joe Cool*. They discussed hunches, possibilities, and scenarios, swinging wildly from hope to despair.

What everyone wanted to know was, where were Jake, Kelley, Scott, and Sammy? The Coast Guard finally provided some additional information to the Branam and Kairy families. The *Joe Cool*'s life raft and two survivors had been found on Monday morning, drifting slightly north of the abandoned *Joe Cool*, which was at least 140 miles south of its intended course. Only two? The families and friends were horrified. Who were the two survivors? The *Joe Cool* had started out with six people aboard. What happened to the others?

Eventually the Coast Guard identified the survivors as Guillermo Zarabozo, nineteen, and Kirby Archer, thirty-five. Those names meant nothing to the family and friends huddled together on Star Island. Apparently the two men told the Coast Guard that they had been the *Joe Cool*'s charter passengers on the Saturday trip to Bimini Bay. But no one had ever heard of them. And there was no more information for the family and friends of the missing crew.

CHAPTER FIVE

Hope

The mysterious "ghost ship" and its missing captain and crew began to attract intense news media interest. Captain Jake Branam, twenty-seven, wife Kelley, thirty, half brother Scott Gamble, thirty-five, and friend Sammy Kairy, twenty-seven, were officially missing at sea. The story was reported on local television stations and newspapers and then picked up by national media: CNN, the Associated Press wire, the *Los Angeles Times*, *Newsweek* magazine, and NBC's *Today* show, among others. On Thursday, September 27, Jon Branam was interviewed by Matt Lauer on *Today*, confirming that the family was operating on the assumption that the captain and crew of the *Joe Cool* might have been thrown or somehow fallen overboard—alive—and left to fend for themselves in the water. "I still have hope," he said. "I'm conducting a private search. I've got planes up in the air searching the islands. I'm hoping they're on an island. . . . My whole family is doing everything in its power to bring them home."

The Coast Guard was keeping a tight lid on information about the *Joe Cool*. They had not told Jeff Branam or the other family members or friends much about the survivors rescued from the life raft, because the FBI didn't want any inadvertent leaks to the news media. With so little information, the families constantly rehashed what they knew and speculated about what they didn't. How could the *Joe Cool* go so far off its track in broad daylight in open water? What was the boat doing so close to the Cuban coast? The *Joe Cool* was plenty fast, especially at cruising speed on the fins Jake had added to the hull. If Jake or any of the crew had had any trouble, they would certainly have called the Coast Guard. But no such calls were ever reported. There was no warning of suspicious vessels in the area. There was a panic button on the instrument panel of the boat that would automatically send a signal if pushed, but it was intact and untouched when the *Joe Cool* was found. The EPIRB would transmit an emergency position signal to the Coast Guard if started manually or even just tossed overboard into salt water. Yet the EPIRB was undisturbed in its rack just above the instrument panel in the cockpit on the boat's fly bridge. In short, there was simply nothing to explain what had happened to the *Joe Cool*.

With nothing else to focus on, the Branam clan was deeply suspicious of the survivors, Kirby Archer and Guillermo Zarabozo, the two mysterious charter passengers who had hired the boat on that sunny Saturday afternoon. Family resentment also began to build against Jeff Branam, since he had given the okay and collected $4,000 in cash for what turned out to be a disastrous, and possibly deadly, trip. But he and Jon agreed that they had seen no cause for concern about the two men who appeared on the dock that day for the trip. They'd seemed pleasant and friendly enough. Nothing out of the ordinary. They had handed over $4,000 in cash for the trip, which might be suspicious in some places, but Miami Beach was awash in cash. Lots of people,

especially tourists, walked around with plenty of cash in
their pockets.

One thing everyone agreed on: Jake, Sammy, Scott, and
Kelley were all young, fit, and strong. The Coast Guard had
not mentioned any guns found on the boat or in the life raft,
but unspoken worries lingered. Perhaps, they discussed,
there had been some mishap and the missing crew members
were on one of the Bahamas' many tiny, uninhabited islands. Maybe they had somehow fallen off the boat. Jake,
Kelley, Sammy, and Scott were excellent swimmers, and
the September water in the area was still warm. Kelley was
afraid of the ocean, but they knew she could swim. Certainly the others would have helped her ashore somewhere
if she panicked in the water. They all clung to the slender
hope that Jake, Kelley, Sammy, and Scott were still alive,
somehow, somewhere. They would be found and all their
families' questions would be answered, the mystery explained. Maybe someday they could all have a laugh at
whatever had stranded them, and everyone would be grateful for a happy ending. Coast Guard and private planes and
boats were still scouring the entire area. No one was giving
up. Soon, they thought, their friends would be found, alive
and well, and they could all put this horrible scare firmly in
the past.

Meanwhile, Jeff Branam had learned from the Coast
Guard that the men picked up in the life raft claimed to be
charter passengers from the *Joe Cool* named Guillermo
Zarabozo and Kirby Archer. He didn't recognize the names.
Jeff Googled them. Nothing turned up for Zarabozo, but
there was a hit on Archer: a flyer from law enforcement in
Independence County, Arkansas, bearing a face that looked
very familiar. It was definitely one of the passengers, the
older one with the Southern drawl. Jeff felt sick when he
learned that the person he now recognized as Kirby Archer
was wanted in Arkansas on a fugitive warrant. Archer was
suspected of stealing $92,000 in cash and checks from the

Wal-Mart where he had worked as a customer service manager in January 2007. The theft could explain Archer's $4,000 cash payment for the charter. He was also under investigation for the sexual abuse of several young boys in Arkansas and Missouri, according to reports Jeff found on the Internet. Apparently, law enforcement authorities in Arkansas had been closing in on Archer in January when he went on the lam. All this was known by the Coast Guard and FBI investigators within minutes of taking the survivors aboard the cutter *Confidence*, but the results of their investigation were not released to the news media.

Somehow, the names Guillermo Zarabozo and Kirby Archer leaked to the press. Soon, information about Archer's sordid past began to appear in media reports as journalists hit the Internet. There was speculation that he had been hiding out in South Florida for months before he and Guillermo Zarabozo had set out on the ill-fated trip to Bimini. What had Archer been doing? And how had he hooked up with Zarabozo, who turned out to be a teenaged Cuban refugee from a rundown neighborhood in the Miami suburb of Hialeah? Since Kirby Archer was accused of the sexual molestation of young boys, had he somehow seduced the nineteen-year-old Guillermo Zarabozo? Were they lovers? The questions were endless, but solid answers were few. As Jon Branam told Matt Lauer during his *Today* interview, "Everybody's very tight-lipped. They're trying to build a case. I know the FBI's working very hard. I know the Coast Guard is working very hard. Right now, they're not releasing any information. I've been giving them all the information I know."

CHAPTER SIX

Moving On

On Thursday, September 27, the Coast Guard search-and-rescue operation was called off. The search had covered 14,850 square miles of Atlantic Ocean, from the Cay Sal Banks just thirty miles from Cuba, north to Daytona Beach, Florida, and east to the waters surrounding the Bahamas islands. According to the online *Coast Guard News*, a vast array of assets had been involved in the search, including the cutter *Pea Island*; the cutter *Confidence* and its deployed HH-65 Dolphin helicopter; the eighty-seven-foot cutter *Cormorant*; the cutter *Reliance*; an HU-25 Falcon jet; two C-130 Hercules aircraft; an HH-60 Jayhawk helicopter; a Coast Guard Auxiliary aircraft; a Good Samaritan aircraft; and even a Navy P-3 Orion patrol plane. Remote, uninhabited islands and atolls had been searched on foot. Nothing was found, and now there was nothing more that the Coast Guard could do. "Our thoughts and prayers are with the families and friends of the *Joe Cool*," Lt. Cmdr. Chris O'Neil was quoted in the article. "If the crew of the *Joe*

Cool was in the areas we searched, we would have found them." With the search officially suspended, Jake and Kelley Branam, Sammy Kairy, and Scott Gamble were now presumed dead.

A tsunami of fear surged through the boating community. It was still terrifying news for those who regularly traveled the ocean in the area. Many charter fishing operators recalled near misses themselves, and word spread that Kirby Archer and Guillermo Zarabozo had contacted several other charter fishing companies from Palm Beach to Fort Lauderdale to Key West, trying to line up the trip to Bimini. For one reason or another, there were no takers—except the *Joe Cool*.

Robert Nolin, a reporter for the *South Florida Sun-Sentinel*, spoke with several charter boat captains in the area and compiled their comments in an article published on September 30, 2007. "Everybody's talking about it," Nolin quoted Rick Brady, captain of the forty-six-foot Hatteras *Marlin My Darlin* and president of the captains' association at the Bahia Mar Marina in Fort Lauderdale. "What happened is kind of scary," David Ide told Nolin for the article. "It's going to change a lot of people in the business." Ide said he planned to take a firearm along on his next Bahamas trip, and according to Nolin, he would "take a real close look" at potential charter clients. "We're definitely going to have to screen them," he said. "We'll definitely search their bags."

Michael Mayo, news columnist with SunSentinel.com, reported the haunting story of Jason Walcott, thirty-five, a Fort Lauderdale boat captain who had been first mate aboard the *Rapscallion*, a sixty-five-foot Hatteras based at Pier 66 Marina in Fort Lauderdale, back in 1995. The details sounded so familiar: The *Rapscallion* had taken a one-way charter to Bimini for a cash payment of $4,000 for two men Walcott referred to only as "the Big Guy" and "the Little Guy," who said they were going to meet girlfriends there. Walcott recalled that at dusk, just before the boat reached Bimini, the

Big Guy commandeered the boat with a MAC-11 subma-
chine gun and ordered Capt. Larry Withall to head south. He
and his partner, the Little Guy, intended to steal the $1.5 mil-
lion boat and take it to South America. There was a struggle,
including gunfire, and Captain Withall managed to ram the
boat aground, damaging the engine, and then leap overboard
in the confusion. The would-be hijackers were enraged. The
Big Guy put the gun to Walcott's head and said, "Don't do
anything stupid. . . . I'll shoot you, open up your stomach,
throw you overboard, and you'll never be found." Walcott
thought he was dead, but he somehow managed to stall them
by trying to fix the disabled engine. With the *Rapscallion*
now grounded and useless, the frustrated hijackers eventually handcuffed Walcott to a railing and took off in the boat's
life raft.

   The Big Guy and the Little Guy were later captured on
Cat Cay in the Bahamas and charged with piracy and kidnapping. But the two men managed to get released before
trial by posting $185,000 bond, and both promptly fled. The
case was within Bahamas, not U.S. jurisdiction, and apparently no one in the Bahamas went looking for them. So far
as anyone knows, they may be still at large. According to
Michael Mayo's article, Captain Withall looked over his
shoulder for the rest of his life because of this violent close
call and took to carrying a .357 Magnum with him in his
truck.

   Jason Walcott told Michael Mayo that he always feared
that the Big Guy and the Little Guy might someday come
after him, too. That's why he wouldn't use their actual
names, even after a dozen years. And while Walcott became
a private boat captain and sportfisherman, he refused to take
charter trips. "When you think of it," he told the reporter,
"it's amazing something like this doesn't happen more
often." According to Michael Mayo's article, the story has
become "a well-known cautionary tale around South Flori-

da's docks." Apparently, it was a tale that the young Branams had never heard.

THE Coast Guard cutter *Pea Island* towed the *Joe Cool* slowly back to the entrance to the Government Cut channel off Miami Beach. The sportfisher was then transferred to a smaller Coast Guard vessel, which towed it through Government Cut, past the channel by Monty's and the Miami Beach Marina, and finally tethered it to the dock at the Coast Guard Miami Beach Station across the water from the D-30 slip where the tragic voyage had begun on that sunny Saturday afternoon. Work and play stopped at the marina as the *Joe Cool* was towed past. By now, everyone had heard the story. Everyone knew why slip D-30 was empty, and seeing the *Joe Cool* limping home under tow was a stark, tangible reminder. Valerie Kevorkian, a dive shop owner and scuba instructor, was quoted in the *Miami Herald*: "Everyone stood there and followed the boat with their eyes, and then there was only emptiness . . . a ghostly feeling. . . . There was no soul in it anymore." Among the charter fishing community, there was also a sense of there but for the grace of God, it could have happened to any of them. Seeing the crippled and abandoned *Joe Cool* every day tethered to the Coast Guard dock was a sad reminder not only of the loss of their friends but also of the vulnerability of those who venture out on the open sea, alone and isolated, beyond the reach of even the United States Coast Guard's mighty arsenal. Even with modern electronics and safety equipment, any boat could fall prey to some purely random misfortune—or evil. That was the lesson of the *Joe Cool*, the beautiful, empty, ghostly boat across the water.

The following week, Branam relatives and friends planned a solemn flotilla memorial to the lost crew. A procession of boats would cruise silently through the waters the

Joe Cool and its captain and crew had known so well, past places where they had spent some of the happiest days of their young lives. They would travel along the Miami Beach Marina, across Government Cut, and through the channel between Fisher Island and Virginia Beach. There would be no funerals since, as Scott Gamble's sister, Amie Gamble, put it, "We don't even have any bodies to bury." Amie desperately wanted closure for the family. "Why don't [Archer and Zarabozo] just tell us what happened so we'll know?" she pleaded. "Just tell us so the family can move on." But no information was forthcoming. Amie and the others resigned themselves to waiting for the answers to their many questions.

EVEN two months later, Kelley Branam's mother, Leanne Van Laar–Uttmark, couldn't relinquish hope that her daughter was still alive, somehow, somewhere, perhaps on some remote island. In a tearful interview, Leanne told reporter Tamara Lush, "I don't think she's gone. I think I would feel it." She had traveled to Miami to investigate what more could be done to find Kelley. Leanne had contacted Texas EquuSearch, a search-and-rescue outfit in Texas that had searched—unsuccessfully—for the young Natalee Holloway on the Dutch island of Aruba in the Caribbean. They were willing to help, Leanne said, but they needed a bigger boat for the search and no one had volunteered. Leanne was distraught. "Isn't my daughter as important as Natalee Holloway?" she asked the reporter.

According to Leanne, her daughter was always "very big on funerals." As a child, she was forever taking in stray animals, in addition to the many pets she kept at home, and whenever an animal died, Kelley would organize a proper funeral. Kelley created a special "family plot" in the backyard as a burial ground for her animals, each of which was placed in a shoe box and buried with great ceremony. Kelley would lead the family in singing "Bringing in the Sheaves" and "Amazing Grace" as part of her funeral services. And now Kelley herself had been lost at sea—her worst fear, according to her mother—and she would never have a proper burial.

CHAPTER SEVEN

Family Court

Even while the Coast Guard search-and-rescue operation was still under way trying to find Jake and Kelley Branam, Scott Gamble, and Sammy Kairy, urgent questions arose as to who should care for Jake and Kelley's two young children. Their parents had entrusted them to Harry Branam and Maria Gagliardo for the planned overnight trip to Bimini, but now more permanent arrangements had to be made. It was a tacit recognition that Jake and Kelley weren't coming back, although their daughter, nearly three years old, continued to ask for them constantly. The couple's baby son, only four months old, had no comprehension of the situation, but their daughter told Maria that she wanted to go home to Star Island to be there "when Mommy and Daddy come back." No one really knew what to tell the young child or how to handle the inevitable trauma she would have to face. Maria and Harry were willing to keep the children indefinitely, but everyone recognized that some coordinated plans needed to be made for their custody and care. As things stood when Jake and Kelley disappeared, no one—not Maria or Harry or anyone else—had the legal authority to make basic decisions for the children, even decisions like consenting to emergency medical treatment, should that become necessary.

It came as no surprise that the children's Branam and Van Laar family members couldn't agree on who should have custody of the two tiny orphans. It was inevitable that the issues would have to be addressed within the legal system. The custody battle over the children began just a few days after the search ended for Kelley and Jake Branam, and even during that first traumatic week, petitions for custody were already being filed in Miami-Dade Family Court.

The complicated, hotly contested case was assigned to family court judge Sandy Karlan, a well-respected, experienced jurist who served as administrative judge for the family court division. All the parties hired lawyers, and hearings soon degenerated into a slugfest among some of the family members. The combatants included Harry Branam, who had frequently taken care of the children with Maria's help when Jake and Kelley were out. Harry and Maria had a strong, continuing relationship with the young children, but Harry was their great-grandfather, a single man in his seventies, and age might be an issue. Was he too old to take over responsibility for such young children?

Harry's former wife, Jeannette, also weighed in seeking custody, as did Jake's uncle, Jeff Branam, which would at least return the children to Star Island and provide a financially secure home for them. But both Maria Gagliardo and Leanne Van Laar–Uttmark, Kelley's mother, said that Kelley had never even wanted Jeannette to look after the children, as there was little relationship between them. Plus, she was nearly Harry's age; and though Jeff was in his fifties, he was divorced and had little experience raising young children alone. Both Jeannette and Jeff also worked long hours at

Alliance Industries and sometimes on weekends, so a nanny would have to be hired for the daily demands of raising such young children.

Leanne, the children's grandmother, also wanted custody, but she lived in St. Louis with her husband, Bob. If the children went with her, would their Branam relatives in Florida have sufficient contact with them, at least while they were so small? And then there was Kelley's older half sister, Genny, who also wanted custody of her niece and nephew. She lived in Michigan in a one-bedroom apartment, had no children, had moved frequently (twenty times in the past twenty-two years, according to her mother), and lived a "single woman's lifestyle." But she also had a teaching certificate, a master's degree in math, and she taught calculus and trigonometry in a high school in Michigan. She claimed to have some experience with younger children. Genny petitioned for custody, but Maria Gagliardo and Leanne Van Laar–Uttmark insisted that Kelley said she would never want Genny to raise her children if something happened to her. According to Leanne, Genny and Kelley did not get along well and sometimes weren't even speaking to each other. By Leanne's estimate, Genny came to visit Kelley in Miami only three times during the years that Kelley lived there, and whenever Genny came to Star Island, there was trouble.

Both Maria Gagliardo and Leanne Van Laar–Uttmark reported disturbing conversations that each had had with Kelley concerning who should raise her young children if "something happened to her," discussions that now haunted them. These talks had seemed strange, since Kelley was young, only thirty, in excellent health, and a married woman. Why was she so concerned about who would raise her children if she weren't there? Perhaps it was because she felt so unhappy in the Branam family compound, with no family support of her own nearby. Whatever the reason, Maria said that Kelley had broached the subject with her out of the blue one day and clearly stated that she did not want her half sister, Genny Van Laar, to have custody of her children "under any circumstances." Maria advised Kelley to think over what her intentions were, discuss it with Jake, and then she and Jake should put something in writing about the children to guide others "just in case."

On the weekend of September 15 and 16, 2007, exactly one week before the tragic charter on the *Joe Cool*, Harry and Maria had taken Jake, Kelley, and the children on a trip to Disney World in Orlando. Maria said that the subject of the children's future came up again during the brief vacation, and she reminded Jake and Kelley that if something happened to both of them—for example, traveling somewhere together or out on the ocean on the *Joe Cool*—there would be nothing in writing about their intentions concerning their young daughter and baby son. After a private discussion, she said that Jake and Kelley announced that their decision was for Harry and Maria to raise their children if something happened to them. Harry and Maria were the only other people with whom the children had a close relationship and the only people their parents ever entrusted them to when they went out. Jake promised to take care of the paperwork during the coming week. Harry already had an appointment with his attorney to revise his estate plan, so he agreed to include provisions concerning his great-grandchildren's custody and care in his plan, if that was what Jake and Kelley wanted. They asked Harry to do so, and he agreed.

But Jake and Kelley never got around to "taking care of the paperwork" during the following week. They could easily have done so, since Florida law provides a fairly simple procedure for designating a "pre-need guardian for minor" in writing and filing the document with the clerk of the court. According to a well-recognized expert in this field of law, the wishes of the natural parents are always honored and enforced "unless the designated guardian is someone like an axe-murderer." This omission proved tragic. By the next weekend, September 22–23, it was too late.

Leanne Van Laar–Uttmark also said that Kelley had requested her mother take over with the children if something happened to her. Leanne recalled that she told Kelley that she loved her grandkids and would definitely want to take care of them, but she was having trouble with both her knees and wasn't sure she would be up to the task, since the children were both so young and their care involved much physical effort. "Why don't we get your knees taken care of?" Kelley told her mother. "Then you would be able to handle them in case something happens to me." They discussed the possibility of Leanne's coming to Miami to have her damaged knees repaired. Leanne recalled that Kelley told her Jake's dad, Joe, had had the procedure done in Miami with an excellent surgeon and that Jake had had "a torn knee" repaired by the same specialist. According to Leanne, she and Kelley were still discussing this possibility when Kelley disappeared. The memory of that conversation brought Leanne to sobs. "Why was I so worried about my knees?" she said. "Why didn't I just tell Kelley to put something in writing immediately, go to a bank and have it notarized, and send it to me?"

Leanne was convinced that Kelley would not have wanted Jeannette or Jeff Branam to raise her children, either. She recalled that in 2006, when Jake was planning to spend several months in South Carolina refurbishing the *Joe Cool*, he called Leanne and asked her if Kelley and their baby daughter could come to stay with her while he was gone. Leanne replied, they'd be delighted to have them come stay. Then, according to Leanne, Jake said something that seemed strange to her. "He didn't think it was safe for Kelley and the baby to be alone on Star without him," Leanne recalled. She was mystified, but she didn't ask for any details.

Kelley and her young daughter came to stay with Leanne and Bob in St. Louis while Jake was in South Carolina. By then, Kelley was pregnant again, and she arrived in St. Louis severely dehydrated and weak. Leanne and Bob promptly had her hospitalized for treatment, and when she was released, Kelley and her daughter stayed on with them in St. Louis. Leanne knew there were problems in her daughter's marriage, and she couldn't help overhearing Kelley and Jake arguing on the phone. Kelley was crying and unhappy much of the time she stayed with her mother. Leanne said that Kelley told her she was thinking about divorce, and they discussed whether Kelley and her daughter should remain in St. Louis. Leanne wanted Kelley and the baby to live with her, but Kelley preferred her own apartment. Leanne, Bob, and Kelley found a nice apartment nearby, and Leanne paid the initial deposit. But then Kelley changed her mind, and she took her daughter back to Star Island.

Allegations of misbehavior aired during Harry and Jeannette Branam's ugly divorce were now dragged back into family court in the context of "who was best for the children," but Judge Sandy Karlan made it clear that she wasn't about to retry that messy case in her courtroom. Her sole concern was which of the competing parties should now have custody of the two tiny orphans, and her focus was on the best interests of the children. But what *were* the children's best interests?

There was no easy answer. None of the candidates who vied for custody was a perfect fit for the small children who had spent their short lives mostly being shuttled between the cottage on Star Island with their parents and the Miami Beach condo shared by Maria and Harry. It appeared that the children had no close, continuing relationships with anyone other than Maria and Harry. The constant conflict with other Branam family members on Star Island also posed a huge problem for the judge in trying to work out a balanced arrangement for these children with so many years ahead of them and so little cooperation among their relatives. In terms of geography, Kelley's Van Laar relatives posed additional problems, given that her mother was in St. Louis and her half sister, Genny, lived in Michigan. If the children went to live with either of them, how could they maintain close contact with their relatives in Florida, especially while they were so young?

Judge Karlan sought professional advice on the difficult issues confronting her. She appointed Margaret C. F. Quinlivan, Esquire, known in the legal community as "Connie," to serve as guardian ad litem to represent "the best interests of the children," and ordered the parties to meet with psychologist Dr. Vanessa Archer immediately to obtain guidance on how best to explain the loss of her parents to Jake and Kelley's daughter. She and her baby brother were still living with Maria and Harry, but now she was asking more and more often to go home to Star Island to await her parents' return. Dr. Andrew Wenger was appointed to provide grief therapy to the little girl. An interim schedule was worked out for the children to spend four days each week with Harry and Maria and the next four days on Star Island.

Dr. Miguel Firpi and Dr. Neena Malik were selected to undertake psychological evaluations of the children and the adults, which was a necessary process in a case of disputed custody. Dr. Firpi was to conduct psychological testing. Dr. Malik's expertise was in children's developmental stages and, in particular, the areas of bonding and attachment as part of their social and psychological development.

Soon, the complex custody case seemed to become an arena within which old family antagonisms, jealousies, long-simmering resentments, and wounds from the past surfaced in what became an ugly competition for the "prize," which was, unfortunately, the fate of two tiny children orphaned by a catastrophe beyond measure. The legal battle became a forum for airing personal attacks on the character and past behavior of family members and pitted daughter against mother, father against son, and former husband against former wife.

Adding to the pressures of this conflict was the adversarial style of some of the attorneys hired by the parties to press their individual cases for an award of custody. The attorneys were advocates for their clients, and it was their duty to zealously represent their clients' stated interests; that is, their professional responsibility was to help their clients "win," within the bounds of the law. The costs of this expensive battalion of experts and lawyers would be borne by the parties seeking custody. The Branam family members had substantial financial means, and Leanne Van Laar–Uttmark and her husband, Bob, were financially comfortable and stable, having been happily married for thirteen years, and living in the pleasant, waterfront home they owned near St. Louis. But how would Genny Van Laar finance what would be a lengthy and expensive legal battle? She worked as a public school teacher in Michigan and earned approximately $45,000 per year. According to her mother, Genny had no assets.

There was talk of a wrongful death suit to be filed against Sissy Baby Sport Fishing Charters, which had operated the *Joe Cool*, and its sole shareholder, Jeff Branam, and his affiliated companies. The theory was that the deaths of the captain, his wife, and the crew members were the direct result of Jeff Branam's negligence in approving the charter without taking basic safety precautions concerning the charter passengers, such as requiring identification, checking their backgrounds, and inspecting their luggage for weapons. The object of the litigation would be financial compensation.

The internecine warfare—and mounting professional fees and expenses—would continue for years. All of the parties would be left emotionally and financially exhausted, and some would be mistrustful of the judicial process in custody cases and embittered by the long and drawn-out conflict. The Branam and Van Laar families' tenuous personal relationships were blown apart forever by the tragic final voyage of the *Joe Cool* and its destructive aftermath.

And what would happen to the lives of the children at the center of this maelstrom, the orphans for whom all the contestants claimed to be seeking "only their best interests"? There was no way to predict their future, no matter where—and with whom—Judge Karlan decided they should live. Under Florida law, family court judges have broad discretion in such matters, and their decisions are given great deference by the appellate courts. This only increased the pressures and hostility within the Branam and Van Laar families, since whatever Judge Karlan decided, whether they believed it was right or wrong, fair or unfair, would likely withstand almost any challenge.

CHAPTER EIGHT

Inside the Investigation

Before the *Joe Cool* made its sad journey home, even before Kirby Archer and Guillermo Zarabozo were picked up from the *Joe Cool*'s life raft and transferred to the Coast Guard cutter *Confidence*, a special interagency federal investigative unit, the Maritime Seaport Squad, was already at work on the case. By eight o'clock on that Monday morning, September 24, FBI special agent David Nuñez had received a call from his squad mate, Agent Herbert "Skip" Hogberg in Miami, about an alert from the United States Coast Guard Station at Miami Beach on an "overdue," the charter fishing vessel *Joe Cool* out of Star Island, Florida. Nuñez and Hogberg had little detail, but they knew something must have gone disastrously wrong on the charter boat, a U.S. flag vessel believed to be carrying six American citizens in international waters. The forty-seven-foot *Joe Cool* had been recovered, empty and abandoned, and many miles south of their intended course, but there was no sign of the missing Americans. The agents knew that whatever evidence might be aboard the boat, it would be exposed to degradation from wind, rain, and sea spray until the *Joe Cool* could be towed safely back to the Coast Guard Station in Miami Beach for a complete forensic examination. And six Americans were still missing at sea. They knew they had to act fast.

David Nuñez quickly assembled his teammates on the squad: Agent Richard Blais of the Coast Guard Investigative Service, Special Agent Scott Hahn of the FBI's Evidence Response Team, and evidence technician Ken Denardo, a forensic photographer, also of the FBI's Evidence Response Team, and they set out to complete a preliminary assessment of the *Joe Cool* and to assist in the search for the missing Americans. It was a long, tiring trip. First, they were transported by Coast Guard jet from the Opa Locka airfield in Miami to the small island of Marathon in the Florida Keys, and then by the HH-65 Dolphin helicopter out to the Coast Guard cutter *Confidence*. Evidence specialists Scott Hahn and Ken Denardo were taken by boat out to the deserted *Joe Cool* to assess the situation and search for, photograph, and collect any evidence they found aboard. The plan was for Agents Nuñez and Blais to remain on the *Confidence*. Throughout that long day, the team was in constant contact with Agent Skip Hogberg, who had remained ashore, and the shoreside command staff.

By 9 A.M. on Monday, September 24, the search-and-rescue helicopter returned to the *Confidence* with Kirby Archer and Guillermo Zarabozo, who had been retrieved from the water adjacent to the *Joe Cool*'s life raft. Aboard the *Confidence*, Paul Baker, executive officer and second in command of the ship, awaited the chopper's return with the survivors before he decided what action should be taken next. When the helicopter landed, it did not immediately power down, because only two survivors had been recovered and Baker had no word about the other four missing Americans from the *Joe Cool*. He might need to send the helicopter out again, so it sat idling on the flight deck of the *Confidence* while Archer and Zarabozo disembarked. The sound of the chopper on deck was so loud that Commander Baker couldn't converse with the survivors to figure out what should be done next to search for the four other missing persons. He escorted them inside the ship to the upper deck to talk.

First, Baker took Zarabozo down the ladder to the cutter's sick bay and handed him off to a medical corpsman, asking him to evaluate the survivor to be sure he was okay. While he awaited the results of that assessment, Baker took Archer into a small dining area called the chief's mess, which is beneath the flight deck. Commander Baker was the first person aboard the *Confidence* to talk with Archer. He needed to know right away whether there were other survivors off the *Joe Cool* to search for, and he used a script of questions approved by the Coast Guard to help determine that. What Baker got in return was "a very discombobulated, a very emotional story," he said. "As a matter of fact, [Archer] was somewhat sobbing. I could not understand the story. I had to break it down."

Through careful questioning, Commander Baker learned that Kirby Archer said he had met Guillermo Zarabozo at Monty's in Miami Beach, and that the two had known each other "for a couple of months." They had chartered a sportfishing boat to take them on a one-way trip from Miami Beach to Bimini, which Archer had paid for. They had left the Miami Beach Marina on the afternoon of Saturday, September 22, on the charter. During the trip, Archer said he became seasick. He had been below in the boat's cabin, he said, when he heard "a commotion" up top and saw a body fall from the fly bridge of the boat. He told Commander Baker that next he had witnessed the shooting of one of the crew members. Archer told Baker that Cuban pirates or hijackers had boarded the boat, shot all those aboard except for Archer and Zarabozo, and then forced Zarabozo to dump their bodies overboard into the ocean. Archer said that he was ordered, at gunpoint, to drive the charter boat south toward Cuba. He did so, until the boat ran out of fuel. Then, he told Baker, another boat arrived and picked up the hijackers, leaving Archer and Zarabozo stranded on the boat. Archer said that he and Zarabozo tried to put the anchor out, but it did not hold, so they decided to take the life raft out with their belongings.

After speaking privately with Guillermo Zarabozo, who told a similar story, Commander Baker concluded that there were no more survivors in the area to search for from the *Joe Cool*. The helicopter powered down. Baker learned from another member of his staff that there was a fugitive warrant outstanding for Kirby Archer from Independence County, Arkansas. He decided to hold Archer and Zarabozo under security watch until the investigators from the Maritime Seaport Squad arrived on the cutter *Confidence*. Both survivors seemed to be in good physical condition, and they were offered dry clothes, food, and water. That afternoon, the helicopter was launched again, this time to pick up the agents from the Maritime Seaport Squad, who by then were waiting in Marathon in the Florida Keys, and bring them back to the *Confidence*.

When Agents David Nuñez and Richard Blais boarded the *Confidence*, they were briefed by the command staff about what they had learned concerning the abandoned *Joe Cool* and the two survivors who had been retrieved from the life raft. The agents were told about the survivors' strange tale of Cuban pirates or hijackers who had ambushed the *Joe Cool* and then abandoned it, leaving Archer and Zarabozo to set out in the boat's life raft. Archer had been carrying $2,200 in American hundred-dollar bills when he was rescued. Zarabozo's wallet and his Florida driver's license were found on the *Joe Cool*, along with a laptop, a cell phone, a camera, various personal items, and equipment worth thousands of dollars. They also learned that an Arkansas fugitive warrant was outstanding for Kirby

Archer for the suspected theft of $92,000 in cash and checks from a Wal-Mart in January 2007. What about the four Americans still unaccounted for? That was the worst news of all. According to the survivors, the charter boat's captain, his wife, and two crew members had been shot and dumped at sea by the Cuban hijackers.

The helicopter rescue crew reported that the survivors had left what appeared to be several pieces of black luggage in the life raft when they were rescued that morning. The life raft was still adrift and might be holding information valuable to the investigation and the whereabouts of the missing four Americans. The cutter *Confidence* would retrieve the life raft and bring it aboard for examination. The cutter *Pea Island* would take the *Joe Cool* under tow in daylight to begin the journey back to the Coast Guard Station at Miami Beach, where the boat would become a floating crime scene for detailed forensic examination.

Special Agent David Nuñez and his partner, Agent Richard Blais, were ready to meet with the survivors separately to hear what they had to say, especially about the four missing Americans. Just after eight o'clock on Monday evening, September 24, they sat down with Guillermo Zarabozo in the wardroom of the cutter *Confidence*. Because of their long, grueling day of travel, the agents were casually dressed. David Nuñez began the interview by introducing himself and his partner and showing their credentials. Then he asked Zarabozo some general questions about his age, his level of education and work experience, his family, and his demographics, to ascertain whether he was coherent, could understand English, and was able to participate in the interview. After ten or fifteen minutes, Nuñez was satisfied. But before they asked specific questions, the agents wanted to Mirandize Zarabozo using a standard printed form and having him read it aloud to be sure he understood his rights. He was not a suspect and there was no open criminal investigation, but Nuñez considered the form a standard precaution for any interviewee. No one could predict what might come out in an interview, so it was only fair that the interviewee be informed of his rights before the interview began. Zarabozo didn't have to answer the agents' questions, but if he did he would be held to his answers. Zarabozo had no difficulty with the form, read it aloud, stated that he understood it, signed it, and began to talk to the agents.

At first, he seemed "calm, cool and collected," according to Nuñez. He told them that he was a security guard with the Pinkerton security company and that he did not own a firearm of his own but used one when he was working security. He said he had met Kirby Archer on a security job, but he couldn't remember any details about their meeting. Zarabozo repeated the story about booking a boat trip to Bimini to meet some girlfriends. But when Nuñez asked him for details about the girlfriends, Zarabozo couldn't provide their cell phone numbers, their physical descriptions, or even one of their names. He couldn't say how they planned to get together in Bimini. The more details Nuñez asked for, the more visibly nervous Zarabozo became. With thirteen years of experience as an investigator, Nuñez found this behavior strange. He later recorded his observations in his FBI report of the interview, "He just gave me the deer in the headlights look. He couldn't even make anything up."

Zarabozo seemed calmer when Nuñez asked him about the captain and crew of the *Joe Cool*, and he gave adequate descriptions of each individual. He described Kelley Branam as having "a good body" and he mentioned the "tribal tattoo" that encircled her upper right arm. He said that he was on the fly bridge with the captain and his wife when he overheard a radio call from a vessel in distress. According to Zarabozo, the captain responded to the call and positioned the boat starboard to starboard with the other vessel. There were three Cuban men on the other boat and two of them boarded the charter fishing boat. One climbed to the fly bridge and shot the captain, who fell to the deck below. At that point, Zarabozo said, the captain's wife "started freaking out, acting hysterically, and lying down in a fetal type position." Then the intruder shot her twice in the side and she also fell off the fly bridge and landed on the deck next to her husband.

While describing this violent, macabre scene, Zarabozo seemed "calm, cool and collected," according to Nuñez. The agent asked for detail about the hijackers' appearance, and Zarabozo gave a generic description of three dark-haired Cuban men. What were they wearing? Nuñez asked. Jeans and polo shirts, Zarabozo answered. He calmly went on to tell the agent that the hijackers shot and killed the remaining two crew members and that he begged them for his life and that of Kirby Archer. He described the fly bridge and the aft deck as very messy, very bloody. At gunpoint, he said, he was made to dump the bodies overboard and then hose down the boat.

Zarabozo told the agents he went back up to the fly bridge where Archer was now driving the boat south, heading for Cuba as the hijackers had ordered. He said he fell asleep for eight hours, which he timed on his stopwatch. When he awoke, Archer was still driving, but the boat was nearly out of fuel. The hijackers then used a cell phone to call another boat to pick them up. After the hijackers left on the other boat, Archer and Zarabozo were alone on the charter fishing boat, which was out of fuel and drifting. They decided to take their belongings and climb aboard the life raft rather than remain on the charter boat. He remembered little else until they were rescued by the Coast Guard helicopter.

Kirby Archer told the agents a similar version when he was interviewed, except for details like what the hijackers were wearing. According to Zarabozo, it was jeans and polo shirts, but Archer said two wore boating clothes, T-shirts and shorts, and another wore long pants and a shirt. There were also significant discrepancies in their accounts of what happened aboard the charter fishing boat and the sequence of events leading up to the trip. They couldn't both be telling the truth, and neither story made any sense, given what the agents already knew. Why would hijackers abandon the valuable *Joe Cool* with all its expensive equipment on board, with another boat—the mysterious third boat—available to tow it the last few miles to Cuba? And if these mysterious Cubans had killed the captain, his wife, and the crew members, why would they leave these two witnesses alive to tell the tale? And wouldn't they at least have taken the $2,200 cash out of Archer's pocket before they let him go?

It was clear to the agents that they wouldn't get a straight story from either Archer or Zarabozo. And four Americans were still missing. They knew they needed time and expert help to investigate the survivors and their stories and to collect and analyze all the physical evidence on the *Joe Cool* and the life raft. The agents could not have predicted the twisted trail the investigation would follow and the mountain of evidence that would eventually be recovered from the *Joe Cool*, the life raft, the luggage, computers, video surveillance tapes, receipts, witnesses, and a seemingly endless stream of electronic messages and cell phone calls.

In the meantime, they wanted to keep their investigation—and Archer and Zarabozo—under wraps. They could arrest Archer and keep him in custody on the Arkansas fugitive warrant, but what about Zarabozo? A quick computer search turned up no criminal conduct in the Hialeah teenager's past.

Agents David Nuñez and Richard Blais and survivors Kirby Archer and Guillermo Zarabozo were transferred to the cutter *Pea Island* for the return to the Miami Beach Coast Guard Station. The cutter *Pea Island* already had the *Joe Cool* in tow for the trip. Suddenly, Guillermo Zarabozo changed his story, telling the agents that he had never been aboard the *Joe Cool*, had never even seen the boat. Baffled, the agents pointed out the *Joe Cool* in tow right behind them, but Zarabozo continued to insist that he didn't recognize it, had never seen it before. Since his wallet and Florida driver's license had been found in the boat's galley and he had been rescued from the *Joe Cool*'s life raft, his denial was an obvious and puzzling lie. But he had just made false statements to federal agents during the course of an official investigation, and that might be enough to keep him in custody while the investigation progressed.

CHAPTER NINE

The Prosecution Begins

On September 24, 2007, just as the Special Maritime Squad's investigation of the *Joe Cool* was ramping up, the FBI alerted Assistant United States Attorney Karen Gilbert, chief of major crimes in the Miami office of the United States Attorney for the Southern District of Florida. Gilbert immediately recognized that this would be a high-profile, challenging case. The *Joe Cool* charter fishing boat had gone missing in international waters with six Americans on board. Although two survivors were later found aboard a life raft, the captain, his wife, and two crew members were still missing despite the Coast Guard's search-and-rescue efforts. And now the only two survivors from the *Joe Cool* were beginning to look like suspects in the disappearance of the other four. After consulting with the United States Attorney for the Southern District of Florida, R. Alexander Acosta, Gilbert quickly assembled her team of experienced, top-notch prosecutors, Assistant United States Attorneys Jeffrey Tsai and Michael Gilfarb, and went to work. They set up their command center in a windowless conference room in their offices in the massive James L. King Federal Justice Building, which faces other federal buildings on a large, open plaza in downtown Miami. The prosecutors were friends as well as colleagues. They would grow to trust and depend upon each other's skills and judgment during their work together on this case. There would also be fierce, hotly contested arguments on strategy and tactics. But there would always be respect.

What they couldn't know on that cloudy Monday in September was that they would spend the next sixteen months together, working nonstop on only the *Joe Cool* case in a windowless room they would soon call "the war room." Holidays, birthdays, celebrations, seasons, personal events, vacation plans, and parties would come and go, but their work together would go on, days, nights, and weekends, until the job was done.

The prosecution team assembled available information about the case and set about formulating strategy and identifying priorities. Everyone recognized that time was running out in the search for the four missing Americans, and the prosecution team had to be ready to deal with this case immediately. Depending upon what the investigation disclosed, if there was evidence that these missing people had been murdered, this would be a capital case, a rarity in federal court. In a capital case, there were only two possible penalties for conviction: life in prison or the death penalty. Such cases were referred to as "death eligible," because the death penalty could be imposed. Most capital cases were murders committed within a state's jurisdiction, and those cases are tried in state courts. In states that permitted the death penalty, the head prosecutor of the district in which the crime was committed would decide whether to seek the death penalty or life in prison in a capital case.

But this case was within federal jurisdiction, because the crimes had occurred on the high seas, in the "special and maritime jurisdiction" of the United States. In a federal capital case, it was the U.S. attorney general who decided which penalty—life in prison or the death penalty—would be sought. There were certain procedural steps that must be taken in federal cases before that decision was made. No one on this newly assembled prosecution team had any prior experience with federal capital cases, but they would all have to learn fast.

But first, they summed up what they knew about the survivors. Guillermo Zarabozo was practically a blank slate, a nineteen-year-old Cuban refugee living with his family in a scruffy neighborhood in the Miami suburb of Hialeah, where many newly arrived Cubans settled. Guillermo, along with his younger sister, mother, and stepfather, had emigrated from Cuba in 1999 after winning an immigration "lottery." Guillermo had graduated from Hialeah High School in 2006 and held a number of part-time jobs since then, sometimes as a private security guard for local companies. He had no criminal record and had apparently never been in trouble.

Kirby Archer, however, had left a long, tangled, sometimes sordid trail during his thirty-five years. When he was picked up by the United States Coast Guard, he was fleeing an Arkansas warrant for his arrest. Archer had served in the United States Army, including a stint as a military police investigator. He was briefly stationed in Guantánamo, Cuba, when fleeing Cuban nationals were housed in tents there awaiting immigration to the United States. Then Archer had gone AWOL from the army and earned a less-than-honorable discharge as a result. There was also a web of bad marriages and charges of domestic violence in his past, and allegations of child sexual abuse in Missouri and Arkansas and possibly Arizona, well before the theft from Wal-Mart leading to the fugitive warrant. By the time he fled Arkansas, Archer was again under investigation for serious child sex abuse charges. He had skipped several appointments to meet with investigators in Independence County, Arkansas, and they were closing in on him. It seemed clear to the prosecutors that Archer had gone on the run in Arkansas in January and somehow turned up in Miami that September for the tragic charter trip on the *Joe Cool*. So far, no records had turned up in Florida in his name. But the missing $92,000 would have been convenient cash to fund his flight from prosecution.

The prosecutors consulted with agents of the Maritime Seaport Squad and learned what evidence had been collected so far, what they were working on, and what theories they had. The *Joe Cool* had run out of fuel very close to the Cuban coast. Cuba could've been a likely destination for Kirby Archer, since there was no extradition treaty between the United States and Cuba. Archer would expect to be safe from arrest and prosecution there. Also, he had served in Guantánamo, and it was believed he spoke Spanish. But why would Guillermo Zarabozo want to return to Cuba, which he had fled with his family just a few years earlier? It didn't make any sense. Everyone in Cuba seemed to be trying to get out, and this guy wants back in? What possible motivation could he have?

How and why would these two seemingly disparate individuals have met and embarked together on the *Joe Cool* for a one-way trip to Bimini? Since the Zarabozo family had briefly lived in a Guantánamo detention camp before immigrating to the United States, perhaps Kirby Archer had met Guillermo Zarabozo during his army hitch in Guantánamo, but they couldn't confirm that hunch. Zarabozo had told FBI agent David Nuñez that they had met each other while both were working a security job together, but that lead wasn't panning out. Zarabozo couldn't provide any details of the job and no records had turned up. Kirby Archer's story was that he had met Zarabozo "a couple of months" earlier at Monty's on Miami Beach.

Investigators were still in the process of obtaining physical evidence in the case, but what they already had was alarming. Guillermo Zarabozo had freely admitted to Nuñez that he'd brought a blowgun and darts aboard the charter fishing boat. Martial arts–type throwing stars or quills, knives, and a large leather whip had been found in the survivors' luggage on the life raft, and Kirby Archer had been carrying a wicked-looking knife. A handcuff key was recovered on the bow of the *Joe Cool,* and there were dried bloodstains on the stern. But there were no bodies—the search for the four missing Americans was still under way and the *Joe Cool* was at sea under tow by the cutter *Pea Island.*

At that point, there was no direct physical evidence tying either Kirby Archer or Guillermo Zarabozo to any crime on the boat. But there were obvious inferences to be drawn from the circumstantial evidence found so far. The captain and crew were missing from the *Joe Cool*; the boat had been found abandoned and drifting far south of its intended course; suspicious bloodstains were seen by investigators on the aft deck of the boat; and the only survivors, Kirby Archer and Guillermo Zarabozo, told investigators strange, inconsistent stories about Cuban pirates or hijackers. For the investigators and prosecutors, this circumstantial evidence provided probable cause to believe that deadly crimes had been committed aboard the *Joe Cool.* Zarabozo and Archer were the best suspects—indeed, the only suspects—they had. They were determined to keep the two men in custody while the investigation proceeded. Archer and Zarabozo had been on the run before, and if they were released, they would likely take off again.

The following day, the cutter *Pea Island* delivered Archer and Zarabozo to the United States Coast Guard Station at Miami Beach, accompanied by Agents David Nuñez and Richard Blais. Archer and Zarabozo were handcuffed and walked the ship's gangway awkwardly, with blankets thrown over them like Mafia dons, in an attempt to shield their faces from the large media pack assembled across the water from the Coast Guard Station. Both were immediately taken into custody by the FBI, Kirby Archer for unlawful flight to avoid prosecution and Guillermo Zarabozo for making false statements to federal agents in the course of an investigation.

Meanwhile, the prosecution team worked feverishly to assure that Archer and Zarabozo wouldn't be released while a thorough investigation was under way. The suspects would soon have counsel working on their behalf, and prosecutors Karen Gilbert, Jeffrey Tsai, and Michael Gilfarb knew they were facing a series of crucial appearances, bond hearings, detention hearings, and arraignments. Defense lawyers would be just as determined to obtain release for Archer and Zarabozo as the prosecution team was to hold them in custody. The prosecutors knew they would have to make some judgment calls now, disclosing just enough of their evolving theory and evidence against Archer and Zarabozo to keep them locked up as suspects in the disappearance of four Americans from the *Joe Cool*, without giving up anything that would tip off the defense before they were ready. It was a race against time, especially since the families were still clinging to the desperate hope that Jake and Kelley Branam, Sammy Kairy, and Scott Gamble were somehow, somewhere still alive.

While maintaining the posture that the victims were still officially missing at sea, the prosecutors decided they had to disclose the basic premise of their allegations against Archer and Zarabozo. The men had booked the trip on the *Joe Cool* under false pretenses, claiming to be surveyors planning to meet up with girlfriends in Bimini, while their real intention was to hijack the boat and drive it to Cuba, disposing of the captain, his wife, and the crew members along the way. These inferences rested upon undisputed evidence that the *Joe Cool* never arrived in Bimini; that Guillermo Zarabozo couldn't name even one of the supposed girlfriends; and that no girls had come forward to verify their story, despite massive publicity since the vessel had gone missing. It was now common knowledge that Kirby Archer was on the run from an Arkansas fugitive warrant, a likely motive for flight to

Cuba to avoid prosecution. Guillermo Zarabozo's odd behavior and strange story about the Cuban hijackers supported the prosecutors' theory, combined with his subsequent baffling falsehood that he had never been aboard the *Joe Cool*. The prosecution team would also have to release more details of the suspicious circumstances surrounding the mystery at sea—details that had not yet been disclosed even to the victims' relatives.

The first test was an appearance before United States Magistrate Judge Robert L. Dube. Allan Kaiser, a former federal prosecutor now in private practice, was appointed to represent Kirby Archer, and Faith Mesnekoff, an experienced lawyer with Miami's prestigious Federal Public Defender's Office, would handle the defense of Guillermo Zarabozo. At the hearing, Kaiser and Mesnekoff argued that there was insufficient evidence that a crime had been committed—and no evidence of their clients' involvement— to justify holding Archer and Zarabozo in custody without bail. In response, prosecutor Michael Gilfarb outlined some of the evidence the government had so far—including details of the strange stories told by Archer and Zarabozo as survivors of the *Joe Cool*. Gilfarb used as much as he felt he needed to win the argument without giving anything away prematurely. The suspects were an obvious flight risk, he told the judge, since they had been picked up practically in Cuba. Until the mysterious disappearance of the others aboard the *Joe Cool* had been resolved, Archer and Zarabozo should also be considered a danger to the community. After hearing the lawyers for both sides, Judge Dube declined to set bail for Kirby Archer and Guillermo Zarabozo. They would remain in custody, at least for the time being. Both sides agreed to postpone further consideration of the matter until October 2, 2007.

Prosecutors had won the first round, but they knew many more lay ahead and they had to win every single one. Kirby Archer and Guillermo Zarabozo had attended the hearing, handcuffed and in prison garb, as Zarabozo's sad-eyed mother, Francisca Alonso, watched from the gallery. They were not allowed to speak to each other, although Zarabozo smiled cheerfully at her. She left the courtroom without speaking to reporters outside. Archer's attorney, Allan Kaiser, told the press that he expected more information about the prosecution's case to be disclosed at the next hearing. "We're going to see what the government has to offer," he told reporter Vanessa Blum of SunSentinel.com. Faith Mesnekoff stated in court that the FBI and prosecutors had been notified not to speak with her client, Guillermo Zarabozo, without her present.

That same day, FBI agents called members of the victims' families in for a conference to update them on the investigation. Kassin Kairy and his younger brother, Ilan, accompanied their parents, Albert and Marian, to the meeting, waiting to hear what the FBI had to say. Kassin was still trying to figure out whether this was, as everyone hoped, a misunderstanding or some kind of mechanical malfunction, or even one of his brother's foolish pranks gone awry. He still couldn't really believe that Sammy and Jake, who had spent their young lives on the ocean and were such capable seamen, could possibly be missing off the *Joe Cool.* His own thoughts and worries he kept private, but he tried to keep the possibility of hope alive for his parents. They were increasingly distraught and "out of it," and Kassin was beginning to worry about them.

Everyone knew that the FBI and Coast Guard had been keeping a tight lid on the case to safeguard the investigation's progress, and little of what the agents and prosecutors now knew had been shared with the families. In addition, the agents didn't know exactly what the prosecution team had decided to reveal in court at this point. The agents were extremely cautious about discussing details for fear of jeopardizing their investigation. Finally, Amie Gamble and other family members complained that they had been called down to the FBI conference for nothing. It was a waste of time, they said, since they were told virtually nothing new. All they knew was that the two charter passengers off the *Joe Cool* had been found, but the other four people— the ones they cared about—were still missing at sea. They were frustrated and unhappy as they left the building in downtown Miami.

Now Kassin began to worry seriously for the first time. If the FBI wasn't telling them anything, he reasoned, it must be really bad. He said nothing to his parents, but he pulled his younger brother, Ilan, aside. "Look, I think something's really wrong here," he said. "This could be very bad. We need to keep a close eye on Mom and Dad."

Unfortunately, some of what the agents omitted from their update to the families had just been made public at the hearing before Judge Robert Dube in federal court, especially the survivors' graphic stories about the murders of Jake, Kelley, Sammy, and Scott. As they left the FBI interview, the friends and family members were blindsided by a pack of reporters shouting questions at them and shoving microphones in their faces. This was a new experience for them, and they had no idea what was going on. Kassin Kairy was now extremely apprehensive, although he tried not to show it in front of his parents. He and his brother, Ilan, quickly hustled their parents off to their car and home, away from the media pack. They all escaped as best they could, then everyone started checking around with friends to find out what was going on.

Their friends told them that there had been breaking news stories all afternoon on TV about the case and that apparently reporters had attended the hearing in federal court before Judge Robert Dube—the hearing that was going on at the very same time that the families were cooped up in their fruitless meeting with the FBI. In court, the reporters had seen the survivors with their newly appointed attorneys. Urging Judge Dube to hold Archer and Zarabozo without bond,

prosecutor Michael Gilfarb had revealed the first public out-
lines of the terrible story about the gruesome murders of the
captain, his wife, and the crew members aboard the *Joe Cool*.

When the Kairy family finally got home and turned on
the TV, they saw the brutal news reports and heard the
pirates/hijackers story for the first time. Reporters said that
all four members of the crew had been murdered, and then
there was Sammy's face on TV, along with Jake, Kelley, and
Scott. Marian Kairy was nearly hysterical, repeating, "Oh
my God! Oh my God! Oh my God!" She was in shock, inconsolable, and her sons were very worried about her.

Friends of the Kairy family began to call, but Marian
was in no condition to speak with anyone. Kassin and Ilan
retreated for a private talk. "Remember what Sammy always said?" Kassin asked his brother. "He said, if anything
ever happens to me, I want you to go out and party for me."
Ilan remembered, but was that really the right thing to do?
Their parents were completely "out of it." Later, when their
parents fell into an exhausted calm, Kassin and Ilan decided
they should go out for a few minutes, just to a neighborhood place to toast their lost brother as he'd wished. When
they arrived, they were surprised to encounter many of
Sammy's friends from high school, from college, from the
docks and boats, from all the places he had known and
loved. Everyone had heard the terrible news. Apparently
Sammy had told all his friends the same thing about going
out to party for him, and with no prearrangement, they were
all there to honor him and to carry out his wish. There was
no joy, no "party," but there was at least a shared tribute to
a life well lived, if far too short. "He always wanted to live
his life to the fullest," Kassin said. "Out on the ocean, he
was exactly where he wanted to be."

THE Branam and Van Laar families were devastated, especially to learn all the grim details secondhand on TV and

from news reports rather than from the FBI team investigating the case, who were supposedly bringing them up to date at the very same time the suspects' hearing was going on in federal court. Even Kelley's grandparents in Kalamazoo saw her picture on the TV news and heard the terrible story. It was hurtful to the families and embarrassing to the federal investigators. FBI spokeswoman Judy Orihuela issued a formal apology to the families for the error. "It shouldn't have happened, but it did and we apologize," she told a reporter. "We have dozens of agents working [o]n the case full-time with very little sleep. That should give the family some sense we're working very hard."

It was a very upsetting faux pas to the family, but the prosecution team had to keep its focus on the coming hurdles in court. They began to draft a criminal complaint, the first official charging document to be filed in federal court in which the government would specify its grounds for probable cause to believe that hijacking, kidnapping, and murders had been committed on the *Joe Cool* and that Kirby Archer and Guillermo Zarabozo had committed these crimes. In this pleading, the prosecutors had to establish a detailed, legally sufficient basis for probable cause. And they would have to do it without weapons, fingerprints, confessions, witnesses to the crimes—even without the victims' bodies.

In fact, federal investigators were already hard at work on several fronts. Immediately after Zarabozo and Archer were arrested, the FBI obtained a search warrant for Zarabozo's car, a loaner, which they had tracked down. A warrant was also obtained to search the *Joe Cool*, as well as the life raft from which Zarabozo and Archer had been rescued. The warrants were executed on September 26 and various evidentiary items were removed from the boat, the life raft, and Zarabozo's car. In addition, the FBI had already obtained videotape from Lou's Police and Security Equipment Store in the Miami suburb of Hialeah, Florida, showing Zarabozo and Archer purchasing a magazine for a Sig Sauer handgun on September 12, ten days before their departure on the *Joe Cool*.

On Thursday, September 27, FBI agents visited Guillermo Zarabozo's home address in Hialeah using the driver's license found on the *Joe Cool*. Home turned out to be a shabby pink stucco second-floor walk-up that Zarabozo shared with his mother, younger sister, and stepfather. FBI special agent Herbert Hogberg and a Spanish-speaking colleague knocked and identified themselves to Zarabozo's mother, Francisca Alonso, who readily admitted them. She spoke no English, so the conversation was conducted in Spanish. She was aware of her son's "situation," but she didn't believe one word of the terrible things they were saying about him on TV. He was a good boy, a son to be proud of, and she believed in him completely. She didn't know "the gringo," Kirby Archer. Her son wanted to be a police officer, Francisca told the agents, and she showed them a letter he had received from the Miami-Dade Police Department admitting him to the orientation class in October 2007. Francisca also showed the agents photos of Zarabozo in the Junior Air Force ROTC at Hialeah High School, where he had graduated in 2006, and another of him in the Boy Scouts. She had no idea how he had turned up on a raft in the ocean. He didn't know anything about boats and had no experience or particular interest in the ocean.

Guillermo Zarabozo's mother told the agents that he worked part time as a private security guard and that he paid her $300 per month to live in the apartment where he shared a bedroom with his younger sister. She added that her son thought she was "nosy" and was "getting in his business," but she had told him that while he lived in her home, he would have to "follow . . . [my] rules and I will be in your business."

According to the FBI agents, Francisca volunteered to let them search Zarabozo's bedroom. One side of the bedroom obviously belonged to a young girl who favored pink, frilly decor and stuffed animals, while Guillermo's side showcased posters of soldiers, bodybuilders, and martial arts trainers. There were framed certificates from the Boy Scouts and the Citizens Police Academy on the wall above the top bunk on his bunk bed. Zarabozo's mother told the agents that he had a lockbox for his handgun that he needed for his work as a security guard. She located it and opened it, using a code that she knew, and the FBI agents peered inside. They saw a cardboard box, and at that point, Agent Hogberg decided it would be prudent to obtain a search warrant before commencing a search.

Once they had a search warrant in hand, the agents returned to Zarabozo's bedroom and seized a number of items, including a receipt from Lou's Police and Security Equipment Store for the purchase of an M19 Glock magazine for a nine-millimeter weapon, as well as boxes of ammunition for the gun. They also seized a computer from the family's living room.

Zarabozo's mother wasn't worried about what the agents had seized from her house. She knew that her son was a good boy. A neighbor confirmed that Zarabozo was "a boy any mother would want to have." Other neighbors told reporters that Zarabozo was polite and friendly, never loud or rowdy, never causing any problems in the neighborhood. A good kid.

Without comment, the FBI agents loaded up what they had retrieved from Guillermo Zarabozo's home for transportation and later forensic analysis. As luck would have it, Zarabozo's computer turned out to contain a treasure trove of evidence regarding the case. But it would take two separate forensic examinations, with two different specialists in two different law enforcement agencies, to unlock all the secrets hidden there.

CHAPTER TEN

October 2–November 13, 2007

The next prosecution hurdle was coming up fast: a pretrial detention hearing set for October 2 before United States Magistrate Judge William Turnoff. This would be a tougher test of the developing case against Kirby Archer and Guillermo Zarabozo. Their court-appointed attorneys, Allan Kaiser and Faith Mesnekoff, had had time to consult their clients, begin their own investigations, and prepare to argue that bail should be set for their clients who were, under law, presumed innocent until proven guilty at trial.

Michael Gilfarb again spoke for the prosecution team, announcing what everyone had already assumed: Kirby Archer and Guillermo Zarabozo "are presently under investigation for murder." The Coast Guard's extensive five-day search for the four missing Americans had finally been called off, and Jake and Kelley Branam, Sammy Kairy, and Scott Gamble were presumed dead. Gilfarb briefly repeated the suspects' tales that pirate/hijacker invaders had murdered the captain, his wife, and the crew, and then commandeered the *Joe Cool*, and went on: "Where the evidence is leading us so far is that these two individuals [Archer and Zarabozo] were involved in and had a hand in" the crimes. They had, in effect, planned the hijacking themselves. They were the hijackers, the kidnappers, and the killers. The mysterious three Cubans—dubbed Cuban #1, Cuban #2, and Cuban #3—were entirely fictitious. No murder weapon had been found, but Gilfarb now confirmed that three spent nine-millimeter shell casings had been recovered from the boat—two of them inside the cabin—contrary to the suspects' original story that all the hijackers' killings had taken place outside on the *Joe Cool*'s fly bridge or on the aft deck. More corroborating evidence had been found in Zarabozo's home: an empty box of nine-millimeter cartridges of the same type as the spent shell casings on the *Joe Cool*, a pistol lockbox, and an empty handcuff box. A handcuff key had been retrieved from the boat's bow. The prosecutors also had a surveillance video from Lou's Police and Security Equipment Store in Hialeah showing Archer and Zarabozo buying magazines for the same type of nine-millimeter ammunition. Gilfarb disclosed that suspected human blood had now been retrieved from the boat, both outside and inside the salon, the galley, and the cabin, and was under analysis for DNA evidence. The evidence was mounting, but obviously the investigators needed more time to follow the trail.

In response, arguing that her client should be released on bail, Faith Mesnekoff told Judge Turnoff that Guillermo Zarabozo was a naturalized citizen who had come to the United States from Cuba with his mother and family in 1999 and had no history of trouble with the law. "He and his family lead a simple, law-abiding life," she said. The prosecutors "have no physical evidence connecting Mr. Zarabozo to the murders that have been alleged."

Allan Kaiser argued that his client, Kirby Archer, was a former military policeman in the United States Army, who also had no criminal record. This was true in the sense that Archer had never been convicted of a crime, even though an arrest warrant had been issued for him in Arkansas for the alleged Wal-Mart theft. Kaiser said, "We haven't heard one shred of evidence that links my client to any homicide."

But Judge Turnoff concluded that each suspect was, indeed, a flight risk and a danger to the community. "There is circumstantial evidence to believe that four homicides took place here," he ruled. Archer and Zarabozo would remain in jail without bond.

On October 10, the prosecutors filed their first charging document, a criminal complaint alleging more formally the hijacking, kidnapping, and multiple murder charges against Kirby Logan Archer and Guillermo Alfonso Zarabozo, both now referred to as "the defendants" instead of "the survivors" or "the suspects." In support of their detailed complaint, the prosecutors relied upon the sworn affidavit of one person: Richard G. Blais, Special Agent, United States Coast Guard Investigative Service. He had accompanied his partner, FBI special agent David Nuñez, on Monday, September 24, on the long trip to the Coast Guard cutter *Confidence* to interview Kirby Archer and Guillermo Zarabozo about what had happened on the *Joe Cool*, and he had participated closely in the ongoing investigation since that day. Blais had a strong law enforcement background, beginning as a federal air marshal during the 1970s and 1980s, when airplane hijackings were more common, and then as a special agent with the United States Drug Enforcement Administration before joining the Coast Guard in 1984.

According to his affidavit, all factual statements contained therein were based upon Blais's own personal knowledge or information provided to him by other law enforcement officials and investigators of the Coast Guard and the FBI during the course of the ongoing investigation. He stated that the affidavit did not include "each and every fact and circumstance known to me, but only the facts and circumstances that I believe are sufficient to establish probable cause" that the crimes were committed by Archer and Zarabozo. This was fair warning to the defendants and their counsel that the government had more evidence than it had chosen to disclose in the complaint.

The affidavit reviewed much that was by then already public knowledge about the defendants' hijacker stories and the inconsistencies in the accounts told separately by Kirby Archer and Guillermo Zarabozo. For example, Archer had told investigators that the hijackers had two Glocks, while Zarabozo said it was one Glock and another weapon that was definitely not a Glock. Other new information included the surveillance video and gun store records establishing that Zarabozo, accompanied by Archer, had purchased two magazines for a Sig Sauer pistol. The Glock and the Sig Sauer were both semiautomatic pistols that could use the same ammunition; accessories such as magazines, however, weren't interchangeable. Another spent shell casing had recently been recovered from inside the *Joe Cool*, this one found inadvertently by Jon Branam when he moved fixtures about in the cabin of the boat after it was released back to the owners. This made a total of three shell casings found inside the *Joe Cool*'s cabin and a fourth that had been found lodged in the side of the aft fishing deck outside. All four were from nine-millimeter cartridges manufactured by Federal Premium. Forensic processing determined that all four were from the same firearm, likely a Glock.

Traces of human blood had been found inside the *Joe Cool* as well as outside on the aft deck. Another handcuff key had been recovered from Guillermo Zarabozo's luggage on the life raft. No distress calls had been received by the Coast Guard on September 22 in the relevant area. There was no evidence of any other vessel nearby at that time.

Raising a subject that would become part of a substantial evidence trail at the trial, Blais referred to a paper receipt found in Zarabozo's belongings from a T-Mobile store in Coral Gables, Florida, for a SIM card and activation kit purchased in the name Michael Zoiou. As would later be explained to a jury, no identification was required to purchase a SIM card. The purchaser simply filled out a standard form and provided payment for a set amount of usage. Thus, a SIM card amounted to an anonymous prepaid card for cell phone service that can be transferred from one phone to another. Using a SIM card, a particular cell phone call could be traced only to the listed purchaser of the card—in this case, the fictional Michael Zoiou—and not to the registered owner of the phone in which it was used. A SIM card purchased in a fictitious name virtually eliminated any traceable record of who actually made the call, much like a prepaid "throwaway" cell phone.

In light of the charges contained in the criminal complaint filed against Zarabozo and Archer, the earlier charges of flight to avoid prosecution and false statements to investigators were dismissed. They would be rearrested on the new, much more serious charges—capital charges—and then proceed to another series of appearances and detention hearings, none of which would result in their release on bond. The defendants would remain in custody in solitary confinement until their trial. They were now being held in an isolated special housing unit, or SHU, at the Federal Detention Center in downtown Miami, cells often used for high-profile defendants like Colombian drug kingpins.

Archer's attorney, Allan Kaiser, told Curt Anderson, a reporter for the Associated Press, that the evidence revealed against his client so far was thin. "It's a very difficult case," he said. "You have no physical evidence, really, linking my client to anything. You have no motive. . . . We're going forward to vigorously defend this case." A few days later, Kaiser told Jay Weaver, top crime reporter for the *Miami Herald*, "There's no question the victims were murdered. But I don't see any circumstantial evidence that impacts my client." Zarabozo's attorney, Mesnekoff, commented, "The government is grasping at straws."

United States Attorney R. Alexander Acosta took an emphatically different view. In a televised press conference, Acosta was surrounded by the top officers of the various federal investigative agencies that had participated in the search-and-rescue and the subsequent ongoing investigation. While Acosta admitted that the evidence was largely circumstantial and forensic, he announced, "We believe the evidence is strong. We shouldn't shy away from a case just because it's not an easy one."

Everyone acknowledged that no weapons had been found, nor any bodies recovered. Even prosecutors admitted it was unlikely that the victims' bodies would ever be found. Could a defendant be convicted of murder in the absence of a body? It was difficult, but not impossible, according to Miami attorneys willing to give opinions on the subject to the press.

One hauntingly familiar case was a murder at sea in 1998 in which there had been no body, no murder weapon, and no direct witnesses to the crime except, of course, the victim and the killer themselves. A New Jersey man, Michael Koblan, was suspected of killing his brother-in-law, Christopher Benedetto of Singer Island, on a boat off Palm Beach County and then dumping the body overboard. When Benedetto's wife was found strangled, her body concealed in her husband's bait freezer, Koblan became a suspect in that murder as well. In Palm Beach County, the case was known as "the Bait Freezer Case." Christopher Benedetto's body was never recovered, and Koblan claimed he was in New Jersey at the time Benedetto and his wife were murdered. Assistant United States Attorney Bruce Reinhart had been enlisted to help the local investigators and prosecutors in obtaining out-of-state subpoenas to further their investigation, but although the local authorities believed Koblan had committed the crimes, they more or less gave up trying to make the case against him. There was very little evidence, and the case seemed like a hopeless task.

Shortly thereafter, on a plane ride to Atlanta to argue an appeal in a public corruption case, Assistant United States Attorney John Kastrenakes asked his colleague Bruce Reinhart for something to read, since he was bored and had already finished his own work. This was typical of Kastrenakes, a high-energy prosecutor who enjoyed the mental exercise of trying to put difficult cases together and obtain convictions. In his own briefcase, Reinhart happened to have the file containing the subpoenas and other information on the Koblan case. He handed the file to Kastrenakes, just to distract him and give him something to read during the rest of the flight. After studying his friend's file, Kastrenakes said, "You know, I think I can make this case. Let's take another look at it."

Kastrenakes took the file from Reinhart and soon took over the case from the local authorities. He went to work. This was just the kind of puzzle Kastrenakes enjoyed, and he became deeply committed to his case and to the family of the victims. "They were just wonderful people," he said, years later, referring to the Benedetto family. He uncovered a motive: it seemed that Koblan owed his brother-in-law about $100,000 for a business loan. Working with the FBI, Kastrenakes eventually determined that during the relevant time period, Koblan had in fact slipped into Palm Beach County under an alias, stayed at a hotel on Singer Island, and made a single traceable phone call back to New Jersey from his hotel room. During the investigation, Koblan had made inconsistent statements about his alibi. At a federal trial more than five years after the crime, Kastrenakes and his trial partner, Steve Carlton, used this circumstantial evidence against Koblan to win a conviction in the murders of both Benedetto and his wife. The case became the subject of a television drama called *The Investigators*.

There were obvious similarities to the *Joe Cool* case, and prosecutors Karen Gilbert, Jeffrey Tsai, and Michael Gilfarb knew John Kastrenakes well as a colleague in the United States Attorneys' Offices. They consulted him about their own case, occasionally discussing strategy and bouncing ideas off him.

When the criminal complaint against Archer and Zarabozo was filed on October 10, 2007, the case was entered into the official criminal docket as *United States of America v. Kirby Logan Archer and Guillermo Alfonso Zarabozo*. By random assignment, the case went to the Honorable Paul C. Huck, United States district judge, who was then charged with managing every aspect of the prosecution until a final conclusion was reached: dismissal, guilty plea, or jury verdict. The official clerk's docket sheet for the case would eventually cover two years, forty-seven typed pages with 448 separate entries, in addition to literally thousands of pages of typed transcript prepared by Judge Huck's official court reporter, Patricia Sanders. A capital criminal case was a crushing responsibility for the judge as well as the lawyers. Judge Huck was an experienced, highly regarded judge known for working long hours and requiring the lawyers appearing before him to do the same. This wasn't his only case, of course, and he managed his lengthy docket of both criminal and civil cases with a firm hand. Judge Huck was regarded as evenhanded, fair, and very intelligent and committed to his work. Huck's assignment to this case put all the lawyers on notice that they would be working extra hard—not to mention, extra fast— and that the judge would demand that they be prepared, prompt, and succinct in their presentations. In his chambers, Judge Huck was assisted by a staff of bright, hardworking young lawyers: law clerks Abigail Corbett, Jason Gould, Aimee Ferrer, and Evelyn Williams, who also served as the courtroom deputy. The prosecutors and defense lawyers were pleased that the case had been assigned to Judge Huck, since they knew that one of the best legal minds on the federal bench would be carefully overseeing the case, and they could count on his experience, his expertise, and his resolute commitment to fairness to all the lawyers and the defendants.

Kirby Archer and Guillermo Zarabozo were formally indicted by a federal grand jury on October 25, 2007. The indictment spelled out the charges against them:

> Count 1: Conspiracy to Commit Violence against Maritime Navigation;
>
> Count 2: Seizing and Exercising Control over a Ship by Force, Threat Thereof, and Intimidation;
>
> Count 3: Performance of an Act of Violence Likely to Endanger the Safe Navigation of a Ship;
>
> Counts 4–7: Murder in the First Degree of Jake H. Branam; Kelley S. Branam; Scott M. Gamble; and Samuel A. Kairy;
>
> Counts 8–11: Kidnapping of each of the four victims; and
>
> Count 12: Robbery (of the *Joe Cool*).

The indictment would later be amended in two separate superseding indictments to include Counts 13–16, Causing Death through Use of a Firearm in a Crime of Violence as to each of the victims. The case finally went to trial almost a year later in September 2008, on the last superseding indictment with a total of sixteen counts.

Speaking for the Branam family, Jon Branam told *Miami Herald* reporter Jay Weaver that the indictment was encouraging. "It won't bring our loved ones back to life, but it's a small battle won," he said. "At least, we now have hope that there will be justice."

Shackled at the wrists and ankles, Kirby Archer and Guillermo Zarabozo were arraigned on the indictment, both entering pleas of not guilty to all charges. The following day, Assistant Federal Public Defender Anthony Natale was added to assist Mesnekoff in defending Kirby Archer.

Now the defense lawyers would have to address a very difficult issue. The indictment charged Archer and Zarabozo with federal capital crimes, for which there were only two possible penalties if they were convicted: life in prison without parole or the death penalty. With the possibility of their clients' very lives hanging in the balance, the lawyers knew they needed help to address the arcane, seldom-used federal procedure to determine whether the death penalty or life in prison would be sought against Kirby Archer or Guillermo Zarabozo. First, they had to find and associate defense lawyers with actual experience in this special procedure in order to defend their clients properly.

MEANWHILE, on Star Island, Jeff Branam received a letter from BOATPIX.com, Inc., a company of professional photographers who took random shots of beautiful boats from helicopters and peddled them to the boat owners. The form letter stated: "We have pictures of your boat JOE COOL taken while photographing" in Miami on September 22, 2007. It was like a voice from the grave. Could the *Joe Cool* have been photographed setting out from the Miami Beach Marina on the fatal trip? The date was the same, but it seemed too much of a coincidence. The photographs could have been taken at any time on September 22, while the *Joe Cool* was out on an early-morning fishing charter, or returning, or simply moving in or out of the Government Cut channel. Jeff called the FBI, told them about the letter, and asked what he should do. The agents told him to order the photographs and let them know when they arrived. Jeff filled out the form at the bottom of the letter with his credit card information and sent it out.

* * *

MICHELLE Rowe, Kirby Archer's second ex-wife and the mother of their two sons, soon read about the tragedy aboard the *Joe Cool* and the association of Kirby Archer's name with that event. She sympathized with the families of the victims, and she decided to write a note of condolence to Scott Gamble's mother. Michelle didn't know Scott's mother—she had never even heard of any of the people she was reading about in the news, and she had had no idea that her ex-husband Kirby Archer had gone to Florida—but she knew firsthand what havoc he could wreak upon a family's life.

Michelle sent an e-mail:

Sorry for you loss

I can't imagine what you are going through there is not a day that goes by that I don't think of you and your family. My name is Michelle Rowe I am the ex-wife of Kirby Archer I have been trying for the past 5 years to get Kirby put away he is an evil evil man and I hope this time he does not get away with this horrific crime. Every person that he has ever come in contact with he has betrayed I am fighting and doing everything I can to make sure that he will no longer slip through the cracks.

May God Bless You and Your Family,
Michelle

CHAPTER ELEVEN

Learned Counsel

United States District Judge Paul C. Huck held a status conference in the case of *United States of America v. Kirby Logan Archer and Guillermo Alfonso Zarabozo* on October 30, 2007, to address some pending issues. Prior to the conference, the prosecution team had been contacted by two separate inmates at the Federal Detention Center in Miami, both of whom claimed to have important information concerning incriminating statements that defendant Guillermo Zarabozo had made to them about the case—statements that amounted to a confession of sorts. The informants, Antwan Hall and Daniel Noel, had been housed together near Zarabozo in SHU, close enough to carry on conversations between their cells. Hall claimed to have had direct conversations with Zarabozo concerning Zarabozo's role in the murders, and Noel told the prosecutors that he could verify Zarabozo's statements to Hall since he had overheard their conversations. Such informants are usually referred to as "cooperating informants" by the prosecution and called "jailhouse snitches" by the defense, off the record.

Prisoners who came forward with such stories were always a big gamble for the prosecution. In the first place, these were people who had already been convicted of, or pled guilty to, serious crimes themselves, so their reliability was "questionable" at best. In addition, they were generally motivated by hope of personal gain, such as a reduced sentence, in exchange for their testimony. In this case, both of the cooperating informants already had a previous connection to prosecutor Michael Gilfarb, and one of them, Antwan Hall, had actually been represented in his own case by Faith Mesnekoff, the same public defender who was now defending Guillermo Zarabozo in this case. The resulting legal triangle was a complicated matter that would be deferred for later determination.

But just in case the government decided to go forward with the informants and the judge allowed them to testify, Faith Mesnekoff asked Judge Huck to permit a private attorney, William Matthewman, to cross-examine Antwan Hall at trial so that she wouldn't have a conflict in her representation of Zarabozo. Matthewman was a well-known criminal defense lawyer in private practice, so he would have to be appointed under the federal Criminal Justice Act (CJA).

Faith Mesnekoff had another reason for wanting Matthewman to be appointed to assist her. He would qualify as "learned counsel" for Guillermo Zarabozo to assist her with the arcane, little-used procedures developed especially for federal capital cases. This was a precise, complex, little-known area of federal law. Since the prosecution team had not yet announced whether they intended to seek the death penalty for Kirby Archer or Guillermo Zarabozo, the defense teams had to proceed on the assumption that the death penalty was still "on the table" for both defendants. That meant, as a practical matter, that lawyers for both Kirby Archer and Guillermo Zarabozo had to seek the appointment of specialist lawyers, "learned counsel," to assist them in preparing for trial in case the prosecutors sought the death penalty for their clients.

The United States Code contains specific provisions in recognition of the fact that few criminal defense lawyers, no matter how capable as public defenders or in private practice, have had actual experience in representing a defendant in a federal capital case. In such a case, the decision of whether to seek the death penalty or life in prison without parole was ultimately made by the U.S. attorney general before the case was tried. This decision must be made in advance of the actual trial for two reasons. First, defendants facing a possible death penalty were entitled to the appointment of learned counsel to assist their attorneys not only in preparation for trial but also to participate in a specific process whereby the defense team was allowed to make its best case on their client's behalf that the death penalty should not be sought against them. Second, if the death penalty was sought against a defendant, the government was entitled to a special jury, a so-called death-qualified jury, in that trial.

In selecting a death-qualified jury, the lawyers or the judge questioned prospective jurors specifically about their opinions concerning the death penalty in order to ascertain, for example, whether they had any moral or religious objections, whether they could agree to impose the death penalty on the defendant if the prosecution proved its case at trial, and so forth. According to criminal defense lawyers—and some studies that they cite—death-qualified juries were more likely to convict a defendant than other criminal juries. According to them, the jurors selected through this process were ready, willing, and able to convict—even predisposed to convict—and likely to favor the prosecution over the defense. They believed that the battle for a defendant's acquittal could be lost as soon as a death-qualified jury was seated.

These were among the reasons that federal law provided some safeguards for a defendant in a death-eligible case. These safeguards included ensuring that a defendant facing a possible death penalty had the opportunity to be represented by counsel with special knowledge and experience in this area, and that such counsel was afforded a specific opportunity for input into the penalty decision—that is, whether the government should seek only life in prison or the death penalty.

IN choosing William Matthewman to assist her as learned counsel, Faith Mesnekoff had found exactly what Guillermo Zarabozo needed if the prosecution team sought the death penalty against him: a highly experienced criminal defense lawyer who had worked on forty to fifty death-eligible cases as learned counsel and knew exactly how to present the best case for life in prison instead of the death penalty. To Matthewman, Zarabozo was just a gullible kid who fell for Kirby Archer's "international man of mystery" ruse hook, line, and sinker and went along for what turned out to be an extremely bad ride. Matthewman believed that Kirby Archer was the real villain of the piece, a ruthless, unscrupulous killer who manipulated Guillermo Zarabozo for his own nefarious purposes.

A former policeman who rose to the rank of sergeant in the Miami Police Department before going to law school, William Matthewman had tried well-known federal capital cases around the country and even in Puerto Rico. He was recognized as smart, thorough, and likable. Even prosecutors respected his legal talent and his professional courtesy. In a Miami federal courtroom, Matthewman had once represented a defendant in the so-called Boulder Boys case; "boulder" referred to the large chunks of crack cocaine that the defendants were accused of making and selling—and fighting and killing over. This was during a time of great societal and legislative conflict over the imposition of the death penalty for federal crimes. Lawyers like Matthewman were beginning to press their claims that the death penalty was being sought—and applied—disproportionately to blacks and minorities over whites convicted of the same crimes.

In 1995, Matthewman raised this objection in a motion to United States District Judge Ursula Ungaro-Benages in Miami, who was presiding over the Boulder Boys case (in which all the defendants were black), asking her to declare the death penalty unconstitutional as applied for this reason. Judge Ungaro-Benages denied the motion, but eventually several respected studies would prove Matthewman's analysis had some merit, and death penalty procedures were refined to ensure fairness in the process of selecting and prosecuting death-eligible cases.

When William Matthewman learned that the Honorable Paul C. Huck was the judge in this case, he thought, *Hmm, this is going to go a bit quicker than usual.* Judge Huck was well known and admired for the brisk pace at which he moved his cases along. Matthewman immediately set to work with Faith Mesnekoff on the enormous challenge of convincing the attorney general of the United States that the death penalty should not be sought against Guillermo Zarabozo. Although Matthewman had a full case load in his private practice, he made time to review Zarabozo and his case thoroughly. And he began to develop a strategy that might save his client's life.

But first, he wanted to go look at the crime scene, the fishing vessel *Joe Cool*, himself. It was something he always did when he represented a client, and Matthewman believed that he learned something important every time he went to a crime scene to experience firsthand the nuances and the feel of the place. As he inspected the interior of the charter fishing boat and climbed around the fly bridge, he was struck by how small the areas were, how close the spaces.

He tried to envision what had happened there. Could a single person, one man acting alone, really murder four people on two different levels on this small boat on the open ocean? It had certainly been an ambush, so the killer would have had surprise on his side. Or would these murders have necessarily required two men and two guns? It was a subject he would ponder often as he worked on the *Joe Cool* case.

KIRBY Archer's CJA attorney, Allan Kaiser, chose Humberto "Bert" Dominguez as learned counsel to assist him in representing Archer, since he knew Dominguez had prior experience in a federal capital case. When Allan Kaiser asked him to assist as learned counsel in representing Kirby Archer, Dominguez knew from experience that it would be an incredible amount of work. He had been following the *Joe Cool* case in the news accounts, and at first he thought the case against the defendants would be difficult to prove unless one "flipped" and testified against the other. He was also concerned about the heavy emotional burden of the case, since he would be, at least in part, responsible for his client's very life. After some reflection, he agreed to take the case. Kaiser and Dominguez went to work.

Kirby Archer's lawyers considered it more likely that the government would seek the death penalty for their client than for Zarabozo, because Archer was older, more experienced, and the presumed mastermind of the crimes. Archer was already on the run from a fugitive warrant when the murders took place on the *Joe Cool*. Kaiser and Dominguez went to meet with Kirby Archer in the Federal Detention Center in downtown Miami. When they met, Dominguez assessed Archer as a fairly clean-cut, reasonably pleasant fellow who was not likely to be a "difficult client." Archer seemed intelligent and he followed his lawyers' instructions fairly well, according to Dominguez. These impressions were weighed in comparison with his prior experience with other federal criminal defendants, a fairly lenient standard by which to judge a man, to say the least. Bert Dominguez knew that Archer was worried about his case because he was smart enough to recognize the severity of the charges against him, and Dominguez agreed that he had good reason to be concerned.

Kaiser and Dominguez also believed that if the defendants were tried together in a joint trial, Zarabozo was likely to testify against Archer, and that would not bode well for their client. In that scenario, it was possible that Zarabozo would be believed by a jury, and maybe even acquitted, while Archer could get the death penalty. Their first step, the lawyers decided, was to meet with United States Attorney Alex Acosta and the prosecutors to determine whether the government would agree not to seek the death penalty for their client. They were also looking for an agreement for "severance," that is, separate trials for Archer and Zarabozo. Kaiser and Dominquez were not hopeful, but they had to try.

The lawyers set up a meeting with Acosta and prosecutors Karen Gilbert, Jeffrey Tsai, and Michael Gilfarb. They made their best case for life in prison instead of the death penalty and separate trials for the two defendants. The prosecution team and the U.S. attorney listened politely. Predictably, however, the prosecutors and their boss would not agree to forgo the death penalty against Archer or to sever the trials of the two defendants. Kirby Archer's lawyers were disappointed but not really surprised. The burden on these two critical issues would rest squarely on the shoulders of Kaiser and Dominguez.

The lawyers decided to proceed along two tracks: First, they would start assembling their "mitigation package" on Kirby Archer's behalf to be presented to the Capital Review Committee in Washington, D.C., concerning the issue of the death penalty or life in prison without parole; second, they would try to identify factors to persuade Judge Huck to order separate trials for the defendants, to lessen the possibility of Zarabozo testifying against Archer at a joint trial.

Kaiser and Dominguez set to work preparing their mitigation package explaining why the death penalty should not be sought against Kirby Archer. The Capital Review Committee, a select, little-known group of government lawyers in Washington, would evaluate the case and then make a recommendation to the U.S. attorney general concerning the appropriate penalty to be sought. The committee would include the deputy attorney general and the assistant attorney general for the criminal division (or their designees). This procedure was instituted by the then U.S. attorney general Janet Reno in 1994 during the passing of legislation significantly expanding the grounds for imposing the death penalty in a federal criminal case. Kaiser and Dominguez intended to use every resource at their disposal to persuade the committee to recommend life in prison rather than the death penalty for Archer. They knew that regardless of the committee's recommendation, the attorney general alone would still make the ultimate decision.

Kaiser and Dominguez marshaled their information about their client and began their task. Much of Kirby Archer's background was already well known. He had served in the army, including time as an investigator with the military police, before going AWOL and earning a less-than-honorable discharge. Since January 2007, Archer had been on the run, accused of stealing $92,000 in cash and checks from his employer, Wal-Mart. He was also facing serious charges of child sexual abuse in Arkansas. Kirby Archer had been in the midst of a third troubled marriage when he went on the lam, and his past wives could be counted on for damning evidence of his character. There were lurid divorce court filings accusing him of adultery, a homosexual relationship, child sexual abuse, and domestic violence. Even a former relative in Arizona had commented to a reporter that he was glad Archer was locked up as "there was something wrong with him."

On the positive side—well, there wasn't much hard evidence for the lawyers to work with. Kirby Archer was a man of extremely humble beginnings. His parents, Betty and Sam Archer, ran a store in a tiny Arkansas town and lived in a small mobile home next door to it; Kirby had lived with them after his most recent divorce. An issue in his divorce from ex-wife Michelle Rowe had been "family resources" available to help care for the couple's two young sons. Although the Arkansas court concluded that Kirby Archer had more family members to help care for the young children than his ex-wife did, in fact, his mother was frequently busy running the store, and after his father became partially disabled, she had to drive a truck part time to make ends meet. The custody decree had been reversed in 2006 and his former wife Michelle was awarded custody of the children.

The fact that Kirby Archer had served in the military and as an investigator for the military police could be interpreted as "helping law enforcement." But his background could also be used against him in an argument that Archer had used his special military police investigator's experience and knowledge in planning and carrying out the heinous crimes on the *Joe Cool*. At least Archer had not actually been convicted of a crime previously, though he had been accused of them. Investigators in three states had been looking at Archer for serious charges of child sexual abuse, but he had not been criminally charged. This was probably due in part to his flight from Arkansas, one step ahead of investigators there.

There was no evidence that Archer had ever killed anyone before, either during his military service or in private life. The only really favorable fact the lawyers had was that his parents—at least his mother—seemed to love and support him completely. When he met them in Miami, Bert Dominguez thought of Betty and Sam Archer as a salt-of-the-earth couple who believed their son.

Kaiser and Dominguez would also argue that the evidence against their client was purely circumstantial and shouldn't be used as a basis upon which to take his life. Would these arguments outweigh the tragic loss of innocent life on the *Joe Cool*? They knew that lawyers for Guillermo Zarabozo were separately preparing their own mitigation memorandum for their client to be presented to the Capital Review Committee, but the separate teams for the defendants did not work together or share information.

Kirby Archer's attorneys recognized that the specter of the death penalty for their client was huge. At some point, they might have to discuss the possibility of a plea agreement with their client.

CHAPTER TWELVE

Jailhouse Snitches

Now that learned counsel had been appointed for both Kirby Archer and Guillermo Zarabozo, their defense teams turned their attention to another crucial issue in the case: the jailhouse snitches. The defense teams already knew who the snitches were—Antwan Hall and Daniel Noel. Both inmates carried a lot of baggage. Antwan Hall had been referred to in the press as "a low-level street thug." He had been found guilty of possession of a firearm by a convicted felon after a jury trial in which he contested his guilt by attacking the credibility of the arresting officers. Hall was serving a sentence of thirty months in prison to be followed by three years of supervised release. Hall had an obvious motive to provide information against Kirby Archer and Guillermo Zarabozo, since he was trying to get his sentence reduced by acting as a cooperating informant for the government.

Hall's cell mate, Daniel Noel, was indicted for conspiracy to deal in firearms without a license; dealing in firearms without a license; false or fictitious statements in connection with the acquisition of a firearm; and false statements to a federal firearms licensee. In other words, Noel was a small-time freelance dealer in weapons of dubious origin. Noel pleaded guilty to conspiracy to engage in the business of dealing in firearms without a license and making false or fictitious statements in connection with the acquisition of a firearm. He was sentenced to twenty-four months of imprisonment to be followed by two years of supervised release. Noel's plea agreement with the government contained standard language requiring him to cooperate with authorities in any investigation.

According to court documents, Hall was caught trying to smuggle contraband into the Federal Detention Center and thereafter placed in SHU as punishment. It is unclear why Noel was also placed in SHU as Hall's cell mate.

Both of the defense teams were also aware that there were complications in the relationships between the snitches, or "confidential informants," as the government preferred to identify them, and lawyers on both sides of this case. According to their information, Antwan Hall was already "working for," or cooperating with, Assistant United States Attorney Michael Gilfarb in other cases in an effort to get his sentence reduced in exchange for helpful information. Since Gilfarb was a prosecutor in this case against their client, Zarabozo's defense team was particularly suspicious. They knew that these incarcerated felons would be highly motivated to cooperate with Gilfarb and the other prosecutors in an attempt to get their own sentences reduced, or at least get moved out of SHU, which is a very restricted prison environment. Zarabozo had been placed in a cell in SHU "in close proximity" to these informants, another fact that made his lawyers wary. Inmates talk to each other in prison, especially to those in nearby cells. If Hall and Noel were housed close to Zarabozo, they would have ample opportunity to try to manipulate him into revealing some information they could use.

To further complicate matters, Assistant Public Defender

Faith Mesnekoff had represented Antwan Hall at his own trial—a trial that he had obviously lost, and consequently he was now serving a lengthy term in the Federal Detention Center. Apparently, there were also some postconviction complaints from Hall that he hadn't really wanted to go to trial—he said that he had wanted to negotiate a plea—but he claimed that he had been persuaded to go to trial instead by his attorney, Faith Mesnekoff. According to Hall, she had told him that she thought he "had a good case" and should go to trial.

Guillermo Zarabozo's defense team conducted discovery and legal research on the issues and eventually addressed the matter in a motion to suppress testimony of the jailhouse informants Hall and Noel and a request for an evidentiary hearing. This motion was filed only by William Matthewman, the CJA co-counsel appointed to represent him. Matthewman's conclusion was that the court should suppress the testimony of both jailhouse informants, now publicly identified in this document as Antwan Hall and Daniel Noel, concerning anything they claimed to have heard from defendant Guillermo Zarabozo.

In support of this position, Matthewman accused the government of at least taking advantage of the lucky proximity of these three men—Hall, Noel, and Zarabozo—if not deliberately setting up the entire situation so that Hall and Noel could get Zarabozo to talk to them about his case. Some courts have ruled that if there is an actual agreement or prearrangement between prosecutors and the jailhouse informants to seek out a particular defendant's testimony, then the informants are virtually "government agents" and their evidence cannot be used.

Matthewman's motion to suppress testimony also noted that Hall and Noel were "practiced criminals" and very experienced in the criminal justice system. By contrast, Guillermo Zarabozo "has never previously been arrested and has no prior experience with the criminal justice system."

The clear implication was that Hall and Noel knew how this particular game was played, having been around the block, so to speak, but Zarabozo didn't really know or understand what was going on. Therefore, he was an easy target from whom to get incriminating information about his case—maybe even a confession of guilt.

If the court granted the motion to suppress testimony, then neither Antwan Hall nor Daniel Noel would be permitted to testify at trial. This would eliminate any potential ethical conflict for both Faith Mesnekoff and William Matthewman and would make the government's prior motion to disqualify Zarabozo's counsel moot.

Matthewman's motion to suppress testimony also disclosed the substance of what Hall and Noel claimed they had heard Zarabozo say. This was the first time that Zarabozo's account—as alleged by Hall and Noel—was made public, and the story was riveting. According to the motion, Zarabozo had told the following story:

Zarabozo and Archer had chartered the *Joe Cool*, which they planned to divert to Cuba so that Archer could "get established there," since Cuba did not extradite criminals or suspects to the United States, and Archer would be safe in Cuba. There would be no risk to Zarabozo of getting stuck in Cuba, he believed, since he could go back home to the United States at any time because he was a U.S. citizen. His Florida driver's license had been found in the abandoned *Joe Cool*. Once aboard the *Joe Cool* and well out to sea, according to Zarabozo's story, Archer got into an argument with "the driver of the boat" (i.e., Jake Branam). Archer wanted Branam to take the boat to Cuba. Branam refused. Zarabozo said that Archer reached into Zarabozo's luggage and retrieved Zarabozo's gun. Then Archer pointed Zarabozo's gun at Jake Branam. While the arguing continued, according to Zarabozo, "the only woman" on the boat (i.e., Kelley Branam) shouted at the other crew members to call the Coast Guard. Then, Zarabozo said, Archer shot and killed Jake Branam, Kelley Branam, and the two remaining crew members, Scott Gamble and Sammy Kairy, with Zarabozo's gun. Zarabozo agreed to throw the four bodies overboard because they had all been shot with his gun, and he was afraid that if they got caught, Archer would blame him for the murders and use the gun as evidence that it was Zarabozo, not Archer, who had killed them.

Zarabozo's remarkable story continued:

> [After Zarabozo] threw the bodies overboard, he cleaned the boat. . . . Archer had difficulty driving the boat. Archer became angry and frustrated and began to search for fired casings, becoming more angry and frustrated because he found only one. . . . Furthermore, Zarabozo advised that they decided to deploy the life raft and unload their luggage into the life raft with the intent to float to Cuba. . . . once on the raft, "they" threw their guns into the ocean.

This was the first public glimpse of what might have happened aboard the *Joe Cool*, and the story was repeated in sensational news accounts. According to Antwan Hall, this was the first time that Zarabozo mentioned the presence of two guns, although the government and investigators had theorized all along that there must have been two weapons— Zarabozo's Glock and Archer's Sig Sauer—because other evidence in the case showed Zarabozo and Archer buying ammunition, clips, and accessories at Lou's Police and Security Equipment Store for both a Glock and a Sig Sauer, equipment that couldn't be used interchangeably in a Sig Sauer and a Glock.

At any rate, Guillermo Zarabozo's story—there were no pirates or hijackers and Kirby Archer did everything—was now out, and it was not really news to Archer's defense team, who had assumed all along that this was likely. A separate trial for their client, Kirby Archer, was even more important now that they knew what Zarabozo would say about him.

At a contentious hearing before Judge Huck, the prosecution team vehemently denied that they had had any "agreement or prearrangement" with Hall or Noel to seek out evidence from Zarabozo. After considering the issues, Judge Huck left open the possibility that at least Hall might be barred from testifying at trial. The judge set another hearing to consider that matter further.

But then the issue became moot because the prosecution team decided not to call the informants to testify at trial. The only exception might be, according to prosecutor Jeffrey Tsai, if Zarabozo testified at trial and told a different story from the one he had told Antwan Hall. In that case, they might call Hall as a rebuttal witness.

In May 2008, Judge Huck denied Archer's motion to sever trial from Zarabozo. The evidence against the codefendants, the judge ruled, was "inextricably intertwined," calling for one trial. He said, "It looks like we're going to trial with both defendants."

While the motions concerning disqualification of Faith Mesnekoff and suppression of the testimony of jailhouse informants Hall and Noel were still pending, Matthewman and Mesnekoff had begun to implement a new strategy for Guillermo Zarabozo's defense. When they considered that the time was right, they would unveil their strategy in a motion trying to persuade Judge Huck to allow certain evidence of their client's innocence to be admitted at trial.

CHAPTER THIRTEEN

Polygraphs

Faith Mesnekoff and William Matthewman continued their preparations for the defense on the assumption that the government would be seeking the death penalty against their client, Guillermo Zarabozo, since they had heard nothing to the contrary. What they knew so far about the case was that the evidence was entirely circumstantial, since there were no eyewitnesses to the killings on the *Joe Cool* except Zarabozo and Archer, both of whom were accused of the crimes. There were no bodies, no fingerprint evidence, and no DNA evidence directly linking either defendant to the crimes with which they were charged. The lack of direct physical evidence—fingerprints and DNA—was not surprising since no weapons had been found and all the surfaces on the *Joe Cool*, both interior and exterior, had been subjected to degradation by wind and saltwater spray for several days before they could be examined.

Since Guillermo Zarabozo was a teenager with no criminal history, his lawyers thought this would be an ideal situation in which to retain polygraph examiners "in an effort to find the truth in this case," as the defense team put it. Because Zarabozo had no previous offenses, he wouldn't have to explain any prior illegal conduct. He was practically a blank slate, which would make it easier for polygraph examiners to focus their inquiry on the circumstances of this single event. Faith Mesnekoff had moved on to another assignment, so the defense team now consisted of William Matthewman and two lawyers from the Federal Public Defender's Office: Anthony J. Natale, supervisory assistant federal public defender, and Brian L. Stekloff, assistant federal public defender.

Working together, the defense team selected "two leading polygraph examination experts": John J. Palmatier, Ph.D., who had worked extensively for the Michigan State Police, and Thomas K. Mote Sr., a forensic polygraph examiner with twenty-six years experience. The team considered both to be highly regarded experts with vast experience in their field, including years of work and hundreds of polygraphs undertaken to assist law enforcement as well as defendants. According to the defense team, they were not "hired guns," meaning they were not examiners selected because of any defense bias; both men "administered their examinations in an objective, professional manner without a preconceived outcome."

On February 21, 2008, Dr. Palmatier conducted a polygraph examination of Guillermo Zarabozo. He began with an extensive pretest interview, asking Zarabozo in detail about the allegations against him in the case. One of the most fundamental issues in the case was whether Zarabozo had been a knowing, willing participant in killing the crew and stealing the *Joe Cool* or whether he was Kirby Archer's innocent dupe who had been taken by surprise when Archer started shooting on the boat. During the lengthy interview, Palmatier reported that Zarabozo "denied knowledge and/or participation in [the crimes] . . . prior to hearing a series of gunshots. . . . [He also denied] being a party to any conspiracy or ever firing a firearm while aboard the *Joe Cool*," although he no longer denied that he had been on the boat.

Dr. Palmatier connected Guillermo Zarabozo to the polygraph machine and began his test. He asked Zarabozo the following questions and obtained the following answers:

1. While on the *Joe Cool*, did you shoot anyone? *Answer—No*.
2. Before hearing the first gunshot, had you talked with Kirby Archer about shooting anyone on board the *Joe Cool*? *Answer—No*.
3. Before hearing the first gunshot, had you talked with Kirby Archer about stealing the *Joe Cool*? *Answer—No*.

After concluding his analysis of Zarabozo's polygraph, Dr. Palmatier concluded that "there is a 99.9 percent chance or greater that Mr. Zarabozo answered the relevant questions truthfully." Palmatier had videotaped his entire examination of Zarabozo.

The second examiner, Thomas K. Mote Sr., had conducted over five hundred polygraph examinations annually for the Miami-Dade Police Department's Homicide Bureau from 1984 to 1997. Mote then entered private practice and had served as a government witness for the State of Florida and in United States District Court for the Southern District of Florida. On March 18, 2008, Mote conducted an examination of Guillermo Zarabozo "to determine whether Mr. Zarabozo is being deceptive when he states he had no prior knowledge of what Mr. Archer planned to do and eventually did do on the *Joe Cool*." Mote began by interviewing Zarabozo about the allegations in the case and the events that took place on the *Joe Cool*. Zarabozo told Mote a bizarre new version of events: Kirby Archer was a former military investigator who was now working as a spy for the

Central Intelligence Agency. He had high government contacts and was planning a big job. Zarabozo met Archer while both were hanging around a Hialeah auto shop, and eventually Archer had recruited him for the new job. They would begin by going to Bimini together to do some bodyguarding work. Then, according to Zarabozo, he and Archer planned to move on to Cuba where they would be conducting high-level intelligence and security work together in Cuba and possibly in Venezuela for the CIA. Zarabozo said that he believed they were going to Bimini first on the *Joe Cool* for the bodyguarding job. He had no idea that anything illegal might happen on the boat until he heard Kirby Archer begin shooting and killing the victims. Acher then threatened Zarabozo with a gun to make him help throw the bodies overboard and clean up the boat. He lied to investigators when he was picked up from the life raft, Zarabozo said, because he was "stressed, confused, and in fear."

After the initial interview with Zarabozo, Mote also used the "probable lie control question" technique and then asked questions relevant to Zarabozo's alleged participation in the crimes. According to the document filed by the defense team, the following questions were asked during the examination and Zarabozo gave the following answers:

Q1: Regarding what you knew before that charter boat the *Joe Cool* crew was killed and the boat hijacked last September 22, 2007: Do you intend to answer truthfully each question about that?

A1: Yes.

Q2: Other than what you now know: At any time before the crew members of the *Joe Cool* were shot: For any reason did you really know that was going to happen?

A2: No.

Q3: When you said that before the shooting occurred on that boat the *Joe Cool*; that the only reason you were on board, was to travel to Bimini and participate in pre-planned security job with Kirby Archer, did you lie about that?

A3: No.

Q4: When you said that you expected to participate in a future CIA assignment with Kirby Archer either in Cuba or Venezuela after the Bimini security job was done: Did you lie about that?

A4: No.

Q5: When you said that you brought your handgun for use on the Bimini security job and that it was never intended to be used by you or Kirby Archer to hijack that boat the *Joe Cool*: Did you lie about that?

A5: No.

Mote analyzed and evaluated Zarabozo's answers to these five questions, according to the defense team, and determined that Zarabozo "was not being deceptive and answered the questions truthfully." But for the time being, the polygraph tests and Zarabozo's strange new story about working with Kirby Archer for the CIA were kept under wraps.

The real question—the first object of this entire exercise—was whether Judge Paul Huck would recognize the polygraph results as reliable scientific evidence and permit the defense team to introduce them at this trial. All the lawyers knew that would be a long shot. It was a basic premise in federal criminal trials that polygraph examination results were not admissible at trial; polygraph tests were still traditionally viewed as unreliable and not sufficiently "scientific" to be considered evidence by a jury in the same way as, for example, fingerprint evidence or DNA analysis. Also, there was the concern that admitting such evidence could be overly persuasive to a jury, usurping their basic function at trial, which was to determine whether witnesses testified truthfully. Otherwise, the argument went, why have a jury trial at all? Why not just give all defendants polygraph tests and rely on the results to resolve the question of guilt or innocence, and let it go at that?

For decades, polygraph examination results had been excluded from federal criminal courts, period. But a tiny chink had appeared in the previously ironclad armor of that rule in 1989 in the case of *United States v. Piccinonna*, in which the court stated that such evidence could be admitted under certain conditions, in summary: (1) where there is a stipulation among the parties that the evidence shall be admitted or (2) where the evidence would be used only to impeach or corroborate the testimony of a witness at trial.

With a June 2008 trial date fast approaching, Zarabozo's defense team decided they were ready to raise this subject with Judge Huck. On May 1, 2008, the defense team filed its motion to admit the polygraph evidence. But rather than asking the court to admit these polygraph examinations to establish Zarabozo's innocence in their case in chief, they wanted Judge Huck to rule that they could introduce the polygraph test results only as rebuttal testimony if—undoubtedly, *when*—the prosecutors attacked Zarabozo's truthfulness in his testimony in his own defense at trial. It was a foregone conclusion that Guillermo Zarabozo would have to testify in his own defense at trial. Under those circumstances, there was simply no alternative for his defense team but to put him on the stand, let him tell his story, and hope for the best.

In response, on May 15, 2008, the prosecution team filed a motion in limine to exclude the results of Zarabozo's polygraphs. In summary, the prosecutors argued that the polygraphs were not admissible because Zarabozo's lawyers had not given notice until after the two polygraphs had been administered, not before, as was necessary according to the government. Also, the evidence was inadmissible under the Federal Rules of Evidence pursuant to the government's analysis, and in any event, the polygraph evidence was unreliable. Both sides had to agree that the entire matter of the admissibility of this evidence was discretionary with Judge Huck.

THE defense lawyers' motion not only raised the issue of the admissibility of polygraph results but also quoted questions and answers from the tests administered to Zarabozo. These test results seemed to exonerate Zarabozo completely. He had clearly and unambiguously denied any advance knowledge of or participation in the crimes aboard the *Joe Cool,* and two experienced examiners analyzed his answers as truthful—according to Dr. Palmatier, a "99.9 percent chance or greater" that Zarabozo was telling the truth. But the prosecutors were skeptical. Over many years of experience with self-serving polygraph results in numerous criminal cases, they had learned never to accept such tests at face value. When the prosecution team first learned of the polygraph evidence, they demanded that the defense lawyers turn over all the test materials, including copies of the videotapes of the examinations. The defense lawyers complied, providing the examination evidence, which turned out to include approximately six hours of videotape, not only of the actual polygraph test administrations but also of the all-important pretest interviews between each examiner and Guillermo Zarabozo.

Prosecutor Karen Gilbert reviewed the videotapes several times. Then she ordered transcripts. Her careful examination of the videotapes and transcripts demonstrated that they contained a wealth of valuable information for the prosecution team. If the prosecutors had harbored any lingering doubts about Zarabozo's role in the crimes, the videotapes must have eliminated them. In the first place, Guillermo Zarabozo had apparently been given at least *four* separate polygraph tests, not just the two that he had "passed." On the videotape of one of the pretest interviews, an examiner was seen telling Guillermo Zarabozo that it was his third test and that he should forget about the other two, that the examiner really wanted him to do well on the latest one, or words to that effect. It was obvious that Zarabozo must have failed the first two polygraph examinations.

Although the motion in limine gave only brief snippets of the two polygraph tests that Zarabozo had passed, the videotapes of the two pretest interviews contained long discussions between the examiners and Guillermo Zarabozo about exactly what Zarabozo claimed had happened aboard the *Joe Cool* on Saturday, September 22, 2007. Interestingly, the two separate discussions differed in details provided by Zarabozo concerning where he was standing and what he was doing at various points before, during, and after the murders, which he claimed had all been committed by Kirby Archer.

To the prosecutors, it appeared that Zarabozo couldn't tell his story the same way twice. What events led up to the first murder? Where was Zarabozo then? Which of the victims had been shot first? Where did the first shooting take place? What happened next? Did he step over the dead body of one of the crew members or not? If so, which one? Did he help Kirby Archer carry all four of the bodies to the side of the boat and throw them overboard? Or did he alone carry one or more of the bodies and toss it over the side? How many shots did he hear when he was, according to him, hiding in the head (i.e., the bathroom) of the boat? Which head was he in? The forward or the aft? Why was he there in the first place? Had he entered to use the facilities, or was he scared and hiding?

Now that prosecutor Karen Gilbert had seen and heard Guillermo Zarabozo tell his different versions of events in the six hours of videotaped interviews—and noted all the inconsistencies—she had a preview of how he was likely to testify at trial. And she was well prepared to cross-examine him no matter what he said.

After a lengthy and exhaustive hearing, Judge Huck denied the motion to admit the polygraph evidence. The jury would never hear about the polygraphs at trial, but during this exercise, the prosecution team had gained an advance look at what Zarabozo's story to the jurors would be.

On the other hand, Zarabozo's lawyers believed they had won a small victory, too. Even though they were disappointed in Judge Huck's ruling, which they had known would be a long shot, they had preserved what they thought was compelling evidence of their client's innocence. They would not be able to get this evidence admitted at trial, but the Capital Review Committee in Washington, D.C., did not operate under the same stringent rules as Judge Huck. They planned to make good use of their polygraph results when they went to Washington to make their presentation on Zarabozo's behalf to the committee. But would it be enough?

CHAPTER FOURTEEN

A Matter of Life or Death

Throughout the spring and summer of 2008, a flurry of motions, responses, replies, hearings, and orders shaped the coming trial in the *Joe Cool* case. The trial date was set, reset, and reset again. Judge Huck made a number of rulings that delineated which evidence would—and would not—be admitted at trial. Among the issues were defendant Guillermo Zarabozo's motion to exclude from the trial all evidence recovered from his bedroom in Hialeah, including forensic analysis of the contents of the computer found in the living room (motion denied—the evidence would be admitted); evidence from the life raft and the defendants' luggage found in the life raft (motion denied); and evidence of statements given by Zarabozo to the Coast Guard and FBI after his rescue (motion denied). As the trial was taking shape—especially since Judge Huck had ruled that both defendants would have a single, joint trial—Kirby Archer's attorneys, Allan Kaiser and Bert Dominguez, recognized that their client's best hope of staying alive depended en-

tirely upon them. It was crucial that their mitigation package
and in-person presentations convince the Capital Review
Committee to recommend a life sentence rather than the
death penalty for their client.

With pressure mounting, Allan Kaiser and Bert Dominguez made their final preparations for travel to Washington,
D.C., to address the committee. What they argued—and the
exact composition of the committee—was not publicly revealed. The lawyers felt confident that they had presented
the best possible case for Kirby Archer at the proceeding.
But there was no guarantee, and their client's life might
well hang in the balance. They began to think more and
more about a guilty plea for Archer and how they would
approach him while he still insisted upon his innocence.

WHEN Guillermo Zarabozo's defense team went to Washington to meet with the committee, it was a very familiar
journey for William Matthewman. He had been there literally dozens of times before, and he even knew whom he
might expect to chair the committee that day (he was right).
Matthewman also knew that the prosecution team would be
there, along with some other "line" federal prosecutors. In
his experience, the committee members usually just listened attentively, thanked the defense attorneys for their
submission, and the hearing was over quickly. But this time
proved to be an exception. The meeting lasted unusually
long, well over an hour, and according to Matthewman, all
of the issues were "vigorously discussed." Questions came
from all around the table, and debates flowed freely.

The centerpiece of the defense team's argument for life in
prison rather than the death penalty was Zarabozo's actual
innocence as indicated by the polygraph evidence, which
they were free to introduce and argue forcefully in this forum.
Should the United States impose the death penalty on a teen-
age Cuban refugee, Matthewman argued, a kid who had

never been in any kind of trouble before and had passed two polygraphs? But what about the heinous nature of the crimes, the murder of four innocent young people in cold blood? A horrible crime, Matthewman agreed. But it was the older, more experienced Kirby Archer who was the killer, not Guillermo Zarabozo, a mere pawn in Archer's plan. Archer was the one who had been fleeing the country to avoid criminal prosecution, not Zarabozo. This kid was just along for the ride—foolishly—but without any knowledge of what was coming. He was duped by his own fantasies and Archer's slick talk about a life of espionage and capers for the CIA. Surely the death penalty—the ultimate sanction—shouldn't be sought against this defendant under these circumstances, he argued.

And then it was over. Matthewman had given it the full-court press, he felt, and he had hammered away on his client's youth, his successful polygraphs, and his lack of priors. He thought they were getting through to the committee members, but he couldn't know for sure. One thing he did know: now that this meeting was over and the defense team was dismissed, the "real" meeting would begin, the one where there would be open and candid discussion, where some members get to vote and some don't. And no matter what the outcome of the committee's secret vote, no matter what their secret recommendation, it was still the U.S. attorney general who would ultimately decide the issue of which penalty the government would seek against Guillermo Zarabozo.

There was no timetable for the attorney general's decision. It would not be communicated by him to the defense lawyers, in any event. In this literal matter of life or death, the ultimate penalty, the announcement from the attorney general would be made in a letter to the U.S. attorney for the Southern District of Florida in a single sentence: "You are [or are not] authorized to seek the death penalty." No reasons or explanations would be given. The deliberations and the recommendation of the Capital Review Committee would remain secret. All the lawyers could do was wait.

Finally, the prosecution team announced in open court that it would *not* seek the death penalty for either Kirby Archer or Guillermo Zarabozo. Matthewman and his co-counsel were delighted, and more than a little surprised. Colleagues called him from around the country to congratulate him and the team on their accomplishment. The talk in legal circles had been that this case would be a slam dunk for the death penalty. The loss of four innocent lives, in cold-blooded murder, aboard a small boat out on the ocean—it certainly seemed like the kind of case that deserved the death penalty, if any case ever did.

There was discussion and speculation about what position the prosecutors might have taken with the Capital Review Committee during the "real meeting." Had they considered pursuing the death penalty for Kirby Archer but not for Guillermo Zarabozo? No one who really knew the answers to these questions was talking.

Kaiser and Dominguez were also relieved. They were certain that they had saved their client's life, and that the committee would have recommended the death penalty for Kirby Archer without any hesitation had they not made their presentation on his behalf. They, too, wondered about the Florida prosecutors' thoughts on the subject. Were they also relieved? Judge Huck had ruled that both defendants would be tried in a single trial. And if the defendants were tried together, surely there was a risk that a jury would blame Archer for all the crimes and acquit the younger, more appealing Zarabozo of everything, especially if the death penalty had been on the table. It was something they could never discuss with the prosecutors, who were busy preparing for trial. But there was something Kaiser and Dominguez had to discuss with their client, and they were not looking forward to the conversation.

On the one hand, Dominguez and Kaiser had saved their

client's life, since even if he was convicted, the penalty would be life in prison without possibility of parole, not death. On the other hand, they knew that Archer had always maintained his complete innocence, especially to his parents, Betty and Sam Archer. Past clients had told Dominguez, "If you want me to bargain for my life in prison, forget it. I'd rather die than live the rest of my life in prison." What would Kirby Archer say now that the death penalty was off the table? Would he insist on going to trial in hopes of an acquittal? Or would he agree to plead guilty and spend the rest of his life in prison without possibility of parole? The discussion promised to be extremely unpleasant, but the lawyers knew they had to broach the subject immediately.

They visited Kirby Archer in the Federal Detention Center, explained the situation, and asked Archer what he wanted to do. After their conversation, Archer decided to think about it overnight before advising his lawyers of his intentions. He knew that if he went to trial, all his dirty laundry would be aired in a very public setting and bandied about in the news, and there would be plenty to talk about. His parents would probably hear terrible things about their son that he'd kept from them, and he might well be convicted, anyway. Guillermo Zarabozo's lawyers were certain to paint a picture of an innocent young kid duped by an older man who was already a criminal on the run from Arkansas. But Kirby Archer had assured his loyal mom and dad all along that he had nothing to do with these horrendous crimes. How could he now admit to them that he was a killer—that he was not the son they believed him to be?

Very reluctantly, Archer agreed to let his lawyers explore the possibility of a guilty plea. Bert Dominguez made his own position clear. If you decide to plead guilty, he told his client, you'll have to be the one to tell your parents about it. I won't do that for you.

Finally, Archer made up his mind and had the conversation with his heartbroken parents. He agreed to plead guilty to two murders—Jake and Kelley Branam—and all the other crimes alleged in the final superseding indictment, including kidnapping, conspiracy, and use of a firearm in the commission of a violent crime. Since he already knew that the death penalty would not be sought against him at trial, there was nothing he could offer in exchange for his guilty plea. The government made it clear that they had no intention of calling him to testify at trial, so he had no bargaining power for his testimony. Despite published reports to the contrary, there was no real "plea bargain." Once the death penalty was off the table, Archer simply decided to plead guilty, as any defendant has the right to do, and received nothing in exchange. He had no leverage to negotiate for lesser charges or for any penalty other than life in prison. There was no quid pro quo. "He'll never see the light of day again," as prosecutor Karen Gilbert put it.

Now that the government would be going to trial against Guillermo Zarabozo alone, they had no intention of muddying the waters by putting Kirby Archer on the stand. He would be a loose cannon at trial, and no matter what he said, it wouldn't help their case against Zarabozo. He could only be trouble. Zarabozo's lawyers would be sure to portray Archer as an evil Svengali who had duped their innocent young client into a bad situation.

But Archer would have to satisfy the government and Judge Huck with a sufficient factual basis to support his plea of guilty to two murders and all the rest of the charges before his plea would be accepted in the case. The prosecution team needed to ensure that there was no "wiggle room" in the factual proffer, the defendant's formal statement of facts and admission of his culpability submitted in support of his guilty plea. Archer's statement would have to nail down unequivocally exactly how the crimes took place and who was responsible for each murder. The prosecution team began to draft the document to be presented in court in support of Kirby Archer's guilty plea.

Archer changed his plea from "not guilty" to "guilty" in open court on July 24, 2008. The government's factual proffer was submitted in a courtroom packed with spectators, including family members of the victims. It was deeply disturbing and also shocking. Although prosecutor Karen Gilbert only summarized the facts in court, the prosecutors filed a formal factual proffer in the court file.

This document contained a lengthy summary of Archer's statements to federal investigators:

ARCHER'S STATEMENTS

ARCHER had made admissions and statements to federal agents. Some of these admissions and statements are summarized as follows:

ARCHER planned to infiltrate Cuba by boat. He wanted another person to travel with him to "assist and watch his back." Sometime in 2007, a mutual acquaintance introduced ARCHER and ZARABOZO to each other. ARCHER learned that ZARABOZO worked as a security guard. He began to talk to ZARABOZO and "test[ed] the waters" to see if ZARABOZO would be a suitable person for the trip. ARCHER told ZARABOZO that he needed someone to accompany him into a country that was hostile to the United States. He expressed to ZARABOZO that the trip could involve danger and violence. ARCHER warned that they could be imprisoned and/or tortured and that the incursion could last for months or, perhaps, years. ARCHER also indicated that he and ZARABOZO may not even return.

ZARABOZO agreed to act as ARCHER's partner. ARCHER then told ZARABOZO that they were going to Cuba. He gave ZARABOZO details of the trip, which included stealing a boat and possibly taking it to the Bahamas and re-fueling there if necessary. ARCHER explained that the purpose of entering Bahamian waters was to reduce suspicion *en route* to Cuba. ARCHER instructed ZARABOZO to gather in a bag some belongings, including a firearm and clothes. He further advised ZARABOZO to start preparing his family for his departure and severing ties with his friends. As they spent more time together, ARCHER advised ZARABOZO that he was a fugitive and that there was a pending warrant for his arrest.

As part of the preparations for leaving, ARCHER purchased a Sig Sauer .380 semi-automatic pistol. (He and ZARABOZO later purchased additional ammunition clips for the gun.) ZARABOZO was already in possession of a Glock 9-millimeter semi-automatic pistol.

ARCHER and ZARABOZO visited numerous South Florida marinas in an attempt to locate a boat to steal for their trip. Finding no success, the men focused on chartering a vessel, which they described as "Plan B." In their Plan B discussions, ARCHER and ZARABOZO considered the fate of any crew members on board a chartered boat. ARCHER suggested that they "corral" any crew members on the bow of the boat and leave them on an uninhabited island. ZARABOZO suggested, however, that they kill any witnesses and throw them into the sea in order to avoid being identified at a later time. Recognizing that missing people would attract more attention than a missing boat, ARCHER convinced ZARABOZO of his idea. If anything went awry, however, the two agreed that they would draw their guns to control the crew members and would, if necessary, kill them.

Eventually, ARCHER and ZARABOZO chartered the *F/V Joe Cool* and believed that the boat had enough fuel to reach Cuba. In securing the charter, ARCHER and ZARABOZO advised the boat's owners that they were going on a one-way trip to Bimini. On the day of the trip, ARCHER and ZARABOZO arrived to learn that the boat planned to carry four—rather than two—crew members. Prior to departure, ARCHER and ZARABOZO discussed what to do with the additional crew members. They decided to adhere to the plan and agreed that ARCHER would make the last-minute call whether the boat's take-over would involve a show of physical strength or the threatened use of firearms.

ARCHER and ZARABOZO boarded the *Joe Cool* with their luggage, their firearms and other weapons. After the boat was underway [*sic*] and when Bimini was within eyesight, ARCHER and ZARABOZO conferred in the boat's salon. ARCHER told ZARABOZO that the captain was acting strangely and that the time to act had come. Thus, they each retrieved their firearms.

ARCHER advised ZARABOZO to wait and listen for his signal. ARCHER climbed the ladder to the fly bridge where the captain was piloting the vessel and where the captain's wife was seated next to him. As he made his way to the fly bridge, ARCHER passed a third crew member who was headed down to the lower deck. The fourth crew member was already located on the lower deck near ZARABOZO.

As he positioned himself near the captain, ARCHER heard a gun shot down below. At that point, ARCHER shot the captain, who fell to the lower deck. ARCHER heard a second shot below as he prepared to shoot the captain's wife. ARCHER shot the captain's wife, who fell to the lower deck.

Following the shootings, the four crew members of the *Joe Cool* were dead. ARCHER told ZARABOZO to throw the four bodies into the ocean and to clean up. ZARABOZO complied. ARCHER located three shell casings on the fly bridge that were expelled from his weapon. The fourth casing was located below, which

ARCHER instructed ZARABOZO to discard overboard. ARCHER advised ZARABOZO to find his gun's shell casings and throw them over, as well. ZARABOZO assured ARCHER that he would. ARCHER immediately turned the *Joe Cool* to the south and headed towards Cuba.

ARCHER and ZARABOZO traveled approximately 140 miles until the vessel ran out of fuel and the boat batteries died. At daybreak on September 23rd, ARCHER and ZARABOZO deployed the *Joe Cool*'s liferaft. ARCHER had hoped that the Cuban border guard—not the United States Coast Guard—would find them in the raft. However, ARCHER and ZARABOZO discussed a plan and story to tell in either scenario.

While in the raft, ARCHER told ZARABOZO to tell a hijacking story if the Coast Guard discovered them. If the Cuban border guard found them, however, ARCHER said that the pair should claim to be American military defectors.

Eventually, the Coast Guard located ARCHER and ZARABOZO and took them to a cutter. As planned, they told authorities the hijacking story that they had rehearsed.

On its face, the factual proffer didn't disclose much that was new to those following the case. But its detailed, almost casual, cold-blooded outline of how the vicious crimes were planned and committed was unsettling. Moreover, according to Archer's statement, Guillermo Zarabozo was the more violent of the two, more willing—even anxious—to shoot and kill the crew on the *Joe Cool*. He had fired the first shot.

THE friends and families of the victims now had more answers—and even more heartbreak. That Kirby Archer would spend the rest of his life in prison without possibility of parole provided little satisfaction, but even the death penalty wouldn't have pacified the grieving families and friends. No matter what happened to Kirby Archer for the rest of his life, nothing would bring back their loved ones. They tried to imagine what the lost crew had gone through in their final moments of life. Had they seen it coming? Were they afraid? Did they suffer? Archer's statement made no mention of Kelley Branam shouting for the crew to call the Coast Guard, nor was there any indication that she had become hysterical and "curled into a fetal position" on the fly bridge as had previously been reported as part of the phony "hijackers" story. No one knew what to believe anymore, except the awful finality that all the crew members aboard the boat had been brutally slaughtered and tossed into the sea.

And now they had to steel themselves for the trial of Guillermo Zarabozo in two months. Everyone dreaded it. They knew they would have to relive the tragedy aboard the *Joe Cool* in a public courtroom. Some were committed to being there every day, hearing every word as a kind of testament to their lost friends and family. But others couldn't bear to watch the trial and sit in the same room with Guillermo Zarabozo.

CHAPTER FIFTEEN

Final Preparations

The revelations in Kirby Archer's factual statement stunned the community. It was no great surprise that he admitted the whole "incursion" to Cuba had been his idea. But he also admitted that he had murdered Jake and Kelley Branam in cold blood and said that Zarabozo shot Sammy Kairy and Scott Gamble with his Glock in the boat's cabin. Archer portrayed Zarabozo as a fully informed and enthusiastic player in their deadly game—even more willing to kill the witnesses than Archer himself. It looked like the perfect student had found the perfect teacher.

Zarabozo's version of events—Kirby Archer did it—was already public knowledge. Indeed, it was the only defense left: the naive, young Zarabozo—never in any kind of trouble before, a "good kid" planning a career in law enforcement—was duped all along by the evil, older, more sophisticated Archer, a criminal who was already on the run when he hit town. Zarabozo claimed that he never imagined any murders would take place on the *Joe Cool*, that he had always believed he and Archer were going to Bimini for some sort of high-level, glamorous, secret security job. In that scenario, it was Archer who committed all four murders, apparently using Zarabozo's Glock since four spent shell casings from the Glock had been found aboard the *Joe Cool*. But how could Zarabozo's lawyers explain their client's strange behavior after he and Archer were picked up by the Coast Guard? If he really had been an innocent young man duped by Archer, wouldn't he have told his rescuers about Archer immediately and sought their protection? And what about his strange denial of ever having been aboard the *Joe Cool* at all?

Guillermo Zarabozo was now represented by Assistant Federal Public Defenders Anthony Natale, Brian Stekloff, and Michael Caruso. Although their CJA co-counsel William Matthewman would have preferred to stay on the case and see it through trial, he had been discharged once the government announced it would not seek the death penalty against Zarabozo. Matthewman considered continuing pro bono but ultimately decided he simply had too much work backed up already.

The reconstituted defense team made its first move by offering Dr. Judy Okawa as an expert to testify at trial that Guillermo Zarabozo suffered from acute stress disorder (ASD) during the time of the murders. According to Okawa, a component of ASD is dissociation, a state in which a person is detached from the reality of a traumatic event. In other words, while Guillermo Zarabozo might have physically been present, the argument was that he wasn't really "there" during the killing spree. This explanation was necessary in order for the jury to fully understand and accurately assess Zarabozo's strange behavior and demeanor after his rescue by the Coast Guard, the defense attorneys argued to Judge Huck. But the government had no trouble finding their own experts to provide a harsh critique of Dr. Okawa's methods and conclusions, including a psychologist, Dr. William J. Stejskal, who had been her mentor during her training. At a hearing on the issue, Dr. Stejskal testified that his former student had not properly evaluated the defendant as he had taught her to do and she did not use testing that he would have used. Another prosecution expert, Dr. Harley Stock, criticized the validity of Okawa's opinion and conclusions. This, obviously, greatly diminished the value of any testimony Dr. Okawa could offer, and in the end, neither side presented expert psychological or psychiatric testimony at trial.

While the prosecutors were now assured of Kirby Archer's life imprisonment for these crimes, they were still determined to convict Guillermo Zarabozo as well. They were convinced of the moral certainty of his guilt, and the families of the victims were counting on them to finish the job they had begun nearly a year before. Zarabozo presented some difficulties as a murder defendant—he might have some jury appeal, being young, good-looking, and apparently never having been in trouble before. He also had a record of Air Force Junior ROTC participation in high school and some "good citizen" certificates from the Boy Scouts and the Citizens Police Academy, a community law enforcement support program he had completed with his best friend, Andy Pla. Before hooking up with Archer, Zarabozo had even been accepted into the Miami-Dade Police Department's training class of October 2007.

For the prosecutors, this was an especially chilling revelation. What if Guillermo Zarabozo had never met Kirby Archer? What if, instead, he had actually taken and passed the police training program and become a police officer? Would he have gone over to the dark side as a bad cop? Also, while prosecutors had Archer's factual proffer as a road map of how the crimes were planned, what happened along the way, and the brutal slaughter on the *Joe Cool*, they couldn't introduce it at trial without putting Archer on the stand, which they adamantly refused to do. How could they be sure what he would say? Even if he would agree to roll over and claim that he had committed all the crimes alone and that Zarabozo was innocent—which he hadn't—Archer had already sworn to the story in his factual proffer in the court file. And that story fully implicated Zarabozo. There was no way Kirby Archer would be called to testify at the trial, period.

They would have to find other ways to get the true story out and discredit Zarabozo as the young "good citizen" whose dream was a career in law enforcement so he could help people.

Zarabozo's defense team was free to argue at trial that Kirby Archer had killed all four victims despite Archer's factual proffer stating that he killed Jake and Kelley Branam, and that it was Zarabozo who murdered Scott Gamble and Sammy Kairy. The prosecution team would not put Kirby Archer on the stand to testify, and so his factual proffer could not be admitted at trial or disclosed to the jury. For the same reason, the prosecutors could argue that Zarabozo himself was responsible for all the murders during the commission of the felonies alleged against him in the indictment.

Both sides had to line up their witnesses for trial, issue witness subpoenas, and make travel arrangements for out-of-town witnesses. For the prosecution, this would include a law enforcement officer from Arkansas, who would tell the jury about the investigation of Kirby Archer and why he was on the run. They had many other witnesses on their list, too, such as Gretel Martinez, a sometime friend of Zarabozo's who was then attending Emory University in Atlanta. She could testify that he had come to visit her in Atlanta just before his departure on the *Joe Cool*, at a time when he had told everyone that he was out of town working as an extra on a film shoot. The prosecutors planned to prove that, in preparation for his new life as an international spy in Cuba, Zarabozo had begun telling friends and family members that he would be gone for some time, that he was going to fake his disappearance, and that they might be seeing him as a missing person "on the news" but not to worry about what they saw, since he would be all right. Zarabozo's mother, Francisca Alonso, later said that her son's last words to her before he set out on his trip were: "Mom, don't worry, because I am going to be doing a decent and safe job for the government."

The prosecution team had witnesses to testify that Zarabozo stopped returning calls for private security guard jobs and failed to contact his supervisor at Pinkerton, who was ready to offer him a higher-paying position as a full-time employee of the company, which would replace the small, part-time jobs he had done for subcontractors. Zarabozo also started tying up loose ends, such as offering his car for sale to his best friend, Andy Pla. In the process, he had told a number of lies, which could be useful in establishing his character as an untruthful person. But the prosecutors had to decide which of these lies were worth bringing out through witnesses who might still think of him as a friend and who might even turn hostile on the witness stand.

In addition, the prosecution had to organize a mountain of circumstantial evidence, including complex forensic analysis, and tell a coherent story to the jury to support their charges against Zarabozo. Every piece of evidence would have to be introduced by a witness—either a fact witness, an investigator, or a forensic expert—and explained and presented in a logical and understandable manner to jurors who probably would have little scientific background. It was a daunting task, and the prosecution team had little time for a break, or even sleep, as the trial date approached.

MIAMI was what's known in the news business as a "hot news town," and many of those newsworthy events wound up on display in the city's busy state and federal courtrooms.

While the prosecution and defense teams were working around the clock to get their presentations ready for opening day in the *Joe Cool* case on September 16, 2008, other trial teams were driving themselves just as hard for other high-profile trials set to go during the same period in Miami federal courts. One of those cases came to be known as "the Suitcase Case." It featured a Venezuelan businessman living in Miami's Key Biscayne who was traveling with a suitcase stuffed with an unexplained $800,000 in cash, which arrived in Argentina on a Cessna Citation jet, and Maria del Lujan Telpuk, a former nursery school teacher who in August 2007 was working as an airport police officer in Argentina and who was the person who discovered the stash. According to an article in the *Miami Herald*, federal prosecutors believed that the cash was "a gift from leftist Venezuelan president Hugo Chavez to the presidential campaign in Argentina of Cristina Fernandez de Kirchner, an ally," setting off an alleged cover-up of the ensuing international political scandal.

The case was big news, especially in Argentina, where it was known as "Valijagate," or "Suitcase-Gate," and Maria del Lujan Telpuk became an overnight sensation. As reported by Casey Woods and Gerardo Reyes for the *Miami Herald*, her celebrity inspired Telpuk "to enlarge her breasts, and ultimately landed her on the cover of both Argentine and Venezuelan Playboy magazines holding a suitcase full of cash under the headline 'Corruption Laid Bare.'" The article further described her as a "27-year-old bombshell." She promptly quit her Venezuelan airport job and began to train for an Argentine TV show called *Skating for a Dream*, a sort of *Dancing with the Stars* but on ice. Telpuk was called as a witness in the federal trial in Miami in September 2008, and her arrival at the Miami International Airport attracted a crowd of journalists from three countries. According to the *Miami Herald* reporters, Telpuk relished her time in the spotlight: "Looking dainty and fresh after her eight hour flight, she posed for photographers, gave a pair of live telephone interviews, and said little about her role in a legal case that could shame" the presidents of both Venezuela and Argentina. "She brought her ice skates—tucked into a hot pink bag—with her to Miami, on the off chance that she might get to practice while she's in town."

At the same time, in the same courthouse where the *Joe Cool* case would be tried, another international scandal was on display, this time involving the American son of Charles Taylor, former Liberian president on trial for war crimes at The Hague. Taylor's son, Charles McArther Emmanuel, had been picked up at the Miami International Airport using a falsified passport. Emmanuel was charged with heading an especially violent paramilitary unit in Liberia called the Demon Forces. The story was reported in the *Miami Herald* by Kelli Kennedy, who described the case as "the first test of a 1994 United States law which makes it a crime for a United States citizen to commit torture overseas." Yet another Miami federal courtroom would soon see the third trial (after two mistrials) in another notorious case, known as "the Liberty City Seven." The number of defendants going to trial had actually been reduced to five (one was acquitted and one dropped), but the original case name stuck. According to Assistant United States Attorney Richard Gregorie, lead prosecutor in the case, a local gang from Liberty City, an often dangerous neighborhood of Miami, conspired with a group calling itself "the Moorish Science Temple" in a plot to blow up the Sears Tower in Chicago and the FBI headquarters in Miami. The conspiracy was founded upon an alleged treaty between the Moorish Science Temple and American Founding Father George Washington, which supposedly gave certain property rights on United States soil to the Moorish Science Temple. According to that group, the U.S. government later reneged on the treaty, so the conspirators decided to retaliate and "take a piece of America back" by blowing up the Sears Tower and

FROM LEFT TO RIGHT: Maria Gagliardo, Captain Jake Branam, his wife, Kelley (holding child), and Jake's grandfather, Harry. *Courtesy of the Branam family*

The *Joe Cool* at the dock behind the Branam family compound on Star Island, Florida. *Courtesy of the author*

Jake Branam,
captain of the *Joe Cool*.

Kelley Branam,
Jake's wife.

Scott Gamble,
Jake's half brother,
and crew of the *Joe Cool*.

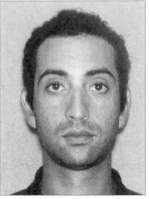

Samuel Kairy,
Jake's best friend
and crew of the *Joe Cool*.

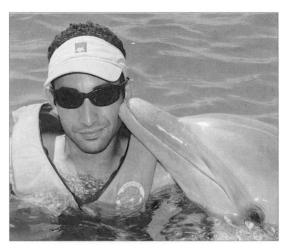

Samuel Kairy, swimming with dolphins. This was one of his most memorable experiences.   *Dolphin Encounters, Blue Lagoon Island, Bahamas*

Amie Gamble, Scott Gamble's sister and Jake Branam's half sister.
*Al Diaz/*Miami Herald

The *Joe Cool* leaving Miami Beach on charter to Bimini, Bahamas, on Saturday, September 22, 2007, with Jon Branam escorting on Jet Ski. *2007 Tom McDermott, BOATPIX.com, Inc.*

Jon Branam
reacts to verdict
on February 19, 2009.
Al Diaz/Miami Herald

Harry Branam
wipes tears after
hearing verdict on
February 19, 2009.
Al Diaz/Miami Herald

The Honorable Paul C. Huck, United States district judge for the Southern District of Florida. *Courtesy of the author*

Wilkie D. Ferguson Jr.
Federal Courthouse,
Miami, Florida.

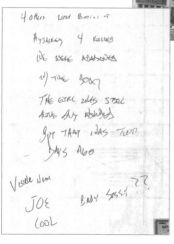

Handwritten note shown at trial from the Coast Guard rescue helicopter on September 24, 2007.

LEFT: Kirby Logan Archer, in an undated photo.

RIGHT: Archer's official booking photo, from September 25, 2007.

LEFT: Guillermo Zarabozo, posing with a prop car while dressed as a police officer for a *telenovela* episode.

BELOW: Zarabozo's security officer license.

Zarabozo's official booking photo, from September 25, 2007.

FROM LEFT: Assistant U.S. Attorney Michael Gilfarb, FBI Special Agent David Nuñez, Assistant U.S. Attorney Karen Gilbert, FBI Special Agent Herbert "Skip" Hogberg, and Assistant U.S. Attorney Jeffrey Tsai. *U.S. Attorney's Office for the Southern District of Florida*

Former Assistant Federal Public Defender Faith Mesnekoff and attorney William Matthewman. *Courtesy of the author*

The Honorable Sandy Karlan, Miami-Dade County Family Court judge.
Courtesy of Daily Business Review

Jeff Branam, uncle of Captain Jake Branam, in Miami-Dade Family Court.
© *Charlotte Southern 2008*

Genny Van Laar, half sister of Kelley Branam, in Miami-Dade Family Court.
© *Charlotte Southern 2008*

the Miami FBI headquarters. After the third trial, the Liberty City Seven (now five) were finally convicted.

But even with all the other action going on in Miami's federal courts, the *Joe Cool* trial would attract major news coverage each day. The media room on the eighth floor of the federal courthouse would be a busy place for weeks to come.

CHAPTER SIXTEEN

―――

Going to Trial

On Monday, September 16, 2008, almost exactly a year after the horrific events aboard the *Joe Cool*, trial began in the case of *United States of America v. Guillermo Alfonso Zarabozo* in Judge Paul C. Huck's cavernous, state-of-the-art courtroom on the thirteenth floor in the new Wilkie D. Ferguson Jr. Federal Courthouse in downtown Miami. Ironically, the $163 million courthouse, completed in 2007, was nicknamed "the boat" because its sleek, all-glass profile and stark modern architecture had been designed by Miami's Arquitectonica firm to resemble a large, oceangoing ship with a prow. Chief Judge Federico Moreno, whose courtroom was across the glass atrium from Judge Huck's, actually had a large, wooden ship's steering wheel mounted in the prow, the glass-enclosed corner of his private chambers, a gift from his law clerks. Even the landscaping was carefully crafted to carry out the nautical theme. Maya Lin, famous for submitting the winning design for the Vietnam Veterans Memorial while still a student at Yale, created a flowing series of graceful, grass-covered mounds that resembled green ocean waves undulating around the building.

All the spaces in Judge Huck's courtroom were oversized: the elaborate, two-tiered brown marble judicial bench, the spacious jury box, the recessed ceiling high above with concealed lighting and free-form, origami-like white panels undulating above the courtroom, and the enormous well of the court. Judge Huck, a trim, middle-aged man with graying hair, presided over the electronic marvels of his courtroom like a pilot in a space-age cockpit. Two computer screens faced him on the bench, with additional screens on the tier below, where his courtroom deputy and court reporter worked. From his solitary perch high above, Judge Huck managed the lawyers' evidentiary presentations by shifting the courtroom monitors to project objects, diagrams, maps, photos, and documents or computer images or videos on the screens for jurors and spectators. He was so far away from the lawyers' tables, the defendant, and the spectators that he seemed to exist on a distant, lofty plane engulfed by the space. But there was never any doubt about who was in control in his courtroom.

This trial could not be likened to a play; it seemed closer to a high-definition 3-D IMAX experience, at least in the modern judicial temple of the Ferguson Federal Courthouse. Each courtroom in the modern building was equipped with an elaborate electronic infrastructure that allowed lawyers to present a play-by-play visual account of evidence to the court using a large electronic podium called "the Elmo" in the center of the well of the court. From their comfortable seats in the jury box, jurors could view evidence presentations on their own individual video screens as if they were first-class passengers on a long transatlantic flight. With large plasma screens suspended at each end of the spectators' gallery, attending a trial was like watching an entrancing mystery movie in a well-equipped home theater.

The trial began in the traditional manner of selecting

twelve jurors and three alternates, who took their oath and settled in for what they expected would be several days. The gallery was packed with spectators, many of them friends and relatives of the victims, including Captain Jake's grandfather Harry Branam, now seventy-five years old, whose loan of $220,000 had made the *Joe Cool* possible. The only ones who did not attend were his former wife, Jeannette, who never came to trial, and his companion, Maria Gagliardo, who was on an extended European vacation with her son that September. Throughout the trial, the rest of the Branam family and friends generally sat together on the right side of the gallery, just behind the prosecutors' table.

Amie Gamble, a tall, attractive young blonde, had lost her brother, Scott Gamble, her half brother, Jake Branam, and her sister-in-law, Kelley Branam, on the *Joe Cool*. She attended the trial nearly every day, often in tears as she relived the tragedy through the witnesses, usually accompanied by John Gibbons, a tall, lanky, tanned young man who wore casual clothes and sunglasses secured by Croakies straps around his neck. Gibbons had been a good friend of Jake's; they'd been fishing pals until Gibbons developed a bad case of seasickness and had to pursue a living on land. Jake had trusted and relied upon Gibbons to look after his wife and children when he was out of town. It was John who would deliver food to Kelley and the children, and John who drove to the airport to pick up Kelley's mother, Leanne, when she came for visits. Leanne adored him and always called him "Big John." He was now dating Amie Gamble and had known the Branam clan nearly his whole life, going back to elementary school days when John, Amie, Scott, and Jake were all classmates at Miami Lakes Elementary School. Outside the courtroom, the Branams' large contingent hugged each other during breaks from the trial and shared family news with Harry.

Albert Kairy, father of Sammy, was also a constant presence at trial, but he had asked Marian, Sammy's mother, not to come with him. He anticipated that some of the testimony would be rough to hear, and he wanted to keep the worst from her if he could. She waited at home to learn from her husband what had happened in court each day. Although Harry and Albert had never met before, they began sitting together during the trial, two gray-haired men who hated being there but couldn't stay away. Sometimes they discussed the evidence presented or the witnesses who flowed past them, in and out of the courtroom. Often they commiserated on their private tragedies, now being replayed in the very public arena of the courtroom. Harry told Albert that Sammy had been like another grandson to him, and Albert believed him. After all, Sammy had spent most of his time with his Branam pals at Star, on the *Joe Cool*, at the Miami Beach Marina, or just hanging out around the water.

On the left side of the gallery sat Guillermo Zarabozo's mother, Francisca Alonso, a small, huddled, dark-haired woman who looked beaten down by life. Her daughter accompanied her every day and, since the mother spoke no English, sometimes translated for her. Occasionally, a few friends or relatives joined them, but mostly they sat alone and apart.

Reporters claimed seats in the rear of the gallery, positioning themselves where they could see the judge and jury and watch the witnesses as they came and went, and then slip out to work when necessary. The collegial group included Vanessa Blum of the *Sun-Sentinel*, Jay Weaver from the *Miami Herald*, and the AP's Curt Anderson. Television news reporters frequently showed up: Peter D'Oench and Ileana Varela from Miami's CBS Channel 4 and Hank Tester from NBC Channel 6. Annette Lopez, an on-camera reporter for a Spanish-language TV station, attended nearly every day, often filming live in front of the courthouse. Word soon circulated that Guillermo Zarabozo had been an occasional bit-part actor in low-budget *telenovelas*, Spanish-language soap opera television dramas very popular in Miami's large Hispanic community. This brought intense Spanish media coverage of the trial, often accompanied on television by stills of the tall, good-looking Zarabozo from episodes of the *telenovelas*. In one shot frequently used, he was costumed as a police officer leaning casually against a faux black-and-white cruiser, a fake gun on his hip. In another, ironically, he was a Coast Guard officer running down an island beach to rescue victims of a shipwreck.

On the opening day of the trial, jurors took their seats in the jury box across from defendant Guillermo Zarabozo, who was already in place at the long defense table, wearing a neat blue shirt and dark tie and suit, looking clean-cut and composed. His team of lawyers surrounded him: Assistant Federal Public Defender Anthony Natale, the gray-haired team leader, and his young trial partners, Michael Caruso and Brian Stekloff. Across the aisle was the prosecution team, headed by the United States Attorneys' Office Chief of Major Crimes Karen Gilbert, a tough, seasoned prosecutor, consistently clad in dark pants suits. She had carefully groomed shoulder-length dark hair, little makeup on her strong features, and a confident, no-nonsense, professional demeanor. When she used the Elmo to present evidence, her bright red, perfectly manicured nails flashed on the video screens in the courtroom, the only sign of feminine whimsy in her appearance. Her assistants, Jeffrey Tsai and Michael Gilfarb, were impeccably dressed each day in dark suits. Gilbert's team also included David Nuñez, the FBI case agent who attended each day at the prosecution table, and various legal assistants who came and went during the trial as needed by the prosecutors to assist with evidence presentation for the Elmo, locate witnesses, carry documents back and forth, perform last-minute research, and take care of the numerous tasks necessary to let the lawyers focus their entire attention on the courtroom proceedings. Counsel tables on both sides of the center aisle held computer screens, monitors, and laptops, as well as the usual notebooks, folders, and files the attorneys used to guide their presentations.

Assistant United States Attorney Jeffrey Tsai, a tall, handsome young Asian man, opened the case for the prosecution. He had a strong, deep voice and made a good impression for the prosecution team. He stated the case in a simple and straightforward manner, describing the heinous crimes and the villains of the piece who had become so familiar in the news: Guillermo Zarabozo, now twenty years old, a guy who dreamed of a life of adventure, action, and excitement and saw his opportunity when he met Kirby Archer. As part of his summary, Tsai added details about Kirby Archer that were previously unreported. On the run from serious charges in Arkansas, Archer used aliases and stolen cash to land in the Miami suburb of Hialeah, where he lived for a time with the Perez family, whom he had known briefly when he served with the United States Army in a refugee camp in Guantánamo, Cuba. At age thirty-five, Archer hung around with a much younger crowd in Hialeah, at a Mustang chop-shop where he was eventually introduced to Zarabozo. Tsai told the jury that Archer portrayed himself as an international man of mystery, a secretive CIA operative who had high-level government contacts and was preparing for a big job coming up.

In Archer, Zarabozo saw a chance to take a shortcut out of his humdrum life in Hialeah and directly into the big-time, glamorous life of an international spy doing espionage and undercover work—and making lots of money. Zarabozo had an eye out for the main chance, and he found it in Archer. He signed on as Archer's partner. They would take a boat to Cuba, where they would use Archer's supposed "high-level contacts" to get work spying, tracking supposed smugglers, whatever turned up, and making millions. Zarabozo knew from the beginning that there might be danger, which attracted the young man who was fascinated by guns, martial arts, knives, money, and the very idea of secret missions.

Tsai emphasized that Zarabozo knew from the beginning that his glamorous new life would begin with deadly crimes.

To implement their plan, Tsai told the jury, Archer and Zarabozo needed a fast boat to take them out of the United States and into Cuba, where the supposed high-level secret missions awaited them. They scouted marinas from Palm Beach to Key West, looking for a boat they could steal. The problem was, neither knew anything about boats—how to choose one, steal one, start the engine, navigate, or even drive one. They moved on to "Plan B": they would charter a large boat with a captain and crew, and, when they were in open water, they would hijack it, disposing of the captain and crew, and then simply head south to Cuba for their life of adventure, glamour, and fortune. Using aliases and an untraceable cell phone SIM card, they scouted marinas for a boat to charter. They finally found one at the Miami Beach Marina: the sportfishing charter boat *Joe Cool*.

Tsai told the jury about the young captain, his wife, and the crew of the *Joe Cool*, innocent young people just beginning their lives with their fledgling charter fishing company. He described the *Joe Cool*'s departure from the Miami Beach Marina on a sunny Saturday afternoon, September 22, 2007, and the brief trip across the Gulf Stream to Bimini. In sight of Bimini Bay, he told them, Zarabozo and Archer turned on the captain, his wife, and the crew, shooting and killing them, dumping their bodies overboard, and driving the boat south until it ran out of gas just thirty miles from Cuba. They almost made it. Tsai told the jury they would hear about the rescue of the "survivors" from the *Joe Cool*'s life raft by the United States Coast Guard and their strange, silent, uncommunicative behavior. He described the cover story the two men first told the Coast Guard and the FBI, the tale of Cuban hijackers/pirates who had overtaken the boat and killed everyone aboard—except them. Tsai outlined the crimes charged against Zarabozo and took the jury through the sixteen-count indictment against him.

Then it was time for Zarabozo's defense team to address the jury. Gray-haired and scholarly Anthony Natale detailed how the young, impressionable Zarabozo had been duped by the older, more sophisticated Archer into what he thought would be a legitimate, if clandestine, bodyguarding job in Bimini. When they departed from Miami Beach Marina on the *Joe Cool*, Zarabozo had no idea that Archer was secretly planning to hijack the boat, kill the crew, and drive the boat to Cuba. He believed they were going to Bimini, not Cuba. He had been young, naive, and foolish, but he had never intended to harm anyone or commit any crimes. Zarabozo had taken his Glock pistol and ammunition aboard the boat because he thought these would be necessary for the body-guarding job in the Bahamas. According to Natale, Zarabozo always planned to work in law enforcement or the military as a career. Everyone who knew him, employed him, or worked with him would tell the jury that he was "a good kid." Kirby Archer had taken advantage of a naive, possibly not-too-bright young man who had only the best intentions. Natale told the jury that Archer alone had killed everyone on the *Joe Cool*, then threatened Zarabozo and forced him to go along with him on the life raft. Zarabozo only told the story about the Cuban hijackers to the Coast Guard and the FBI out of fear of Archer. Natale concluded, "This is a case of how the fantasy of a young man, in a matter of seconds, turned into a nightmare."

Following a short break, the government opened its case with some of its strongest witnesses: the Coast Guard officers who had rescued the defendants from the *Joe Cool*'s life raft and the FBI agents who'd interviewed them aboard the Coast Guard cutter *Confidence*. The prosecution team had decided on a reverse-chronology timeline for their presentation. They would begin with law enforcement's first encounter with the case, the same way the *Joe Cool* mystery had unfolded in the news media and in the investigation of the crimes. Then they would backtrack through preparations for the trip and how Archer and Zarabozo had met and planned to get to Cuba on a hijacked boat.

It seemed a logical and persuasive order in which to present their voluminous evidence against Guillermo Zarabozo.

CHAPTER SEVENTEEN

The ERT Is the CSI of the FBI

The prosecution team opened their case with the location and rescue of Kirby Archer and Guillermo Zarabozo from the *Joe Cool*'s life raft, just twelve miles *north* of where the abandoned boat had been found, more than 140 miles south of their supposed destination in Bimini, and very close to the Cuban coast. They had several white-uniformed, clean-cut United States Coast Guard officers sequestered in their private counsel room just outside the courtroom waiting to be called to testify. Lt. Andrew Baines, pilot of the rescue helicopter, described how they had launched at dawn from the cutter *Confidence* on Monday, September 24, 2007. He was an exchange pilot from the Royal Navy, and between his crisp uniform and his authoritative British accent, Lieutenant Baines easily held the attention of the jury and spectators as he described how they had located the bright orange life raft drifting along on the current near the Cay Sal Banks. His testimony covered the retrieval of the two men from the life raft and the note that his flight mechanic had passed him, as well as his conclusion that there were no more survivors to be rescued, and the helicopter's return to the cutter *Confidence*.

Lieutenant Baines also told the jury about the strange, emotionless demeanor of the survivors. After all of the missions he had flown—more than one hundred—and all of the overjoyed people he had helped to rescue from life-threatening disasters on the ocean, this behavior struck him as unusual. Archer and Zarabozo had seemed withdrawn, even sullen, and refused to make eye contact with their rescuers. It was puzzling to everyone aboard the helicopter and, later, aboard the cutter *Confidence*.

Beginning what would be a long trail of visual evidence for the jury to follow, the next witness, Christopher Janisko, one of the flight mechanics on the rescue helicopter, gave the jury a play-by-play commentary of video he had taken during the rescue from the ocean. There, right in front of them on their individual video screens, the jury could see Archer and Zarabozo in the bright blue water, churned into blasting tumult by the rotor blades of the hovering helicopter, swimming one by one to the rescue basket with its bright orange flotation gear, and then being hauled up to the cramped interior of the helicopter. The spectators could also see the video on the large screens at either end of the gallery. It was vivid and dramatic, almost like actually being there.

In the days to come, the jury and spectators would see many surveillance videos of Zarabozo and Archer checking into and out of various motels; their approaching and entering Lou's Police and Security Equipment Store in Hialeah, purchasing ammunition and magazines; Zarabozo in the Coral Gables T-Mobile store with a clerk, filling out a form with the alias Michael Zoiou and buying a SIM card for his cell phone; Zarabozo buying a black backpack, underwear, and travel gear at Wal-Mart and driving through tollbooths on the Florida Turnpike. From the abundance of detailed surveillance video presented by the prosecution team, it almost began to seem Big Brother–like, driving home how frequently anyone could be captured on camera and on tape, all the time, from the minute one left home, approached or entered a store, restaurant, or hotel, bought something, used an ATM, drove through an automated toll lane on the expressway, or left one's car in a parking lot.

The government obtained much of its evidence through the old-fashioned legwork of the many investigators working the case and subpoenas for records from the stores involved, such as T-Mobile, Wal-Mart, Lou's Police and Security Equipment Store, and many other places Zarabozo and Archer had visited during their lengthy preparations for their big trip. The prosecutors knew exactly where to look for this evidence because Zarabozo had carefully saved many paper receipts from these stops showing when they had been there, what they had purchased, and how the transaction was paid for. Investigators found a wealth of detail and were able to follow their trail through dated receipts Zarabozo had saved in his wallet, which he had then left on the *Joe Cool*, as well as from his backpack from the life raft, from the trunk of his car, and from his bedroom and lockbox. Through long experience, investigators knew that speed was essential in following this trail. Insurers usually required businesses to maintain videotapes of all customers and transactions for specified periods, but tapes were routinely recorded over when the period expired. They had to get subpoenas and personally track down all these leads before valuable evidence was inadvertently lost.

The luggage from the life raft also proved to contain valuable information. By the time the life raft was towed by small boat back to the cutter *Confidence* in the open ocean, the weather was worsening, the sea choppy and the leaden skies spitting rain. The life raft was so heavy and waterlogged that before it could be lifted aboard the cutter, its contents had to be removed lest the raft disintegrate and sink all evidence into the deep water below. Once the defendants' luggage, drenched with salt water and foul smelling, was retrieved from the raft, it was taken to a covered aft deck, opened, unpacked, photographed, inventoried, and identified at trial by Special Agent Scott Hahn, a forensic specialist from the FBI's Evidence Response Team. He facetiously referred to their special forensic unit, the ERT, as "the CSI of the FBI." But their job was deadly serious.

At trial, Hahn identified photographs and explained to the jury what they had recovered from the luggage and the life raft: spears, a leather whip, two knives, a long blowgun and darts, a computer case, a camera, maps and charts, a handcuff key, a lock-pick tool, a survival kit, unused flares, binoculars, and a compass. A Motorola cell phone was found, but it was soaked with salt spray and seemed useless. However, the ship's cook had suggested that if the cell phone was packed inside a bag of ordinary rice, it would dry out enough for later analysis. Amazingly, the simple suggestion worked. The government had a wealth of indisputable detail even before other specialists mined the electronic information they would find in Zarabozo's cell phone and laptop, the computer seized from his living room in Hialeah, and the *Joe Cool*'s sophisticated electronic devices, especially its GPS. And there was also forensic analysis of physical evidence found on the *Joe Cool*, ballistic analysis of the four spent shell casings, and especially, the trail of human blood and the tragic story it told.

The prosecution team wanted the jury to see not only photographs of this evidence but also the actual items, which were wheeled into the well of the court on a large white plastic cart. During a break in the trial, the prosecution team laid out the larger items—the backpack, spears, blowgun, maps and charts, and so forth—for dramatic display on the carpeted floor in front of the jury box. They wanted to pass some of the smaller items—darts and two vicious-looking knives—around the jury, to demonstrate how ugly and dangerous these things were. But Judge Huck was concerned that the jury could potentially hurt themselves with the items, so a compromise was reached whereby the knives and other weapons were secured by plastic ties inside small, open boxes so they could safely be viewed by the jury up close.

The physical evidence seemed insurmountable, and the defense team wasted little effort in trying to discredit it. The government could prove exactly when and where Zarabozo had purchased things, stayed overnight in motels with Archer, and told his employers a few lies along the way. But all that evidence wouldn't get them to the crux of the matter: what was in Zarabozo's head, what he knew, and what his intention was in taking the fatal trip aboard the *Joe Cool* with Archer. It was the prosecution's burden to establish his knowledge and criminal intent, and the defense only had to provide a plausible, innocent alternative explanation. Since the prosecution had determined not to call co-conspirator Kirby Archer to testify, and Zarabozo wasn't about to admit his own culpability, prosecutors would have to rely on the jury to draw the correct inferences from the mountain of evidence in their arsenal.

They called the FBI case agent, Special Agent David Nuñez, to the stand to describe his interviews with Kirby Archer and Guillermo Zarabozo on Monday, September 24, aboard the Coast Guard cutter *Confidence*. In a clear, dispassionate voice, Nuñez described how he had been called early that Monday morning to assemble his Special Maritime Squad and travel by jet and then helicopter to the cutter *Confidence* to meet with Zarabozo and Archer. By now, the story of the search for the overdue fishing vessel was well known and the "pirates of the Caribbean" tale had been widely publicized and then recanted by both Archer and Zarabozo. What no one knew yet were the details of Nuñez's interviews with them and his observations of them.

Nuñez described Zarabozo as calm, cool, and collected throughout most of the interview, "just as he is now." The only time he seemed nervous was when Nuñez asked him for details he obviously wasn't prepared for, such as how and when he'd met Kirby Archer, and, most surprising of all, his apparent panic when he was asked about the girlfriends he and Archer were supposedly going to Bimini to meet. Nuñez asked him why he brought a blowgun, darts, knives, and a handcuff key on the trip, and Zarabozo had replied, "Just for fun."

Zarabozo's most disturbing behavior was his absolute calm, as Nuñez described it, when he told the special agent about the bloody killing spree aboard the *Joe Cool*. He had showed no emotion when talking about the slaughter, not even when he described how he had dumped Captain Jake Branam over the side of the charter fishing boat *while he was still alive*. This was the first public revelation of the horrific scenario of Jake Branam, shot, grievously wounded, bleeding and struggling, being heaved off his boat into deep water. Not even family members sitting in the courtroom had ever heard this shocking detail. It was a traumatic, wrenching moment for them, during what had been a tragic year since the loss of those aboard the *Joe Cool*. The courtroom was dead quiet as Amie Gamble and others struggled to control their tears.

When Nuñez moved on to describe his interview with Kirby Archer, it seemed that nothing worse could be revealed, but that turned out to be wrong. Nuñez told the silent courtroom that in Archer's version of events it was not the captain but *his wife who was still alive* when she was tossed overboard. It was another horrendous surprise for those in the courtroom, even worse, if possible, to imagine Kelley Branam floundering, bleeding, and dying alone in the deep ocean waters she had always feared. Nuñez said that Archer started laughing nervously when he spoke about it in the interview. "Do you think that's funny?" Nuñez had asked him. Archer shook his head but continued to laugh.

During this shattering testimony, it was impossible for spectators and jurors to avoid looking at Guillermo Zarabozo for a reaction. But he remained "calm, cool and collected" throughout, just as Nuñez described him. Indeed, the defendant showed almost no emotion during the entire trial. He sometimes chewed gum, sometimes sat slack-jawed, and he rarely made eye contact with the judge, the jurors, or anyone else. He wrote no notes to the defense team sitting around him and never conferred with them. Zarabozo seemed oddly disinterested, detached, even bored by the proceedings that would determine whether or not he would spend the rest of his life behind bars. The only time he reacted at all was when a witness was asked to identify him in court, and then he jumped up, eager, it seemed, to be recognized.

Judge Huck called for a break and the jurors filed silently out to the jury room. In the atrium, family members of the victims clung together, sobbing. Harry Branam said he couldn't get out of his mind the awful image of his grandson Jake, mortally wounded and thrashing around in the water, trying to save his wife as she, too, was tossed overboard. "Jake would have done anything to save her," Harry said. When Harry's girlfriend, Maria Gagliardo, learned about this testimony, she had nightmares for months afterward, dreaming that Jake was alive in the water and being torn apart by sharks.

IT had already been an exhausting, emotionally overwhelming day for the victims' families in the courtroom, and there was more to come. After the break, the government called an FBI specialist to introduce forensic evidence obtained in serology and DNA analysis and to describe the blood spatters found on the *Joe Cool*. Having long abandoned the hijackers story, Zarabozo's attorneys now claimed that Archer had done all the killing by himself on the fly bridge and the aft deck, all outdoors, and that none of the murders took place inside the salon while their client supposedly huddled in fear for his life in the bathroom.

But the spent shell casings and blood specks found on the *Joe Cool* told a different story. Three of the four casings, all from the same gun, had been found inside the salon of the boat, and one was embedded in the aft deck outside. Tiny blood flecks had been found on numerous vertical surfaces inside the salon and had been collected and analyzed. Since the defense team couldn't contest the results, they stipulated with the government to certain admitted facts that government experts wouldn't have to prove at trial. Among these was that the FBI had properly collected and preserved the evidence from the *Joe Cool*, which the Miami-Dade Police Crime Laboratory properly tested. This established the necessary chain of custody for the evidence to be admitted at trial.

The stipulations were contained in a written document agreed to by both prosecution and defense lawyers and filed with the court. These stipulations were read aloud to the jury at trial by prosecutor Michael Gilfarb. His deliberately dry, uninflected reading couldn't obscure the horrendous mental image the words created: blood flying in all directions, speckling, sticking to horizontal surfaces throughout the salon and galley, in what seemed to have been a desperate, bloody struggle. Because of the familial relationship between Jake Branam and his half brother, Scott Gamble, some of the blood specks couldn't be positively identified as belonging to either of them alone. There was blood found on the aft deck on the water hose used to wash down the boat, and some smears of blood found nearby along the companionway, blood that must have been transferred as the boat was being washed down and cleaned at sea.

But most of the blood identified was that of Samuel Kairy. Blood collected from vertical risers on the steps between the salon and the galley in photographs shown to the jury "tested positive for the blood of Samuel Kairy," Michael Gilfarb read aloud. The courtroom was absolutely silent.

On and on the grim list continued: blood on the stove, on the starboard and port-side engine compartments, from the steps between the berth and the bathrooms, and from the galley all tested positive for the blood of Samuel Kairy. It went on like a drumbeat in the silent courtroom: Samuel Kairy, Samuel Kairy, Samuel Kairy. His father, Albert, sitting next to Harry Branam, had never heard this before. His eyes reddened and teared as he listened quietly, imagining his son shot and bleeding, still fighting for his life. Harry patted Albert's arm consolingly and told him, "He went down hard."

Judge Huck ordered another short break in the proceedings, and the jury went back to the jury room. Spectators filed silently out to the atrium again. Harry said, "Sometimes I just can't believe it happened, then it all comes rushing back at me."

After the break, the government introduced George Hertel, of the Miami-Dade Police Department crime lab, to describe his evaluation of the spent shell casings found on the *Joe Cool*. The testimony was dry and routine, which was a relief after the emotional shocks of earlier in the day. Hertel concluded that all four shells had been fired from the same gun, likely a Glock. A single photograph from a forensic comparison microscope showing all four shell casings was placed on the Elmo and projected for the jurors and the spectators. When discussing his analysis, Hertel touched a finger to different portions of the photographs, making a bright pink line on the screens that disappeared at the conclusion of his testimony when he tapped lightly on the corner of the screen before him. Hertel concluded that the two magazines purchased by Archer and Zarabozo were for two different weapons, a Glock and a Sig Sauer, and couldn't be used interchangeably. Even though no shell casings were recovered from a Sig Sauer, prosecutors believed both had been used on the *Joe Cool*. The ammunition used was the deadliest kind, Hydra-Shok Federal Premium, jacketed hollow-point bullets restricted to law enforcement use only, because of their particularly fatal effect. Inside the body, the bullets exploded, tearing through bone, muscle, and tissue, destroying everything in their path.

Then finally, the long day in court was over.

CHAPTER EIGHTEEN

—————

Hialeah

The character of the Miami suburb of Hialeah has changed over the years. It used to be a middle-class neighborhood of hardworking families who raised some of South Florida's best-known lawyers, doctors, and bankers, a place that even the Branam family had once called home before their big leap to Star Island. In 2007, it had become an enclave where gun shops, shooting ranges, pawn shops, private security companies, and car repair shops seemed to be on every block. Newly arrived Cuban refugees often went straight to Hialeah, where they likely knew someone, or knew someone who knew someone, who could help them get settled, get a job, find an apartment. It was where Guillermo Zarabozo and his family settled when they arrived from Cuba and where Kirby Archer wound up living with the Perez family, whom he had known briefly during his tour of duty in Guantánamo, Cuba.

The jury learned through testimony at trial that Zarabozo had graduated from Hialeah High School and then held sporadic part-time jobs with many of the private security companies in Hialeah, which seemed to be mostly Hispanic-owned family enterprises, as were many of the used-car lots, pawn shops, and shooting ranges. Guillermo Zarabozo had worked part time as an independent contractor for several private security companies: All-American Security Services, Inc., Pinkerton, and Diplomatic Tactical Services (later known as Diplomatic Protective Services). Several of Zarabozo's employers testified at trial. This was a very public forum for the private security companies, and their licenses, their very livelihoods, depended upon a clean record of operations. Not surprisingly, all the witnesses spoke about their strict observance of the regulatory system that governed their businesses. In Florida, private security companies were governed by a web of state laws and by licenses issued, curiously, by the Florida Department of Agriculture.

But occasional missteps hinted that the system might not be as ironclad as it was portrayed to be. For example, one young woman testified that their security guards, who were all independent contractors rather than direct employees for liability reasons, were issued firearms only for a specific job for "armed security" and that their personnel were required to turn in the company's weapons immediately at the end of the job. No weapons were allowed to be taken home.

What if someone failed to return a firearm? she was asked.

If a guard failed to return a company weapon, the company would call the guard and "remind" him to turn in his weapon.

What if the gun still wasn't returned to the company?

If necessary, the company would follow up with the guard and send him a letter threatening to report the gun as stolen if it was not returned.

And if the gun never turned up?

There was no clear answer. According to the witness, if a gun wasn't returned after a job, it could take weeks, if not months, to find it. And apparently some weapons simply "went missing."

The prosecution could not prove that Zarabozo had acquired his Glock from one of his private security company employers, but the implication was there. All the employers confirmed that the young man was very careful and "a good kid." Obviously, Zarabozo was fascinated by guns, enjoyed handling them, and liked to practice at one of the conveniently located shooting ranges in Hialeah.

Guillermo Zarabozo had also worked on occasion as an extra or stuntman for J.C.B. Productions, the production company behind some of the Spanish-language *telenovelas,* run on the side by a Hialeah police officer. Stills of Zarabozo in a fake police uniform, with a fake gun, leaning against a prop patrol car were projected on-screen for the jury and the spectators. His employer had no complaints about Zarabozo, but he had just stopped returning calls for work sometime in late August or early September.

Prosecutor Karen Gilbert called the government's "star" witness: Carlos Mulet, who owned an auto repair shop in Hialeah. Short, dark, stocky, and surly, Mulet didn't bother to dress up for court; he wore a wrinkled polo shirt, untucked, over baggy jeans and rundown boots. His longish dark hair had begun to recede, and he was unshaven. Speaking with a heavy Spanish accent, he was a reluctant, sometimes sullen, witness at trial since he freely admitted that he liked Zarabozo and "didn't want to get him in trouble." But Mulet had little latitude in his testimony, despite his friendly feeling for Zarabozo, since he himself had narrowly escaped a jail term for running a chop-shop specializing in theft to order of Mustang Cobras, possession of a motor vehicle with altered identification, and grand theft. He had been arrested by the Miami-Dade Police Department on October 16, 2007, and first met with FBI agents investigating the *Joe Cool* case on October 25. As part of his agreement with the Miami-Dade prosecutors on the chop-shop case, he had agreed to testify truthfully before a federal grand jury. Carlos Mulet was hemmed in. He was currently on probation for the state charges, so he would have to testify truthfully in this case or risk revocation of his probation and a quick trip to jail.

Mulet testified that Zarabozo was fascinated by fast cars, specifically Mustang Cobras, the hot car of choice for young men in Hialeah. He and some pals hung around Mulet's auto repair shop, he said. "The kids at school used to go to my house to see how I make the Mustangs go fast." Mulet admitted that Zarabozo had twice worked for him as a "spotter," someone who spots a Mustang parked somewhere and relays that information to Mulet in exchange for a fee. Mulet had paid Zarabozo $250 for spotting a Mustang that was later stolen, and admitted collecting $500 from someone else for the same tip, then splitting the take with his good friend, Guillermo. But Mulet denied taking part in the actual theft of the Mustang.

In his shop, Mulet stocked "Cobra kits," emblems and fixtures used to make an ordinary Mustang look like a Cobra, a more expensive car. He used such fixtures to tart up Zarabozo's own Mustang. During a break, Amie Gamble remarked, "Even his car was fake."

Mulet also admitted that he knew Kirby Archer, whom he called "the Gringo," and believed that Archer had some "high government contacts" and could help him "clean up" his driving record, which was so bad that he couldn't get auto insurance at any price. Mulet also did some auto repair work for Archer, who paid him in cash and always used the name Anoris Perez on the receipts. Anoris Perez was a member of the Perez family, with whom Archer was then living. The Gringo, Mulet recalled, never used his own name for anything.

Unfortunately for Mulet, he became deeply involved in Archer and Zarabozo's affairs. He was lucky not to be charged as an accomplice in the deadly rampage aboard the

Joe Cool. It was Carlos Mulet who introduced Kirby Archer to Guillermo Zarabozo. When Archer asked Mulet sometime in March 2007 if he knew where Archer could get a gun, Mulet recommended Zarabozo, who occasionally brought his Glock into the auto shop and practiced shooting at a range located conveniently only a half block away from Mulet's shop. Mulet made the introduction and Zarabozo somehow procured a handgun, believed to be the Sig Sauer, and sold it to Archer for $400. Then Archer told Mulet that he needed someone to help him with "a big job." Mulet thought Zarabozo would be ideal; he was a tall, strapping young man who, Mulet knew from personal experience, would be willing to do something illegal to make a buck.

Whenever Zarabozo and Archer came to Mulet's shop together, they parked out of range of the sixteen surveillance video cameras that they knew Mulet had installed inside and outside around the perimeter of his shop.

The plan began to develop, Mulet testified in court, shortly thereafter. Archer started to talk about needing a big, fast boat that could take heavy seas. He said he wanted a sixty- to seventy-foot boat to go to the Bahamas, refuel, and then go somewhere else. Archer asked Mulet where to find such a boat. Prior to his auto repair business, Mulet had worked for Detroit Diesel as a mechanic, and so he was very familiar with diesel engines on cars and boats. He recommended some marinas, and the three of them went out scouting together. Mulet took Archer and Zarabozo to Detroit Diesel's engine repair shop on the Miami River, and they all wore Detroit Diesel T-shirts, which Mulet had left over from his employment there. It was no problem getting past security, since the guard at the gate was someone Mulet knew. While they made small talk, Archer and Zarabozo took a look at the boats on the dock to get an idea of what they were looking for. When they left, Mulet told them that stealing a boat from Detroit Diesel would be too difficult, since there were too many drawbridges between the repair shop on the Miami

River and Government Cut, the channel that led to deep water.

They discussed other marinas, especially the one at the posh neighborhood of Cocoplum. There were no bridges between the Cocoplum Yacht Club's docks and open water, but there was too much security on duty, according to Mulet. The boats were big and expensive, just like the homes, and they were heavily guarded. Archer and Zarabozo mentioned Pier 66 in Fort Lauderdale. Same problem, Mulet told them. Too much security. Zarabozo asked about the marina near Monty's. Mulet told him it was no good because the boats were too small and too old—not up to the speed they needed.

As they toured a few marinas and discussed the plan in more detail, it became obvious to Mulet that Archer and Zarabozo knew nothing about boats, not even how to start one. He tried to tutor them in the basics, but there were too many possibilities for error, since the very sophisticated electronic and mechanical systems on big boats required specialized knowledge and experience. Why don't you come along and just start a boat for us? they asked Mulet. But he declined. It was too risky and definitely out of his territory.

Next Archer asked Mulet to go with them all the way and be part of the planned big job, which would make them all rich. Rich enough, Archer said, that he could retire on a yacht in Miami Beach when they returned. Zarabozo chimed in, telling Mulet that Archer worked for the FBI. Then he said it was the CIA and then the Secret Service. The story kept changing. Zarabozo said he expected to make $1 million on this job. In court, Mulet recalled that he told Zarabozo, "If it's that much money, it must be something illegal." Apparently undeterred by that factor, Mulet finally got down to practicalities. How long would the job take? he asked. From three to six months, Archer told him. Again, Mulet declined, but he did ask for more details about the job.

You'll find out when you get there, Archer replied. But in the end, Mulet decided not to go.

At that point, Mulet recalled in court, Archer said to Zarabozo, "We'll have to go to Plan B." According to Mulet, Zarabozo looked surprised but said nothing. Neither he nor Zarabozo asked Archer any questions about Plan B.

Mulet concluded by telling the jury that he "did not think it was possible" that Archer and Zarabozo could pull off stealing a boat by starting it and then driving it themselves. He wasn't sure when Archer and Zarabozo actually left the Miami Beach Marina. Mulet received a voice message on his cell phone from Zarabozo, telling Mulet that "he was out on the sea, and for me to go pick up [his] car at Miami Beach Marina somewhere between 20th and 22nd of September." On September 22, Mulet retrieved Zarabozo's car from the Miami Beach Marina parking lot as they had agreed. That night, he left it parked outside his garage with the keys in a wheel well. The next morning, it was gone, as expected. Things were going according to plan.

"When the news of the defendant's—of the case and the boat, when all that made the news, why didn't you come forward to law enforcement and tell them what you knew?" prosecutor Karen Gilbert asked.

"I prefer law enforcement to come forward to me," Mulet answered.

Federal Public Defender Anthony Natale began his cross-examination, initiating a line of questioning concerning the timing of Mulet's interviews with the FBI, whether the FBI attempted to interfere with the police department's handling of Mulet's case, and the implication that Mulet had been offered something in exchange for his testimony. Karen Gilbert objected, and Judge Huck called the lawyers to sidebar for discussion.

The judge turned on the "white noise" sound system so that no one but the judge, the lawyers, and the court reporter could hear their discussion. In the modern federal courtroom, a judge didn't simply put his hand over a microphone to keep sidebars confidential. Technology took care of that.

THE long, stressful days of trial were not without their lighter moments, however.

One morning during the trial, a meticulously dressed and coiffed blond woman appeared in the gallery sitting directly behind prosecutor Karen Gilbert. She was new to the trial scene, and during a break, she identified herself, in a smooth Southern drawl, as Karen Gilbert's mother. She said she was here "on probation" with her daughter, since in an earlier trial observation, she had chastised the defense team for "being so mean to her daughter," and Gilbert had banned her from the courtroom. She was charming and delightful, with a sharp wit and a keen sense of what was transpiring in the trial. At one point, with the jury out of the courtroom, Judge Huck asked the lawyers what time it was as he was planning the trial schedule for the day. In a stage whisper that reached every corner of the courtroom, she said, "The judge doesn't even know what time it is?" This drew a sharp look from Judge Huck, a whispered rebuke from Karen Gilbert, and smiles from everyone else. That was the last time Karen Gilbert's mother attended the trial.

On another occasion, Cuban coffee was somehow distributed to spectators sitting in the gallery behind the defense team. This very potent brew was usually drunk as "shots" in tiny, white, pleated paper cups, and suddenly they were everywhere on the "Cuban side" of the courtroom. Just as suddenly, a courtroom security officer swooped in, removed all the coffee, and hustled a spectator out the door. No reference was ever made to the brief episode. Cuban coffee was available throughout the surrounding neighborhood through restaurant windows open to the sidewalks, but no one ever disclosed—publicly—how the forbidden shots mysteriously wound up inside the courtroom. It never happened again.

Such small incidents occasionally leavened the mood in the courtroom, but diversions were only brief and temporary respites from the grim business of the case.

CHAPTER NINETEEN

The *CSI* Factor

The phenomenal success of the *CSI* television programs has led to much serious speculation in the legal community about whether modern jurors must be dazzled by sophisticated, definitive, almost magical forensic evidence in order to convict a defendant of anything at all. Judges talked about it, lawyers held professional seminars on the subject, and law professors charted evidentiary presentations at criminal trials.

The *Joe Cool* trial provided grist for this discussion, since so much scientific evidence was on display daily in the courtroom. Several hours of expert testimony were devoted to the intricacies of the SIM card, and how cell towers, or cell sites, triangulate cell phone signals to determine where and when a particular cell phone or SIM card was used, the exact length of the call, the number to which the call was made, whether a connection was established, and if so, how long the connection lasted. Cell service provider records also show whether a transmission from a cell phone was oral conversation or a text message. At trial, an expert used a detailed map of South Florida to demonstrate where each cell site was located and exactly what information was learned about Zarabozo's and Archer's cell phone use in the planning stage of the crimes. It was a long, tedious procedure, and jurors sometimes looked bored or even swiveled aimlessly in their chairs. Every single one of the many cell phone transmissions was displayed and described in detail using printed and coded records produced by T-Mobile, Sprint Nextel, and AT&T during the investigation.

The cell phone evidence verified what the jury already knew from other witnesses: Archer and Zarabozo called several marinas and charter fishing companies throughout South Florida and even Key West searching for a boat for their fatal trip. But something interesting also turned up. Carlos Mulet had testified that Archer always carried at least two or three disposable cell phones with him. On one occasion, he used one to call his "supervisor at the CIA," apparently to establish his bona fides as a spy to Mulet. Forensic analysis of the cell phone records showed, however, that Archer had actually called the public information number of CIA headquarters and heard only the answering machine outgoing announcement before he hung up.

A forensic computer expert reviewed the information he had extracted from Zarabozo's computer and laptop and explained how the evidence was analyzed. Although similarly detailed, this presentation proved more interesting. The jury and spectators learned that Archer and Zarabozo left an indelible trail of their activities and their physical location in every hotel or motel room or cybercafe in which they used their laptop. As is standard everywhere, as soon as Zarabozo booted up his own laptop in his hotel room, either using a physical connection or the hotel's wireless system, a record was created not only of which laptop was being used and which Internet sites were visited but also which hotel room the laptop was used in, when, and for how long. Hotels often have more than one Internet address dedicated for customer use; some assign a separate address to each room and others bundle rooms together for use on several different Internet addresses. Either way, providers maintained records of these Internet address assignments, which created an electronic footprint that could be retrieved by someone who knew how to do it.

Through Zarabozo's carefully saved receipts, investigators had tracked his and Archer's movements in the days immediately preceding the trip on the *Joe Cool*. They were on the move constantly, never staying in the same motel on consecutive nights. The places they chose weren't fancy; they stayed in several Holiday Inns, one near the University of Miami and one on Miami Beach, and a Days Inn and, in Key West, an El Rancho Motel.

The criminal investigation revealed that in some instances, Archer used a laptop in a motel room first to check his MySpace page, then logged off, and next Zarabozo used the same laptop in the same room and logged on to his own MySpace page. Sometimes this happened several times in the course of a single night. The evidence documented that Archer and Zarabozo always shared a room in these motels and that Zarabozo always paid, either in cash or using his Bank of America debit card. Video surveillance of these motels showed Zarabozo at the reception counter checking in, often with the barrel of his long blowgun clearly visible protruding from his backpack, while Archer skulked in the background wearing sunglasses until check-in was complete. The videos confirmed witnesses' descriptions of Archer as a man who held himself aloof, wore sunglasses even at night and indoors, and cultivated an air of superiority and mystery. After Zarabozo finished check-in, he and Archer boarded the motel elevators together to locate their room.

The MySpace pages from the laptop records were also illuminating, especially Archer's, since he used his to enhance his self-made reputation as an international man of mystery. He had only twelve friends listed and photos mostly of members of the Perez family with whom he was living, but he also had an elaborate page featuring a picture of a white tiger instead of his face and including a long description of himself in the form of a bizarre, self-aggrandizing poem called "My Mask." In it, Archer adopts the pose of a world-weary, noble old samurai, a self-sacrificing hero who must live behind "a mask" in painful isolation to protect his "loved ones" as he "strides and fights for others, though violence is [his] reward," in some sort of epic battle that is "never ending." Everyone admires him, but no one really knows him or understands his secret pain. The poem addresses an unidentified "you," likely Zarabozo, perhaps as part of his recruiting pitch for their fantasy future together of glamorous international intrigue. It begins: "You think my life is amazing. It's a line you have never crossed. You say I'm on top of the world, but you don't know what I have lost." He seems to invite Zarabozo to join him in his lonely but grand enterprise: "Another to take the task at hand, and do my work in kind." In the poem, Archer claims he wants to "live a life like yours," presumably the boring, inferior, mundane life of ordinary people, as soon as his noble task is completed: "I pray it will soon be over, and I shall be free from this task. Then I can be a man again, and throw away this mask." Next to the picture of the white tiger labeled "Archie," he wrote: "I don't want to be remembered at all . . . . [I]f I'm being remembered, then I'm dead!!!"

But what was the all-consuming "task" that compelled Archer to live behind a mask and "stride and fight for others," with violence as his only reward? The poem gave no clue.

Archer's final MySpace entry was shown as September

22, 2007, the day that he and Zarabozo embarked on the
Joe Cool. In a lengthy farewell to the Perez family, he refers
to leaving for some sort of mysterious job and declares
"I'm good at what I do and I'll be fine." His propensity for
secrecy, misdirection, and illusion is apparent throughout
his farewell: "I know I've been secretive, that's the way I
am and there's no changing that, especially now. If curios-
ity has gotten the better of you and you are still wondering
who that 'special someone' is . . . well, there is no such person." He alludes to a game of deceiving and manipulating
his hosts to divert attention from his real intentions. Archer
concludes: "[S]orry for the deception, but your reactions
were fun. However, all of you have affected me in one way
or another and I'd do most anything for any of you. I'll miss
you all very much . . . Keep a light on for me. Live well my
friends . . . . Goodbye!"

THE *Joe Cool*'s departure from Miami Beach Marina on
September 22 was thoroughly documented by the marina's
elaborate video surveillance system, which compiles record-
ings from multiple camera angles. The system is designed
to automatically alternate between camera angles approximately every ten seconds. Each video was time-stamped.
The *Joe Cool* left its slip at the marina on September 22 at
3:49 P.M., according to the video produced at trial. Another
video showed the *Joe Cool* traveling east through Government Cut toward open water at 3:51 P.M.

When Jake's uncle Jeff Branam took the stand, he provided much more emotional evidence of the *Joe Cool*'s departure on that sunny Saturday afternoon. In response to the
letter from BOATPIX, the company that contacted him
about purchasing what they described as pictures taken of
the *Joe Cool* in Miami on September 22, 2007, Jeff had been
advised by the prosecution to go ahead and order the photos.

The photos might have been shots of the boat sitting in the slip or shoving off from the marina, or pictures taken from their early-morning fishing trip that same day. But what Jeff received was like a stab in the heart. The photos were obviously taken from a helicopter from several angles, just as the boat was picking up speed after passing the bright red bouy en route to Bimini. Jeff's son, Jon, was visible, riding his Jet Ski along the portside wake. The *Joe Cool* was lifting to its cruising plane, throwing a foamy white wake, in clear, bright sunshine, heading east to Bimini.

Under the cover on the fly bridge, clearly visible from several angles in the photos, were Captain Jake at the controls and his wife, Kelley, sitting on the starboard side. Beside her, just as Jon had told the FBI, sat Guillermo Zarabozo.

The government had one more piece of forensic evidence for the jury: the meticulous records kept by the GPS aboard the *Joe Cool*. The prosecutors' expert witness described how the GPS continually bounced signals off orbiting satellites and recorded the boat's exact position on a series of "way points," which were then overlaid on a map of the part of the ocean through which the boat traveled. The GPS also correlated the exact time each way point was created. Using a diagram, he illustrated how and when the *Joe Cool* left a clear GPS track from the moment it pulled out of the slip in Miami Beach Marina on September 22 until it was found abandoned and drifting on September 23 just thirty miles from Cuba, over 140 miles south of its original track.

The record of the *Joe Cool*'s travel track was exact and dramatic. First, the GPS showed a straight line of travel beginning right at the Miami Beach Marina slip, passing through Government Cut, and heading directly for Bimini, as displayed in a bright pink line traced by the witness on the map. According to the witness, at that time, the *Joe*

Cool was piloted by "someone who knows what they're doing." Just short of Bimini, however, the GPS track became erratic, stopping dead in the water, drifting on the northeast current briefly, then turning south in a wobbly line when speed is resumed. The *Joe Cool* continued a generally southern course into the Gulf Stream under the control of someone who apparently didn't know how to pilot the boat, according to the witness. The jury learned that the Gulf Stream is a deep, pulsing river of water within the ocean, larger in volume than all the other rivers in the world combined. It creates a powerful, unrelenting current that pushes everything in its path to the north. The GPS readings showed exactly when the boat finally stopped its forward progress, very close to the Cuban coast, and began to drift slowly on the Gulf Stream back toward the north. This was when the *Joe Cool* had run out of fuel. Finally, the boat lost battery power to the GPS. The track simply stopped at that point, although the *Joe Cool* continued to drift slowly northward. When the *Joe Cool*'s life raft was recovered, it was actually north of the boat, moving more quickly on the Gulf Stream current because it was lighter.

Using his calculations of the boat's speed, the current in the Bimini area, and the GPS track, the witness determined precisely when and where Captain Jake Branam had lost control of his boat. There was a period of exactly one minute eighteen seconds when the *Joe Cool*'s engines still had power, but the throttles had been cut back and no one was at the helm steering the boat. The *Joe Cool* was simply adrift, moving slightly north on the Gulf Stream current near Bimini. The GPS was an unimpeachable witness. The tragedy that had befallen Jake, Kelley, Sammy, and Scott had taken only one minute eighteen seconds just outside Bimini Bay shortly before 6 P.M. on Saturday, September 22. What had happened to four strong, vibrant, healthy young adults during that brief time?

According to Zarabozo's lawyers, Kirby Archer climbed down from the fly bridge, entered the cabin, took Zarabozo's Glock out of his luggage down in the salon, then climbed back up the ladder to the fly bridge, killed Jake and Kelley, cut the throttles back, then climbed back down the ladder and shot Sammy and Scott on the lower deck, all while Zarabozo was hiding in fear in the bathroom and the boat was adrift, wallowing in the Gulf Stream. Then Archer found Zarabozo and ordered him at gunpoint to throw the four bodies over the side of the boat and wash down the decks. Archer climbed back up to the fly bridge, took over the controls of the *Joe Cool,* and tried to steer it south to Cuba, heading directly against the northbound current.

But prosecutor Karen Gilbert told the jury that scenario was physically impossible within the brief period of one minute eighteen seconds when the *Joe Cool* was adrift. Obviously, to kill four strong, young people on two separate deck locations in such a short time, toss their bodies overboard, clean up the decks, and then take over the boat's controls and turn it south, there must have been two men and two guns: Archer with his Sig Sauer on the fly bridge killing Jake and Kelley, and Zarabozo with his Glock killing Sammy and Scott on the deck below. Then Archer and Zarabozo, working together, dumped the four bodies overboard. Zarabozo got out the boat's freshwater hose and began to wash down the carnage left on the *Joe Cool*'s bloody decks, up on the fly bridge and on the aft deck below. Then Kirby Archer climbed back up the ladder to the fly bridge to take over the controls, throttle the engines up, and turn the boat south at a point and time clearly established by the GPS.

FINALLY, Guillermo Zarabozo took the stand in his own defense. It was somewhat anticlimactic, as Zarabozo merely

repeated what had already been testified to by other witnesses and claimed to have forgotten much. Anthony Natale
walked him through his background, his plan to become a
police officer, and how he was duped by the nefarious Kirby
Archer with promises of a lucrative security job in Bimini.
Zarabozo said he was using the bathroom when he heard
gunshots, and when he opened the door, he saw Archer
standing over Sammy Kairy's lifeless body. Then Natale
told Zarabozo to look directly at the jury.

"Did you shoot anyone on that boat?" Natale asked.

"No," Zarabozo replied.

Throughout his testimony, Zarabozo had maintained his
curious demeanor of detachment and disinterest close to the
point of boredom. Even when describing the bloodbath on
the *Joe Cool*, he was brief and matter-of-fact, apparently
emotionless. His testimony was monotonous. Even Karen
Gilbert couldn't provoke him during her tough, detailed
cross-examination. In one exchange, she asked him how
many shots he heard fired on the *Joe Cool*, and he replied that
he didn't remember. Obviously frustrated, Gilbert responded,
"Sir, it's not hard to remember if it really happened." Even
this got little response from Guillermo Zarabozo.

Finally, the trial wound to a close. Outside the presence
of the jury, Judge Huck and the lawyers hammered out the
wording of the jury instructions, and time frames for the lawyers' closing arguments were set. The judge wanted no inter-
ruptions or objections during closing arguments, and the
attorneys agreed to adhere to his ground rules.

Closing arguments summarized the evidence and the arguments for each party at trial. There were no surprises, just
a careful ordering of what had been presented and which
inferences each lawyer wanted the jury to draw from all the
circumstantial and forensic evidence that had been presented at trial. The judge read aloud a large stack of instructions on the legal definitions of the crimes charged and how

the jury should apply the law in evaluating the evidence and reaching their verdict. He explained the verdict form they would take with them to the jury room. Finally, they adjourned to deliberate. There was nothing more to be done except wait for a verdict.

CHAPTER TWENTY

Trouble

Handwritten notes from the jury foreman to Judge Huck began to rumble into the courtroom soon after the jury retired to begin their deliberations. Whenever a note was received, Judge Huck assembled the lawyers and read it aloud to them, inviting discussion and proposals for his response to the jury. The first note asked the following question: "If Zarabozo brought the gun on board not knowing that a crime was going to happen, does that make 'Z' automatically a participant [in] a crime because a gun was used?"

The prosecution team was alarmed. Obviously, the jury was considering the legal effect of Zarabozo's carrying his Glock aboard the *Joe Cool* even if he didn't know what was going to happen. They seemed to be buying the idea that Zarabozo had no advance knowledge of the criminal plan, that Archer alone was the architect and the perpetrator of the crimes, and that Zarabozo was simply an innocent dupe who happened to bring his gun along on what he thought was a trip to Bimini for a bodyguarding job. The note implied that the jury was adopting the defense version completely, a very good sign for Zarabozo's lawyers. The only thing the jury seemed confused about was whether simply bringing the gun on board was enough to convict Zarabozo of all the crimes.

With the jury still sequestered in the jury room, the prosecution argued to Judge Huck that the question was vague and that the judge should respond by referring the jury back to the set of printed jury instructions, the superseding indictment, and their own memories of all the evidence that had been presented at trial. The defense team, however, urged Judge Huck to answer the question directly by telling the jury that, under the law, Zarabozo was not "automatically" guilty of the crimes aboard the *Joe Cool* just because he brought the gun. Anthony Natale told Judge Huck, "Jurors should not be led to believe a defendant is an automatic participant of a crime just because he brought a firearm on board."

In the end, Judge Huck declined to answer the jury's question directly and sent a note telling them to review the charges, the jury instructions, the superseding indictment, and the evidence presented at trial. This was how judges usually responded to inquiries from the jury, since the precise wording of each instruction was developed over years of legal precedent to reflect exactly how the law should be applied to the facts the jury finds in a case. In preparation for jury deliberations, the prosecution and defense teams had submitted their separate sets of instructions correlated to the law on each crime charged, and Judge Huck had ruled on every legal instruction presented to the jury in a "charge conference," a hearing in which the judge rules on which instructions correctly represent the state of the law on each element of each crime charged. This jury question was unique only in its suggestion that deliberations might be developing in an unforeseen, perhaps illogical, and maybe even legally incorrect direction. But Judge Huck believed that the answer the jury sought was contained in the instructions they had already been given, and that they should continue their work. Deliberations resumed.

The next note advised the judge that the jury was deadlocked: "As a jury, we feel stuck in the sand [and we] have no hope or expectation that we will be able to move to a consensus." Again, Judge Huck urged them to continue their work. Finally, after four days of deliberation, the jury sent another note stating that they had reached a partial verdict and could go no further. After consulting with the attorneys, Judge Huck recalled the jury to the courtroom to hear their verdict.

Of the sixteen counts in the superseding indictment— four first-degree murders, four kidnapping counts, the hijacking, the robbery of the *Joe Cool*, interfering with safe navigation of a vessel, conspiracy to commit the crimes, and four counts of using a firearm in the commission of a violent crime—the jury was deadlocked on the first twelve counts and found Guillermo Zarabozo guilty only on the last four counts, that is, guilty of using a firearm in the commission of a violent crime. Ironically, these last four counts were the ones subsequently added to the original indictment. But the verdict seemed logically inconsistent. How could the jury have found Zarabozo guilty of using a firearm in committing a violent crime yet not find that he had in fact committed any crime at all?

Under the law, these were "partial verdicts" since the jury was unanimous in finding Guillermo Zarabozo guilty on only four counts out of the sixteen counts charged. Federal criminal law required that a jury be unanimous in order to render a verdict, either guilty or not guilty. There was no unanimous verdict on any of the other twelve counts. Therefore, the case was deemed a mistrial on the other twelve counts on which no unanimous verdict was reached. The defense argued that even the four verdicts on which the jury unanimously convicted Zarabozo were logically inconsistent, because if Zarabozo wasn't convicted of committing *any* crimes, then he couldn't be convicted of using a firearm in committing a violent crime. But were the verdicts *legally* inconsistent as well as *logcially* inconsistent? Only Judge Huck could decide. The judge accepted the four partial verdicts, declared a mistrial as to the remaining twelve counts, and the jury was dismissed. He ordered the lawyers to begin immediate preparation for a retrial and forbade them from speaking with any members of the jury. Whether the retrial would also include the final four counts of the partial verdict was a matter for another day. Judge Huck wanted briefs and legal citations from the lawyers before making that decision.

Then the next battle began.

For the defense team, this was a big victory. The jury's verdict meant that they had persuaded at least some of the jurors that their client was an innocent young man duped by the evil Kirby Archer, and so Guillermo Zarabozo was not culpable in the bloodbath aboard the *Joe Cool*. As it turned out, the law was on their side regarding the legal posture of the inconsistent verdicts. If all Zarabozo had done was bring a gun aboard the boat, and he was innocent (or at least, not convicted) of the knowledge, conspiracy, planning, and execution of any of the violent crimes alleged, then he couldn't be convicted on the gun charge alone. Under legal precedent cited by the defense team, Zarabozo was not "automatically" responsible for what Archer had done with his gun if Zarabozo had no knowledge of or participation in the crimes.

THE partial verdict was a bitter blow for the victims' families. They couldn't understand it. The prosecution team had carefully presented what had seemed an insurmountable mountain of circumstantial and forensic evidence in the case. They had tracked Zarabozo and Archer's every move, every

phone call, every purchase, every step they took in the long
path of preparation for the hijacking and the execution of
their deadly plan. How could the jury have failed to understand that throughout the weeks and months of planning and
preparation, followed by the commission of the final, horrendous crimes and the subsequent attempted cover-up with
the Cuban pirates tale, Zarabozo had knowingly and willfully
participated with Archer? What had the prosecutors missed?
And what should they do now?

Amie Gamble, sister to Scott, half sister to Jake, and
sister-in-law to Kelley, broke down in sobs as soon as she
heard the partial verdicts. Reporters sought Amie out for
reactions throughout the trial, and she was a recognizable
figure on local television news. A tall, pretty blonde, Amie
was approachable, telegenic, articulate, and open with reporters about her feelings without being maudlin or shrill.
She seemed to be a kind, gracious, and thoughtful person,
even under the grueling pressure of the tragedy that had
ripped through her family. There was a certain restraint and
elegance about her. Amie distanced herself from the parti-
san warfare of the Branam clan and kept her focus on justice for the victims aboard the *Joe Cool*. She told reporters
that she was relieved that Zarabozo had at least been convicted of something, but she was "hugely disappointed"
that the families would have to endure another wrenching
trial.

Meanwhile, three jurors discussed with reporters what
had happened during deliberations in the jury room. They
were free to do so, since the trial was over and the prohibi-
tion against speaking with jurors applied only to the lawyers
in the case, not to reporters. Apparently these three jurors had
been the holdouts, reluctant to convict Guillermo Zarabozo
of anything. They told reporters that another juror had attempted to bully them into voting for conviction, ridiculing
and shouting at them and slamming his hand down on the

table. Two of the holdouts said they felt intimidated and finally voted to convict on the four firearm charges just to end the deliberations. When they later learned that the charges carried a life in prison penalty, they were dismayed and expressed a desire to "unconvict," believing that Zarabozo hadn't really done anything wrong and shouldn't be subjected to such harsh punishment. "I never believed for a minute that he was guilty of any of the charges, not even the ones we convicted him of," one juror told reporter Vanessa Blum of the *South Florida Sun-Sentinel*. "That's something I'll have to live with."

The jurors' feelings and public comments would play no part in Judge Huck's decision about the verdicts. But they shocked the families of the victims and the prosecution team. It seemed as if the holdouts had attended a completely different trial than everyone else. Had something been lacking in the prosecutors' presentation, or was it simply a fluke, a case of intense, personal antagonism among jurors resulting in a disastrous deliberation and an incomprehensible verdict? Trial lawyers often took one of two positions regarding the selection and composition of a jury. The first was, just give me the first twelve people off the street; I can convince anyone of anything. The second was, trials are won or lost in jury selection, and what happens during a trial doesn't really change any minds. The present scenario seemed to present a third alternative: unpredictable personal interaction and antagonism in the jury room could wreck even the most carefully presented trial.

The prosecutors ruminated about the case. What should their strategy be for the next trial? And what about the partial verdicts? Judge Huck would ultimately decide whether to vacate them or let them stand, and the prosecution team was reluctant to relinquish even that slim victory. If Judge Huck vacated the verdicts, should the government appeal his decision? An appeal could take months, even years, and meanwhile Zarabozo would be retried on at least the first twelve counts. Where would they be if he was acquitted at the next trial? Since there was going to be a retrial, anyway, should the prosecutors forgo an appeal and retry Zarabozo on all sixteen counts? The discussions went round and round.

CHAPTER TWENTY-ONE

Inside the Jury Room

Several of the jurors who were selected to hear the *Joe Cool* murder case had already heard or read about the highly publicized crimes, but three of them—Eve Tolley, Venora Gray, and Raul Garcia—knew very little about the case in advance, according to Tolley. Most of the others seemed to have at least some information about it before they were selected to hear the case. This was not unusual, especially with a notorious, high-profile quadruple-murder case like the *Joe Cool*. In this case, as in most similar cases, prospective jurors were asked whether they could set aside what they thought they already knew and rely entirely upon the evidence presented in court when deliberating and reaching their verdict in the case. All of the jurors and alternates who were selected had promised to do that.

According to juror Eve Tolley, a married woman who lived on nearby Key Biscayne, divisions began to form among the jurors almost immediately. Since the jurors were permitted (i.e., required) to leave the courthouse each day for their lunch break, groups quickly formed among certain jurors who developed the habit of going out to lunch together—exclusively—on a daily basis. This led, inevitably, to the formation of tight subgroups that became solidified over the several days of trial, causing problems when deliberations began among all the jurors inside the jury room. Also, despite every precaution taken by Judge Huck to keep others detained in the courtroom while the jurors left the building each day for lunch, the jurors were easily accessible to anyone in the limited surrounding area where food was available. At least one juror actively sought out some who were regular spectators in the gallery during the trial, perhaps assuming they were journalists.

Other courthouses had developed better methods for dealing with these problems. For example, Miami's state criminal courthouse, the Richard E. Gerstein Justice Building, had a cafeteria on the ground floor where jurors were seated together in an area separated from the rest of the lunch customers. A court employee conducted the jurors to the cafeteria, made sure they had everything they needed, prevented anyone else from entering the area, and then escorted the jury back upstairs to the jury room after lunch. This kept the jurors together as a single unit and reduced the opportunity for the formation of cliques or for others to interact with the jurors. Some courts took jurors' lunch orders and had food delivered to the jury room, where the jurors ate together as a group.

Lunch breaks for jurors, judges, and employees who worked at the beautiful new Wilkie D. Ferguson Jr. Federal Courthouse in downtown Miami were a big problem. The building's ground floor contained an expansive space for a cafeteria and kitchen, but even three years after the building's occupation, dedication, and naming for the late federal judge, it remained empty. There wasn't even a place to get a cup of bad vending machine coffee anywhere in the building. As Miami lawyer, author, and trial judge Milton

Hirsch put it, "Any accurate depiction of the criminal justice microcosm must include the vital role of the coffee shop."

The lack of on-site provisions for the jury's lunch breaks was more than an inconvenience in this case. It probably contributed to the breakdown of the jury's deliberations inside the courtroom by creating a situation conducive to the formation of subgroups, a breakdown in the unity of the jury as a working group, and a complete loss of control over whom or what jurors might come into contact with outside during their lunch breaks.

Unlike some others, Eve Tolley said that she avoided teaming up with any of the jury's subgroups for lunch each day. "I was in a solo orbit," she claimed. Returning home each evening from the long days of trial, "I was comatose," she recalled. She said that her husband always asked her "how it went in court today," and she always replied, "I can't talk about it." She took her obligations as a juror very seriously and believed that, on the whole, the others did as well.

But she felt it was clear from their first day of deliberations that several minds were already made up for conviction. One juror told the others, "If you ever read a newspaper, you'd know [Zarabozo] was guilty." But reading daily accounts of the trial was just what Judge Paul Huck had instructed the jurors not to do. Tolley and others wondered whether some of their colleagues on the jury were still reading or hearing about press accounts, or even watching the extensive daily television coverage, but she never raised the subject with anyone. One juror told the others that as soon as he got home from court each day, his wife brought him up-to-date on the day's news coverage of the trial.

Everyone knew that one of the jurors, later identified in press reports as a man named Jackie Warner, was totally convinced that Guillermo Zarabozo was guilty on every count, from the first day of their deliberations, right down the line.

Warner often seemed frustrated that others didn't agree with his analysis of the case. There was shouting, yelling, and sometimes belligerent pounding on the table and even lunging across the table to make a point. At least one juror told reporters that she felt intimidated into convicting Guillermo Zarabozo of even the weapons charges on which the jury returned a verdict against him. Tolley didn't see it that way. Yes, there was loud, belligerent talk, but she didn't feel intimidated, even though she often disagreed with Warner. Judge Huck had assigned his courtroom deputy to keep an eye on the jury room—from the outside—and step in if the deliberations became too heated. The entry to the jury room was actually two separate doors with a space between them intended as a noise buffer. But even with this structural precaution, loud arguing could be heard outside the room. On a few occasions, the deputy knocked and reminded the jurors to "keep it cool" and continue their deliberations. This helped for a while, Tolley said, but soon the old arguments and antagonisms resurfaced.

But there was agreement on some points. All the jurors accepted that the mysterious Kirby Archer had been the mastermind of the crime spree and that he had recruited the younger, less experienced Guillermo Zarabozo. But some wondered why the prosecutors didn't call Archer to testify at trial. If he was such an important part of the plan—and such an important witness against Zarabozo—why wasn't he in the witness seat testifying? Judge Huck had specifically told the jury not to consider why certain people were not called to testify at trial. But they couldn't help speculating.

"A big sticking point for the jury," according to Tolley, "was whether the [prosecution] had proved a conspiracy" to hijack the boat. There was acknowledgment that Zarabozo had brought a gun on board, which he had admitted at trial. But there was no consensus about what that fact meant in terms of the charges against him in the case. If Zarabozo really believed that he and Archer were going to Bimini for a bodyguarding job, it seemed logical to some of them that he would bring a weapon along for the work. The discussion went round and round, and finally the jury decided to send the note to Judge Huck asking for guidance on the question.

As speculated by others during the jury's deliberations, that scenario is exactly what some of the jurors were wrestling with. Everyone knew that Zarabozo had brought his Glock aboard, but they weren't sure whether that fact alone made him part of a conspiracy to steal the boat and thus guilty of the four murders. This was not a problem for the jurors who were already convinced that Zarabozo was guilty of all charges: stealing the boat, kidnapping the four victims, four first-degree murders, and using a firearm to commit four violent crimes. But it proved a big problem for at least five of the jurors. Eventually two of them got tired of the constant wrangling and "went along with" Warner's adamant opinion that Zarabozo had been part of the plan from the get-go. But three others still wouldn't budge. Ironically, these holdouts, Eve Tolley, Raul Garcia, and Venora Gray, were the same three jurors who seemed "completely naïve" about the case, and said that they had no real prior knowledge about it.

Judge Huck's response to the jury's note—advising them to rely upon the jury instructions that they had been given—was unsatisfying to the jurors and had the effect of merely fueling the internal debate. Eventually, the jury moved on to other factors that might be considered to establish or refute Guillermo Zarabozo's willing participation in Archer's deadly plan. One of the factors in Zarabozo's favor was what some of the jurors perceived as his lack of attempt to disguise his identity during the run-up to the charter trip. What about the government's evidence that Zarabozo used a fake name to purchase the SIM card at the T-Mobile store? At least some of the jurors bought the defense's explanation that the store clerk simply couldn't understand what Zarabozo was telling her about how to spell his name. They were persuaded by the prosecution's careful, detailed presentation of videotape surveillance from the motels and from Lou's Police and Security Equipment Store that Zarabozo had made no effort to use a false name or disguise his identity in any way—proof, for some, that he had nothing to hide because he didn't think he was doing anything wrong. This was not the inference that the prosecution hoped the jury would draw from its presentation.

Although this was a grisly quadruple murder leaving two tiny orphans in its wake, some of the jurors felt "emotionally distanced" from the horror of the crimes since there were no gruesome photos of the bodies, or blood on the decks, or bullet wounds. Of course, no such photos existed because the killers had disposed of the bodies at sea and hosed down the decks.

At least some of the jurors thought Guillermo Zarabozo was really "a good kid," and "smart, or at least of average intelligence," who simply "didn't really understanding what he was getting himself into" with Kirby Archer. As they watched him testify in his own defense, some thought he was "lying through his teeth," but others saw him as very nervous, "maybe still in shock" about all that had happened. Eve Tolley wasn't sure that Zarabozo "really understood the full implications" of what he was up against, although he seemed "scared to death" about the outcome. She thought he was honest. She saw no reason not to believe his testimony. And she believed he was very remorseful: "I think he felt terrible about it."

One of the other jurors, Venora Gray, had served on the jury at a murder trial once before and on another jury at a trial for armed robbery. She had voted for conviction in both of those cases, but said she just didn't see the same type of conclusive evidence in this case. "I've had experience on both sides" of the criminal justice system, she said. One of Gray's brothers had been murdered, and another brother had been convicted of a felony murder, for which he served nearly twenty-three years before his release. She tried to look at all the evidence in this case dispassionately, since she knew from personal experience what it felt like to be on both sides. She also felt "very intimidated" by Jackie Warner. At times, she recalled, he told everyone that he wanted to go home—they all did—and that Gray and the other hold-outs were making it impossible for them to leave. Turning an already difficult situation into a personal tragedy, Venora Gray's mother died during the jury deliberations. Judge Huck inquired whether Gray would be able to continue deliberating with the jury or ask to be excused. She decided to continue her work on the jury, and after a recess to attend her mother's funeral, she returned and deliberations continued. But the work was no less contentious than it had been before the brief recess.

Venora Gray was bothered by what she saw as the absence of evidence as to who had actually committed the murders. She recognized that it was easy to convince a young man to follow along on a dangerous path—she'd seen her own brother fall prey to a similar bad decision and pay for it with over two decades of his life. But she couldn't see why Zarabozo would "want to waste his life" by knowingly going along with Archer's murderous scheme. She saw the defendant as "a young fellow just trying to find his way and got caught up with [Kirby Archer]." When Zarabozo testified, she said, "I believed him. I thought he was telling the truth. I liked him."

Some of the jurors struggled to understand the concept of "reasonable doubt." Several discussed how to quantify the concept. Could it be reduced to a percentage? Did "reasonable doubt" mean 1 percent doubt? Did it mean that they had to be 99 percent sure of something? The standard jury instructions addressed all these legal concepts, but apparently this jury hadn't found the instructions understandable or helpful in their deliberations.

Eventually, this discordant group of jurors found one thing they could agree upon: that Guillermo Zarabozo had brought a gun aboard the *Joe Cool* without any kind of permit to take it into a foreign country, and that must be illegal. So they voted unanimously to convict him of the four firearm counts, which meant he was guilty of "using a firearm in the commission of a crime of violence" under the law. Some jurors didn't seem to be bothered by the fact that they had not been able to reach unanimity on which, if any, "crime of violence" Zarabozo had committed using a firearm. Everyone was more than ready to go home.

Venora Gray probably echoed the sentiments of most jurors when she said, "I hope I never have to go through anything like that again." She was bothered for some time about the aggressive behavior Jackie Warner displayed during the jury deliberations. While sitting on a jury, "you shouldn't have to be afraid to express your opinions," she felt.

All the jurors moved on with their lives, and the details of the crimes and some of the deliberations faded from their memories. "It took me a long time to put the whole thing out of my mind," Gray said. "It was a horrible thing." She later moved out of Miami to a more rural area that she described as being "very peaceful."

Other jurors stayed more plugged in. Eve Tolley, for example, followed news reports and discussions of the upcoming second trial. She was especially interested to learn about the "new evidence" that would be presented by the government, according to press accounts.

CHAPTER TWENTY-TWO

———

Sentencing Kirby Archer

Even though Kirby Archer's sentence of life in prison was a foregone conclusion, there was a formal sentencing process that Judge Huck had to preside over. After Archer's guilty plea, Judge Huck had ordered the United States Probation and Pretrial Services agency to investigate Archer's background and review the circumstances and the crimes he had committed. The resulting presentence investigation report (PSI) made determinations concerning aggravating and mitigating factors and recommended sentencing for each crime in connection with the guidelines established for sentencing in federal court. Judge Huck and the lawyers had received and reviewed the PSI in preparation for the sentencing hearing. The families and friends of the victims had the right to address the court—and Kirby Archer— at the hearing if they chose to do so. And Archer had the right to speak on his own behalf. On October 14, 2008, Kirby Archer appeared in court wearing a prison-issue beige jumpsuit. Jail had not been kind to him. He looked pudgy, doughy, his face puffy and pale, reducing his eyes to slits.

Amie Gamble spoke for her lost brothers, Jake and Scott, her sister-in-law, Kelley, and her dear friend, Sammy. "Our hell is on earth," she told Archer, "and it began with you." She told him about her relatives and friend, what wonderful people they had been, and what a huge part was now missing from her life and the lives of the broken families. She talked about Kelley, what a kind person and good mother she was, how much she loved her kids. Amie had brought two large photographs of the children with her, and she placed them on the defense table directly in front of Kirby Archer. He glanced at them but didn't touch them. During her speech, Amie tried to meet Archer's eyes directly, to impress upon him the suffering he had created. She occasionally stumbled, then recovered herself and went on.

Last summer, she told Archer, Jake and Kelley's three-year-old daughter pretended to call her mother on her play telephone. "Mommy, why don't you come home?" the child asked. She wanted to know why she didn't have a mommy like her friends in preschool. She was told, "Your mommy and daddy will always live in your heart." The tiny girl replied, "I don't have a heart."

Archer rested his chin in his hands, stoic and emotionless, giving no indication he had even heard what was said, while Harry Branam sobbed quietly.

Amie Gamble collected her notes and turned to walk back to her seat in the gallery. She glanced at prosecutor Karen Gilbert as she passed and saw Gilbert wiping tears from her face. It was a moment Amie would never forget. To her, this symbolized how much the prosecution team cared not just about their work but also about the victims and the friends and families who suffered so much. They knew that they were dealing with the real lives of real people, not just dry legal theories, arguments in court, and their win/loss records. It was a comfort to Amie to recall this moment with Karen Gilbert, and to feel so strongly that Gilbert and the other prosecutors really knew, really understood, and really cared, even though they had never known Jake and Kelley Branam, Scott Gamble, and Sammy Kairy in their all-too-brief lives.

Then it was Kirby Archer's turn to speak. He rose to his feet at the defense table and said:

I will be very brief. For the family, I wish that I could take back what happened. Of course, even more, I wish that I could show a little bit more emotion about it. I am not built that way. But what I will say is that of course I take full responsibility for my actions. Though I didn't— and I will try not to mention their names. I know the families don't want to hear their names from me. Though I didn't physically kill Scott and Sam I am no less responsible. I was just as responsible for their deaths as I am directly responsible for Jake and Kelley's death. I will say that having the Atlantic Ocean as a burial point is not good. That's another thing I regret, not being able to—their families not being able to give them a proper burial. That's a thing they will never have. I just don't know—there's nothing I can say to fix it, to take it back. I won't ask for leniency I will not ask for any compassion. I won't ask for forgiveness. I am not that simple. I deserve to sit in jail for the rest of my life, there's no question of that. I deserve the death penalty, there's no question of that. This is probably the only case I have ever seen where I would not want the death penalty in a situation like this. That's only because it's me. And the only reason that I requested life in lieu of the death penalty is for my family. And I know that's selfish but that's the way it is. So I'm sorry for everything. These people were good people. I knew them a very short time obviously. They didn't do anything wrong. They didn't do anything wrong to anyone. I will say that they did not suffer. Contrary to what has been said in the media, and probably through the trial, there was none of that. It was instantaneous. I'm sorry to be as graphic about it, but I think it's important. It may help the family cope a little bit. That's all.

He spoke in a flat, unemotional voice, not making eye contact with anyone in the courtroom as the victims' families wept openly.

Judge Huck commented on the horrible, multiple crimes for which Kirby Archer was responsible. He imposed a sentence of five life terms in prison, one for each of the murders and one for the conspiracy to overtake the vessel resulting in their deaths, the five counts to which Archer had pleaded guilty. The judge ordered that the terms be served consecutively, without possibility of parole, thus ensuring that Archer would spend the rest of his life behind bars. Judge Huck also ordered a fine and restitution in the amount of $794,184. Then it was over—at least for Kirby Archer.

CHAPTER TWENTY-THREE

New Directions

Three weeks later, on November 6, 2008, Judge Huck vacated Zarabozo's four guilty verdicts for using a firearm in a violent felony. After reviewing the legal authority cited by the lawyers, he concluded that the guilty verdicts could not stand under a precedent established by a United States Supreme Court case. Although he agreed with prosecutors that they had presented enough evidence to support the guilty verdicts, the judge ultimately concluded that the jury was confused by his instructions to them and that their confusion led to the inconsistent verdicts.

Published reactions to the judge's decision were predictable. Amie Gamble said, "We had some type of guilty verdicts, and now they've been taken away from us." The holdout jurors were relieved. One told *Miami Herald* reporters, "I'm so grateful that the judge has taken this action. I have felt guilty every day since the trial knowing that I played a part in this verdict, which I never thought would lead to a life sentence." Another juror's comments were perhaps more prescient: "I want [Zarabozo] to get a whole new trial and have the other verdict erased."

The *Miami Herald* published an op-ed piece on November 11, 2008, lauding Judge Huck because he "showed courage in admitting and fixing [a] trial mistake." The sentiment was shared in the Miami legal community. But Judge Huck was referred to throughout the article as "Judge Hulk." The obvious blooper in the language of the article quickly became fodder for humorous legal blogs. One even superimposed Judge Huck's face on the bulging green mass of the *Incredible Hulk* cartoon character.

The prosecution team decided not to pursue an appeal of Judge Huck's ruling vacating the four guilty verdicts, and the retrial of Guillermo Zarabozo on all sixteen counts was scheduled for January 2009. There had been no breaks for the prosecutors between the original trial and preparation for the retrial, and there would be none, even though the holiday season was almost upon them. There would be no celebrations or days off, just more grinding work to prepare for the next trial.

The prosecutors had several important issues to resolve and a very short time frame within which to work. What had gone wrong in the first trial? What, if anything, could they learn from it? What should they do differently in the retrial? The last question provoked heated arguments among the lawyers as they mulled over how best to make their presentation the second time around. Should they stick to the reverse-chronological order beginning with the rescue of the "survivors" and backtracking through the elaborate investigation and mountains of forensic evidence? And how would they "get inside Zarabozo's head" to show the jury that he knew exactly what was going on all along and was a willing participant?

In a case already replete with remarkable coincidences, yet another one was on the way: a new expert provided updated forensic analysis of the electronic evidence from

Guillermo Zarabozo's computer. Just before Christmas 2008, results of the new analysis began to trickle into the war room, with dramatic effect on the prosecution's work.

THE defense team got its first hint of the prosecution's new trial strategy on December 23, 2008, when they learned that the prosecutors intended to introduce as evidence at the retrial "a few instant messaging chat sessions" found on Zarabozo's computer. The following day, Christmas Eve, the prosecutors delivered written transcriptions of those chat sessions to the defense. They explained that their original forensic computer examiner, an FBI expert, hadn't been able to locate all of the relevant information on Zarabozo's hard drive, so the prosecutors turned to another computer examiner, Francisco Perez, a detective with the Miami-Dade Police Department, to re-search the computer's hard drive. He had begun his work on December 16, 2008.

On January 6, 2009, prosecutors turned over a CD to the defense containing more information from the new computer examination, a summary of the type of work performed on the hard drive, and photographs, chat sessions, and other information obtained that the prosecutors planned to introduce at trial. The prosecutors also notified the defense of their intention to call two new witnesses at the retrial: Gretel Martinez and Andy Pla. They were known to be good friends with Zarabozo, and they would be called to testify regarding chat sessions and other conversations they had had with Zarabozo before his trip on the *Joe Cool*.

After reviewing the new material provided to them, the defense team was alarmed. This information came from Zarabozo himself, either directly from his own computer or through his conversations and electronic "chats" with his best friends, and it was damning. They would try everything in their power to keep this out of trial.

On January 13, 2009, just a few days before the retrial

was set to begin, the defense team filed a motion to exclude newly disclosed evidence or, as an alternative, a continuance. The new evidence should be excluded from trial, they argued, since it was disclosed to them too late, in violation of the court's standing discovery order requiring that counsel for the parties continually update and exchange their evidence to be presented at trial. The motion contained a succinct summary of the new evidence and, hence, of the government's new approach to the trial. It also revealed why the defense team was so anxious to keep the new evidence out. It read:

> Overall, the evidence produced by the government since December 24, 2008, goes to the heart of this dispute in this case—what Mr. Zarabozo knew and intended before boarding the *Joe Cool*. The government intends on using the evidence to demonstrate its position that Mr. Zarabozo did not intend on traveling to Bimini for a security mission. Based on the newly produced evidence the Government intends on calling at least two new fact witnesses at the second trial—Andy Pla and Gretel Martinez.

The prosecution countered that it had not violated the judge's standing order, since the evidence was in fact newly discovered, and they had provided it to the defense as soon as they acquired it. As to their two new fact witnesses, both had been on the original witness list at the first trial. Andy Pla had even previously testified (about other matters), and the prosecutors had only decided at the last minute not to call Gretel Martinez. The defense had known about these witnesses all along, the government argued, so they couldn't claim to be unfairly surprised.

But the defense team was right that the prosecutors intended to use the new evidence to "get inside Zarabozo's head" and establish that his intent all along had been to go to Cuba, not the Bahamas. If they could prove that, then it followed that the Bimini trip was a ruse, which would necessarily mean that Zarabozo was part of the conspiracy with Kirby Archer to hijack the *Joe Cool* to Cuba all along. After months of argument, analysis, research, presentation, and evaluation on both sides, the case was coming down to a single factual issue: when he boarded the *Joe Cool*, did Zarabozo intend to go to the Bahamas or Cuba? Everything else in the second trial would flow directly from that central question. If the prosecution could convince the jury that Zarabozo's intent was to go to Cuba, then they had him on at least the conspiracy charge. And conspiracy was a potent weapon in criminal trials and usually much easier to prove than the details of how the actual crime had been committed. The prosecution had not been able to establish who shot whom in the first trial, and that wasn't likely to change. But under their new trial strategy, they didn't have to prove that. If Zarabozo was part of the conspiracy that resulted in the murders of those aboard the *Joe Cool*, then he was guilty, no matter who actually pulled which trigger and killed each victim.

The newly disclosed evidence was hot and responsive to the single most important issue at the second trial. Try as they might, the defense couldn't get it excluded. Judge Huck gave them their continuance and reset the new trial date to February 9, 2009. But when that trial commenced, the government would be free to use its new evidence and fact witnesses—and whatever other strategy they had developed since the last trial—to try to convict Guillermo Zarabozo on all sixteen counts against him.

Jay Weaver, the *Miami Herald*'s top crime reporter, predicted, "This time, he's toast." Maybe. But many people had thought so the last time around.

CHAPTER TWENTY-FOUR

New Trial

On Monday morning, February 9, 2009, a new panel was brought into Judge Huck's thirteenth-floor courtroom to begin jury selection for the retrial of Guillermo Zarabozo, now twenty, on all sixteen counts against him in the superseding indictment. Several prospective jurors had read or heard something about the case but said they could be fair and judge the case solely on the evidence presented at trial. Others mentioned an aversion to violence, especially guns. One man described himself as a Buddhist and said he was "bothered by violence," then added, "Maybe I've seen too much *Law & Order* or something," referring to the perennial television crime program. Prosecutor Karen Gilbert asked how many people watched *CSI*, and most raised their hands. "This is not *CSI*," she cautioned. She explained the difference between "direct" and "circumstantial" evidence in a criminal trial, and the concepts of "premeditation" and "felony murder," a murder that occurs during the commission of a felony whether the murder was intentional or not.

Out of forty prospective jurors, thirteen told the court that they, or a family member, owned one or more guns. These included a Beretta, several .45s, .22s, and .38s, shotguns, rifles, pistols, a Sig Sauer, a Magnum .357, and a Walther PPK. Miamians, it seemed, loved their guns.

Shortly after 4 P.M., the lawyers and Judge Huck were satisfied that a fair and impartial jury of twelve, plus three alternates, had been selected to hear the case. The jury was sworn and the judge explained the charges contained in the indictment and gave preliminary instructions prohibiting watching, reading, or talking about the case, even among themselves, until they were instructed to do so.

Prosecutor Jeffrey Tsai began the government's opening statement, and it was immediately clear that the prosecution had determined to follow a new timeline for the retrial. Instead of opening with the rescue of Archer and Zarabozo from the life raft, as they had in the first trial, the prosecution team laid out a sequential chronology of the crime spree in three separate parts:

> Part 1, Tsai told the jury, would establish how Zarabozo and Archer met and developed their plan to hijack a boat and take it to Cuba;
> Part 2 would prove the lengthy and elaborate preparations they made for their murderous expedition, including purchases of ammunition and magazines for their guns, Zarabozo's saying good-bye to friends for his year-long trip to Cuba, and Archer's putting his car up for sale on ebay;
> Part 3 was the culmination, the tragic implementation of their plan aboard the Joe Cool on September 22, 2007.

And the price for this plan? "Four innocent young lives lost," Tsai told the jury. This three-part timeline, he said, was the framework within which the government would prove its case. This is what the jury should use as a guide for listening to the evidence presented at trial and, later, for its deliberations on the verdict.

Assistant Federal Public Defender Anthony Natale's response was brief. It was already 5 P.M. and the day in court had been demanding and stressful. Four innocent persons were murdered for no reason, Natale told the jury, and now a fifth innocent person's life hung in the balance: Guillermo Zarabozo's. Kirby Archer alone was responsible for all the crimes, he said, because Archer was "a trained killer" who had served in the United States Army as a military police investigator in Guantánamo, Cuba. The implication was clear. Young Zarabozo was no match for Archer's secret, nefarious scheme.

At last, Judge Huck recessed court for the day and, reminding the jury about avoiding information or discussion concerning the trial, bid them a good evening.

The following morning, the prosecution team called its first witness: Carlos Mulet, the chop-shop proprietor who had introduced Guillermo Zarabozo to Kirby Archer in March 2007. This was the beginning of Part 1, as Jeffrey Tsai had described it for the jury, which outlined how Archer and Zarabozo met and began to develop their plan. Karen Gilbert took Mulet through his testimony, essentially the same as at the previous trial, about the defendant's fascination with guns, fast cars, a life of excitement and adventure, and his brief career as a Mustang Cobra "spotter" for Mulet's chop-shop. He described Archer, "the Gringo," and told the jury how Zarabozo had supplied Archer with a gun and how Archer and Zarabozo developed a plan to steal a large boat. When it became obvious that neither Archer nor Zarabozo would be able to start a large boat by themselves, Archer asked Mulet to do it for them. Mulet refused. Then, according to Mulet, Archer said, "We'll have to go to Plan B." Plan B, of course, was hijacking a charter boat out on the ocean.

Then the government called its bombshell witness: Gretel Martinez, a twenty-one-year-old student at Emory University in Atlanta and sometime girlfriend of Zarabozo. She was a pretty blonde with long, straight, heavily highlighted hair who strode into the courtroom, swinging her skirt and tossing her hair, brimming with sassy self-confidence. At the defense table, Zarabozo showed emotion for the first time in either trial by grinning broadly at her and jumping up to be recognized without waiting to be asked. This time around, the prosecutors were armed with important new information about Gretel Martinez's relationship with Guillermo Zarabozo and what he had told her about his plans. Martinez told the jury that she had been a year ahead of the defendant at Hialeah High School, so she hadn't really known him there. It was during a year she took off from school that they became friends and "workout buddies." Throughout her testimony, Martinez and the defendant openly flirted and smirked at each other, as if they shared a secret. In fact, she was still in almost constant contact with Zarabozo and his family by telephone, and she readily admitted that she "didn't want anything bad to happen to him." On the other hand, she had been extensively interviewed by the FBI and she didn't want to face a perjury charge, either. Gretel Martinez would have to tread carefully.

About two or three weeks before Zarabozo left on the *Joe Cool*, he began to discuss his plans with Martinez while they were working out together at Bally's in Hialeah. As she explained it to the jury, he was very enthusiastic about pursuing "an important government job," and he "might have mentioned the CIA." He said he was going with a friend who had contacts for the big job. "It would eventually head to Hemingway Marina in Cuba," she testified. "The mission could last months to a year." What did Martinez think about what he had told her?

"I thought it was bizarre," she replied. "I questioned—I

asked him how is it that the CIA is choosing you out of a pool of highly qualified individuals and he explained. . . . He said usually out of a group of two people, one should be highly qualified or I guess more dominant and the other one sort of not so experienced so they won't clash and the mission could be productive."

Prosecutor Karen Gilbert took Gretel Martinez through some of the new evidence the team had obtained since the prior trial. Much of the new material consisted of their electronic communications and conversations carried on through so-called social media like MySpace, the online service to which Gretel Martinez, Zarabozo, and Archer all subscribed. Gilbert used Martinez's communications with Zarabozo to educate the jury about Internet slang and acronyms. For example, LMAO, as defined by Martinez for the jury, meant "laughing my ass off" and FOFL meant "falling on the floor laughing." OMG meant "oh my God" and LOL was "laughing out loud." "Muah" was "a kiss."

Gretel Martinez referred to Zarabozo in electronic messages as "Mongo," slang for "dummy" in Spanish, and she also called him "Blacky . . . a term of endearment because he is like tan." Zarabozo's screen name was "Guillez1111," and Martinez identified her own screen name as "HHSVAL2005," which she defined as "Hialeah High School Valedictorian 2005." Prosecutors had learned that her valedictorian award had been somehow controversial, and that this was referred to by some of her classmates as "Gretelgate."

Fifteen pages of transcription of AIM (AOL Instant Messenger) communications back and forth between Zarabozo and Martinez were admitted as evidence, provided to the jury in tabbed binders, and displayed on the screens in the courtroom. The transcription was recorded automatically on Zarabozo's computer and had been retrieved by the prosecution's new computer expert. This particular service provider, AOL, used Pacific standard time to record all messages and kept contemporaneous records of everything that was transmitted, whether text or photographs. Adjusting for the different time zones, some of their AIM chats carried on until nearly 5 A.M. local time. Guillermo Zarabozo also communicated with Gretel Martinez by e-mail, via their MySpace pages, and by cell phone (including via text, photographs, and video). Apparently, these communications were never erased or purged. Some of them were mildly embarrassing.

On the stand, Gretel Martinez had to explain that her AIM reference to "my ex" meant a woman with whom she had had an intimate relationship and how she and Zarabozo commiserated over their failed romances. Later, she said, she and Zarabozo began an intimate relationship. Most of the AIM messages were tedious, repetitive, and banal, communicating such information as "I'm blow drying my hair" and "I pee now."

The keystone of the government's strategy soon became evident to spectators when Karen Gilbert questioned Martinez closely regarding exactly what Zarabozo had told her about the destination of his planned trip. The prosecution team had always believed that the charter to Bimini was a ruse, a cover story for what Archer and Zarabozo had always planned to be "an incursion" directly into Cuba, not the Bahamas. Now they had some solid evidence from Zarabozo himself to confirm what had really been in his mind. And they would use his own words, on his own computer, and to his own best friends, to prove it.

Karen Gilbert directed Gretel Martinez's attention to transcriptions of Guillermo Zarabozo's message to her concerning his big trip. He wrote, "I do [miss you] a lot and I need to tell you now that I cant because when I leave I wont be able to talk to you an tell you that I miss you but you will know that I do." He waffled on when he would leave on his trip: "ileave in a week for sure."

Martinez pressed him, writing, "U SGTIL HAVENT TOLD ME WHEN Y LEAVE!"

Zarabozo replied, "if not this weekend some time during

next week." Finally, he wrote: "an by the way im still leaving next week we got top clearance . . . preaty cool. . . . i
miss you alot guy but this time next year will behaving fun
some place with lots off money lol . . . miss you alot. . . .
bye muah."

On September 30, 2007, Martinez wrote Zarabozo a
farewell letter:

Dear Blacky,

I wanted to take a few minutes to write to you for the
sake of knowing that I've verbally given you my all.

Let this be my farewell letter—a modern one, thanks
to myspace. . . .

Not once before had I considered the possibility of
ultimately choosing a man over a woman, but I don't
know. . . .

I wish you a year full of laughs, joys, adventure and
self-improvement.

Remember to learn how to dance salsa, so you can
blow me away with your moves once your back. . . .

The messages clearly established that Zarabozo told one
of his best friends that he was going on a clandestine mission and would be gone for a year. But what the prosecution
was most interested in was his statement about his destination. In a discussion about the pain of getting over their
failed romances, Zarabozo had written to Martinez: "It does
to me too, but, whatever I will get over it on Cuba lol."

Gretel Martinez had been interviewed by the FBI on December 31, 2008—New Year's Eve—about what Zarabozo
had told her. She was interviewed again, just before trial.
At first, she denied any knowledge of his trip except what
she saw on television, which she later admitted was a lie.
She revised the story: she had lied to the FBI only because
Zarabozo had told her to because his secret mission was for

the CIA, and now she could "tell the truth" since his trip had made headlines, the pirate story was commonly known to be fake, and he had, after all, spent more than a year in jail by that time. In her last interview with the FBI, Gretel Martinez stated that Guillermo Zarabozo had told her he was going to Cuba all along. "And maybe a Caribbean island first," she added later. Karen Gilbert tried to pin her down on this crucial point. Did he ever mention the Bahamas as a destination? Martinez couldn't remember. How about Bimini? No, definitely not Bimini. But maybe the Bahamas as "an island in the Caribbean." Gilbert and Martinez fenced back and forth over the point. It was obvious that Gretel Martinez was evasive, trying to find an answer that would leave some wiggle room about where Zarabozo had said he was going on this trip.

"There's no mention of Bimini or the Bahamas in any of those chats, messages, texts, or e-mails, right?" Karen Gilbert asked, exasperated. "Are you now trying to say that the Bahamas are in the Caribbean?"

Finally, even Judge Huck lost patience and asked the witness directly: "Do you know whether the Bahamas are in the Caribbean?"

"I would say no," Gretel Martinez admitted reluctantly. She had proved an adroit, slippery witness, but the prosecution got what it needed: Zarabozo told her all along that he was going on a long trip to Cuba. His AIM text to her specifically said, "I will get over it on Cuba." He had never mentioned Bimini during all their chats, posts, conversations, and talks.

On cross-examination, Gretel Martinez told the court that she was proud of going to Emory University on a full scholarship, and that her high school GPA was "6.44." Most of the observers in the courtroom thought a perfect GPA was 4.0. Apparently things had changed. When asked about her plans after her undergraduate education, Martinez announced that she was "thinking of law school." No one was surprised, given her glib performance on the stand. Watching from the gallery, however, Amie Gamble speculated that Martinez must be taking acting classes, since she had treated her sworn testimony in court as "an audition for a role."

When she stepped down and crossed the courtroom, Gretel Martinez passed through the center aisle between the prosecution and defense tables. Her back was to the jury and the judge, but spectators clearly saw her smirk at Guillermo Zarabozo as she passed.

After lunch, with the jury still outside in the jury room, prosecutor Karen Gilbert raised an urgent matter with Judge Huck. During the break, Gilbert told the judge, she had learned that defendant Guillermo Zarabozo's father, also named Guillermo Zarabozo, had approached Mr. Andy Pla, the government's next witness, right outside the courtroom door. The elder Zarabozo had asked Pla if he "was still Guillermo's brother." When Andy Pla replied yes, the older man said something like, "Let's see if you still love him," apparently referring to Pla's forthcoming testimony after the lunch break, when trial resumed. He then asked Pla if he wanted anything to eat and offered to pay.

Judge Huck was angry and concerned. He decided that the case should proceed as planned, but he announced that he wanted to question both Andy Pla and the elder Mr. Zarabozo after the jury adjourned for the day. Anthony Natale, the defendant's lawyer, sent an assistant out to scout for the elder Mr. Zarabozo, since he wasn't in the courtroom.

The jury returned and the government called Andy Pla to the stand. He was a slight, quiet young man who had been best friends with Guillermo Zarabozo. "We call each other brothers," he said, and they shared their ambitions and plans for their future careers. They went to Boy Scouts together, participated in Air Force Junior ROTC in high school, and took a Miami Beach Citizens Police Academy course together. Pla and Zarabozo had planned to become police officers and sometimes worked on private security jobs at the W and the Clevelander, both hotels on Miami Beach, and at Home Depot. They both worked as private contractors for Pinkerton and All-American Security. Pla and Zarabozo had similar tattoos resembling the DNA double helix, and Zarabozo's incorporated Andy Pla's birthdate.

Zarabozo had told Pla about his new friend, Kirby Archer, sometimes known as "R. C.," and the long trip they were planning to take together as part of a CIA mission.

"He told me that they were going to go on a mission to Cuba and pretend to be rich people to sell weapons to the Cuban government so that the CIA could track those weapons to see if they were going to Venezuela," Pla said.

Zarabozo also told him about a "briefing they had in downtown Miami, a CIA briefing with R. C. and himself. He described other people being there dressed in formal wear, suits, some guy asking them questions, things like that."

Zarabozo had never mentioned Bimini to his friend.

But Andy Pla had to keep the mission secret, he testified, because Zarabozo told him that if anyone talked about the mission, the CIA would track them down and kill them and their family. It seemed weird to Pla, a little bit unethical, not the career in law enforcement that he and Guillermo Zarabozo had previously planned together. But Pla was very clear and definite about what Zarabozo told him about the destination of the trip: they were going to Cuba.

Andy Pla was with Guillermo Zaramozo when he went to T-Mobile to get a new cell phone. Pla testified that Zarabozo asked the sales representative "whether or not his cell phone would work in Cuba. The representative of T-Mobile told him, yes, but he would have to activate it in the airport of Cuba." Zarabozo never asked anything about whether his phone would work in Bimini, according to Pla.

One day, Andy Pla stopped by Zarabozo's house and

saw him researching "something related to Marina Hemingway" in Cuba on his computer. They discussed it briefly. Pla
still wasn't sure this CIA trip was for real until he learned
that R. C. had "cleaned up Carlos Mulet's driving record."

"When I heard that," Pla testified, "[t]hat's what did it for
me. From that point on, yeah, I completely believed him."

Then Zarabozo told him what was going to happen when
he and Archer left on their trip: "He told me that when he
left his face was going to come out on the news as a missing
person. And that's related to the threat of before. He said
that if anyone called, once again the CIA would track them
down and kill them and their family. So he was going to
come out as a missing person."

In fact, when the news broke, Andy Pla said that he was
terrified of the CIA threat. He went to Zarabozo's parents'
house and told them not to worry, that Guillermo was working for the CIA.

The jury was dismissed for the day and Judge Huck
asked Andy Pla to remain behind. Pla now had an attorney
with him. Under questioning, Andy Pla repeated the basics
of what Karen Gilbert had told Judge Huck earlier, and he
said that he was "uncomfortable" about what the elder Mr.
Zarabozo had said to him. Judge Huck was furious and told
the defense team to get Mr. Zarabozo into the courtroom
immediately to explain. Anthony Natale disavowed any
knowledge of his actions. He sent an assistant out to find
Mr. Zarabozo and bring him to the courtroom.

Mr. Zarabozo was located and waiting in the counsel room outside. Judge Huck asked Natale to bring Mr.
Zarabozo into the courtroom. Natale offered to instruct the
defendant's family that they are not to have contact with
the witnesses. No response from Judge Huck. While the
judge fumed, Natale quickly sent someone to bring Mr.
Zarabozo into court.

Guillermo Zarabozo was a short, stocky, swarthy man
wearing an ill-fitting dark suit, shirt, and tie. He swaggered

belligerently into the courtroom, seeming not in the least concerned about the judge, which only infuriated Judge Huck more. Federal Public Defender Michael Caruso, a member of Zarabozo's defense team, told the judge that Mr. Zarabozo didn't speak or understand English. If the judge wanted to question him, they would need an interpreter and counsel to represent him separately, since the Federal Public Defender's Office had a conflict because they already represented his son.

Judge Huck responded angrily: "I am going to ask you to take as many lawyers, one from each side at least, to meet with the interpreter, with Mr. Zarabozo. Tell Mr. Zarabozo I am very concerned about what I heard from Mr. Pla. I think it's totally inappropriate. I think if it's not tampering with a witness, it comes close to it, trying to influence him before he testifies. I don't know where it will go, but he better not do it again. Please tell everybody and anyone that might have the same inclination that if I hear there's anything close to tampering with a witness, there will be some repercussions."

The judge stood up and left through his private door, and then, black robe swirling around him, he came back with more: "I don't want anyone getting within 30 feet of Mr. Pla. If I see anyone approach him, I am going to put them right behind that door." He gestured to the door to the lockup outside the courtroom. "If I hear the slightest suggestion that there has been any attempt to intimidate them, Mr. Caruso is going to be correct. That person better get a lawyer. If you get a hint, call my office. If anyone looks at you improperly." Here he glanced at Andy Pla. "Everybody understand that? Okay. See you in the morning."

Judge Huck left the courtroom with an audible bang of the door. Still glowering, Mr. Zarabozo shrugged and walked out. He probably hadn't understood a word, but the judge's outrage really needed no translation.

CHAPTER TWENTY-FIVE

Justice

After repeating its evidence concerning the rescue at sea, the FBI investigation, and a review of the physical evidence found aboard the *Joe Cool*, including blood analysis and the GPS track, prosecutors moved on to a new witness and a new topic. Francisco Perez, the Miami-Dade Police Department detective who ran their forensic computer lab, was the new expert whose work led to documentation of the chats, messages, texts, computer searches, and conversations that had proved so useful to the prosecution in this retrial. He was obviously a very talented investigator who thoroughly understood forensic computer examination. The only issue was whether he could make the complex subject understandable to the jury.

Based upon his examination of more than three hundred computers, Perez outlined the procedure he used in such searches: "We take the hard drive [out of a computer] and make what we call a forensic image of the hard drive and do

it in a manner that does not change anything in the original."
The forensic image is an identical copy of the original. To
make it, Perez used a "hardware block, which does not allow
us to write to the hard drive to make sure it stays the same
as it was originally." This method was used to maintain the
original in unaltered condition while a search was done on
the "read-only" hardware block.

Once Perez had that forensic image, he examined it using
forensic software and a key word list. "We tell the software
to look on the hard drive for the keywords and let it run.
When it's done, we get X amount of what we call hits. It
could be 100, could be 1,000."

Then Perez examined every single hit to see if it was
relevant to what he was searching for. The composition of
the key word list was, of course, crucial. Perez met with the
investigator and prosecutor on the case to develop the key
word list. In the case at trial, important key words included
"Cuba," "marina," "Bimini," and "Hemingway Marina."

He turned up many hits on "Cuba" and "Hemingway Marina," for instance, but none on "Bimini." Some of the hits
were on chat messages, others on research of Web sites or
e-mail messages. Perez thoroughly examined each one.

"Basically, when we review the hits and we find something that we determine is relevant to the case, then we do
something called book marking," he explained for the jury.
"Basically we tell the software to save the information so
we can later report it. We tell them what to save, date, and
time, date of creation, path, name of the file, etc."

In this case, the computer Perez examined was the one
removed by the FBI from Guillermo Zarabozo's living
room right after he was taken into custody. "This was a 200
gigabyte hard drive that can contain millions of pieces of
information. . . . It was running Windows Vista . . . [which
had been] installed on August 1st, 2007. . . . [Prior to that]
it was [running] Windows XP." Perez testified that the pro-

file of Osvaldo Ramirez, Guillermo Zarabozo's stepfather, was on the computer. Apparently Guillermo's younger sister also logged on occasionally.

But the information concerning Guillermo Zarabozo was the target of the investigation. The analysis uncovered Zarabozo's history of chats and electronic conversations using AIM Pro, a paid version of AOL Instant Messenger. "What happens when the person connects to the internet and chats with someone else, it automatically creates an HTML file containing all of the chat information," Perez said. "It's created in the name of the person that logged in, in this case it was Guillez1111."

Perez identified various streams of data that were unintelligible to observers watching the presentation on the large video screens in the gallery. These were necessary foundation documents, but they meant nothing to the average person.

Prosecutor Karen Gilbert singled out one entry: "What we know from this is that on August 28, 2007 at 3:22 in the morning, Guillez1111 began an instant chat with HHS VAL2005?"

"Yes," Perez said. The jury already knew that HHS VAL2005 was Gretel Martinez. The content of Zarabozo's various chats had already been explored with Gretel Martinez and Andy Pla and presented to the jury in a tabbed binder.

"[Zarabozo and Martinez] continued the chat over time and the last time they chatted under this user name was on September 11th, 2007 at 4:25 in the morning, is that right?"

"Correct."

When Perez was finished, the new evidence the government had introduced about the electronic chats, searches, messages, and communications seemed indisputable. Taken together, the evidence clearly demonstrated that Guillermo Zarabozo had researched, chatted, messaged, and communicated about Cuba, not Bimini. He had told his best friends that he was leaving on a yearlong mission to Cuba for the CIA. Would he be able to talk his way out of it this time?

The defense case was brief. The most they could do with the computer expert was to get an admission that Perez couldn't actually say whose fingers were on the computer keys at the time any particular piece of data was recorded, although the inference was clear. A few character witnesses later took the stand to say that Zarabozo had been a good employee and "was a good kid." Defense attorneys read into the record the previous trial testimony of Sam Sutton, Kirby Archer's uncle who let Archer borrow his van on that night in January 2007 in Arkansas when Archer absconded with $92,000 stolen from his employer. Sutton was too ill to travel to this trial, so his previous testimony was read to the jury. Not surprisingly, Sutton had a strong opinion as to Archer's truthfulness: "He was a liar."

Finally, Guillermo Zarabozo took the stand again in his own defense. As he had during his previous testimony, he appeared somewhat lethargic, occasionally bored, generally disinterested in the procedure. His lawyer, Public Defender Anthony Natale, led him carefully through the details, setting up the best possible scenario for his client. In his heavy Cuban accent and garbled grammar, Zarabozo repeated the now-familiar story about being duped by Kirby Archer into believing that they were heading off on a super-secret CIA mission and that he would be coming back to Miami. Zarabozo said that Archer told him they had a two-week bodyguarding job in Bimini. That's why they took the charter. Zarabozo had absolutely no idea Archer would be hijacking the boat to take it to Cuba. They might be going to work later in Cuba, he testified, but first they had this two-week job in Bimini.

Finally, it was time for the showdown on cross-examination, and prosecutor Karen Gilbert was ready.

From her first questions, she easily tripped up Zarabozo on the many inconsistencies in his story, even within the same line of testimony. Either he didn't really understand her questions, or he "couldn't even make up a story," as Nuñez had testified about Zarabozo earlier. Gilbert had a lot to work with. Not only had Zarabozo testified at his first trial, he had also given long, videotaped interviews to the polygraph examiners who tested him for his defense team. She also had the testimony of his friends, Andy Pla and Gretel Martinez, and everything that Carlos Mulet had said under oath at both trials. In addition, thanks to Detective Perez and his sophisticated computer analysis, Gilbert had transcripts of the many messages, chats, and Internet searches during August and September 2007, just before the ill-fated trip on the *Joe Cool*.

Gilbert began with various versions of the stories Zarabozo had told about Kirby Archer being a spy and how Archer had hoodwinked Zarabozo by telling him that he "worked for the CIA."

Q: Now, Kirby Archer never told you that he worked for the CIA, right?

A: Yes, he did.

Q: That's not what you said previously, sir. You said that he never told you he in fact worked for the CIA?

A: Yes. I said he had said to me he worked for the CIA.

Q: No, sir. You said "he may have worked for the government, but that he was not a CIA agent." Do you recall that?

A: I can't remember. I know he said he worked as a freelancer for the CIA.

Q: So a freelancer. He didn't work for the CIA?

A: A freelancer for the CIA.

Gilbert moved on to the details of the big job Archer and Zarabozo were planning and the testimony of Carlos Mulet at this and the previous trial.

Q: When you told Carlos Mulet that you were going to make a million dollars, he said to you, if it's that much money, it can't be legit.

A: No, Carlos Mulet never said that to me.

Q: You heard him testify to that, "I said to Guillermo if it's a million dollars, it must not be legit." You heard that testimony from Mr. Mulet, right?

A: I do not remember him saying that here or saying that to me either.

Q: So are you saying that when he testified, "I told Zarabozo if it's a million dollars it must not be legit," are you saying that Carlos Mulet is making that up?

A: I am not saying he is making that up. I am just saying he never said it to me and I don't recall it at all. . . .

Q: You are saying that when Carlos Mulet took the witness stand and said "I told Guillermo Zarabozo a million dollars, that must not be legit," you are saying that never happened?

A: Yes, I am. Because Carlos Mulet never said a million dollars when he was on the stand here.

Q: Whatever term he used, maybe hundreds or thousands of dollars or a huge amount, he said he confronted you and said, "if it's that much money, it must not be legit." Do you remember that testimony?

A: I still don't remember him saying it here, but not to me.

Q: It's your position that Carlos Mulet is making that up?

A: I am not saying he is making it up. I am saying he did not say it to me.

Q: I don't understand the difference between he didn't say it and he is making it up. What's the difference?

A: I don't know. Maybe he said it to someone else and not to me.

Karen Gilbert moved on to Andy Pla's testimony that he had seen the defendant looking up Marina Hemingway on his computer when Pla stopped by his house one day. Andy Pla had said: "One time I went to his house and he was on the computer researching something related to Marina Hemingway. It had some pictures. It was like an Expedia type website. . . . He was talking to me about it."

At his previous trial, Zarabozo had denied looking up Marina Hemingway on his computer, even though his best friend Andy Pla had testified to it in the first trial and again in this trial. As everyone now knew, the search was reflected on the recent reexamination of his computer. Zarabozo eventually realized he couldn't deny looking up Hemingway Marina, because of the computer record, but he now claimed he was confused by Gilbert's question because, he said, Pla wasn't present at the time of the computer search. But Andy Pla had just testified in this trial that he *was* present, Gilbert told Zarabozo, "sitting right where you are now."

Q: You saw when the detective [Perez] testified that there was a Google search for Marina Hemingway, correct?

A: Yes.

Q: You did that, right?

A: Yes.

Q: Previously though you denied looking up Marina Hemingway when you were asked?

A: If I am not mistaken, before you asked me if I ever

looked up the Hemingway Marina with Andy looking
over my shoulder and Andy saying something to me. I
don't remember that happening. I don't remember Andy
being there.

Q: When you testified previously under oath and when you
were asked did you look up the Marina Hemingway with
Andy present, you are telling this jury under oath that
you said no because it was about Andy, not because of
Marina Hemingway?

A: I thought you were asking me if Andy was there. I remember you saying if he mentioned something to me
like what I was doing and I said no.

Q: Here are the questions, sir. [Gilbert began to read from
the trial transcript.] "Question, when speaking of places
you have been on the computer with Andy looking over
your shoulder, you were looking at Marina Hemingway in Cuba, right? Answer, No. You were never on
his or your computer looking up Marina Hemingway
and him saying what are you looking at Cuba for? Answer, No."

Gilbert continued:

Q: So you are telling the ladies and gentlemen of the jury
that you denied it because Andy was there, not because
you didn't look it up? . . . So your testimony now though
is that it was you that searched Marina Hemingway in
Cuba?

A: Yes.

Q: Because you were going there, right?

A: I believe Archer mentioned it to me at one point and I
looked it up.

Gilbert moved on to issues concerning when Zarabozo claimed to have learned details of Archer's plan, such as when and where they would be going and what they would be doing. She reminded him of his testimony at his earlier trial that he had gone to visit Gretel Martinez in Atlanta on September 3, 2007. He had then testified that he had "no details" about the plan until *after* his visit to Atlanta. But the computer analysis showed that he had in fact searched for Marina Hemingway in August 2007, *before* his trip to Atlanta.

Q: When you previously say, I didn't know any details be-
    fore I went to Atlanta, that's not true?
A: That is true because I didn't know any details. . . .

Q: This was your testimony in September [in trial], no de-
    tails by Archer before Atlanta and details after, right?
A: Yes.

Q: Then they search your computer, you heard that testi-
    mony, in December of 2008. That's the first time those
    things were found on your computer, right, December of
    2008?
A: Right.

Q: They find the stuff on Cuba and Marina Hemingway.
    Now there's a chat to Gretel, August 30th. You would
    agree that's before Atlanta?
A: Yes.

Q: You mention Cuba?
A: Yes.

Q: You mention being away for a year?
A: Yes.

Q: With Reymet [a friend] on August 30th, you tell him, I am going somewhere I can't talk about. I'll be back in a year. Before Atlanta, right?

A: Right.

Q: You Google Marina Hemingway in August of 2007, again before Atlanta?

A: Right.

Q: So you knew all of that information before you go to Atlanta?

A: Yes.

Q: So in September [2008, at trial] before you know about the computer, you are denying all of that?

A: I wasn't denying nothing. I am not denying this. I am just saying what I knew and the little things [Archer] had told me, to when he actually sat down with me and explained what was going to happen.

Q: You are saying the destination of where you are going, how long you are going to be gone, who you are going to pose as, you are telling the jury that it is not details? . . .

On and on it went, with Karen Gilbert confronting Zarabozo with specific references to his testimony at the prior trial whenever he changed his story in response to the prosecution's new specific, detailed, and irrefutable computer analysis and the testimony from his best friends, Andy Pla and Gretel Martinez.

In response to Gilbert's relentless questions, Zarabozo dodged this way and that, sometimes contradicting himself in the middle of his answer. He claimed his best friend Andy Pla "was making up" most of his testimony about the going-to-Cuba conversations because he "has a big imagination." Same with Gretel Martinez and his chat message to her about his trip to Cuba. She must be making it up. But again, Gilbert showed Zarabozo not only Gretel's testimony but also the chat message recovered from his computer.

On cross-examination, Zarabozo now testified that his Glock—the one he took aboard the *Joe Cool*—was actually a weapon that he had been "loaned" by one of his employers, DTS, and he had not returned at the end of his employment. He was merely "borrowing" it, because he intended to return to DTS and would need it again.

> **Q:** You quit at DTS because you have a better job now with Pinkerton and Ernesto Clark [his supervisor], right?
> **A:** I never quit with DTS.

Karen Gilbert showed the witness and the jury a document prepared by DTS.

> **Q:** So the paperwork that says, quit, family reasons, that's not accurate?
> **A:** That's not accurate. We have been over that.
>
> **Q:** No, sir, we have not. The DTS records are in evidence. When you are terminated on July 4th, 2007, it says quit, family reasons. . . .
> **A:** I am saying I never signed the paper, I never saw the paper.

Cross-examination moved on. Without identifying the source of her information, Karen Gilbert referred to the substance of the videotaped polygraph pretest interviews in which Zarabozo had given various narrative versions of what had happened aboard the *Joe Cool*. During those videotaped interviews, Zarabozo discussed with the polygraph examiners events that occurred after the killings. First Zarabozo had said that he had to move Sammy Kairy's dead body by himself and throw it overboard. Then he changed the story to say that he took the body's legs and Archer took the arms, and together they dumped him over the side. In some versions of Zarabozo's narrative, Archer forced him to wash down the aft deck. Sometimes Zarabozo said that Archer started washing it down himself. Karen Gilbert vigorously pursued every inconsistency in Zarabozo's numerous statements. There was no opportunity to claim that the polygraph examiners chosen by his lawyers were "making things up," like his friends Andy Pla and Gretel Martinez. Zarabozo was forced to fall back on the explanation that the people who conducted the interviews didn't understand what he was saying.

Zarabozo seemed hopelessly confused—or a very inept liar. At one point, he said: "I am saying about what happened [on the *Joe Cool*] was when I went in the bathroom was when [Archer] got my gun. Maybe if I never went to the bathroom nothing would have ever happened."

"If you didn't have to go to the bathroom, nobody gets hurt?" Gilbert sounded incredulous.

"Maybe that wouldn't have happened," Zarabozo said.

"Isn't that a huge coincidence, that you just so happened to absent yourself when all of these [murders] happened?"

"I think that's the reason I am still alive," Zarabozo said, again stubbornly.

"You are still alive because you entered into an agreement with [Archer] and he didn't kill you because you did what you were supposed to," Gilbert said.

At the conclusion of exhaustive hours of conflicting testimony, Zarabozo summarized as follows: "I feel sad. I feel ashamed for what happened. I feel I was not man enough to try to fight Archer. I had nothing to do with what happened that day. I didn't know Archer was planning to do nothing unlawful."

He also claimed that Archer had wrecked his life and that of his family. The families and friends of the *Joe Cool* murder victims found it extremely difficult to listen to that. But Harry Branam remarked that the Zarabozo family had lost a son also. He had some compassion for them, especially for Zarabozo's mother, a small, dark, huddled woman who attended the trial every day with her daughter. Amie Gamble and John Gibbons passed her each morning on their drive through Hialeah to the courthouse, waiting for a bus to take her downtown to the trial. They knew who she was but they never offered her a ride. It would have been too hard.

Now the trial was over, except for closing statements, jury instructions, jury deliberations, and hopefully, a verdict. While the jurors were on a break outside the courtroom, Judge Huck determined that the prosecutors and defense lawyers each would get two and a half hours for closing statements. The jury instructions were discussed and approved. The jury returned and Judge Huck explained the procedure.

Karen Gilbert spoke for the prosecution, relating the government's evidence closely back to the three-part timeline Jeffrey Tsai had explained in his opening statement. Her summary was logical, tightly structured, and cohesive and demonstrated that the evidence consistently supported each phase of the defendants' plan. She emphasized Zarabozo's inept struggles to reconcile his prior testimony at trial, to the investigators, to his friends, and in his pretest interviews, with what he now was forced to try to explain as a result of the new computer evidence and the additional witnesses, his best friends Andy Pla and Gretel Martinez.

Gilbert carefully explained the law of conspiracy, that as long as a common plan was proved, it wasn't necessary that each conspirator commit every single act in the plan. All the evidence—from Zarabozo's best friends and even his own words in electronic messages—demonstrated that his destination was Cuba all along. The Bimini trip was a ruse from the beginning, and Guillermo Zarabozo had been a willing participant. It was a strong closing, methodical and detailed.

For the defense, Anthony Natale painted a picture of a young man who was headed for a career in law enforcement until he was tragically derailed by Kirby Archer's deceit and manipulation. Everyone he had ever worked for said he was a good kid. But he was young, and Archer had duped him into believing his lies about a glamorous and lucrative career in espionage for Archer's own nefarious purposes. Guillermo Zarabozo had no part in the tragic killings aboard the *Joe Cool* and he was terrified of Kirby Archer. Afterward, he was afraid to tell the truth to the Coast Guard or the FBI because he believed Archer had high government connections who would kill him if he talked. Guillermo Zarabozo had never been in trouble in his life, never caused any problems for his family or anyone else. Natale saw more than enough reasonable doubt in the case to justify an acquittal for his young client.

Finally, Judge Huck read the voluminous jury instructions and sent the jury back to the jury room to deliberate. Soon the jurors' notes began to flow into the courtroom again. The first one announced their lunch break. The lawyers relaxed.

The second note read:

1. We would like to see Zarbozo's [*sic*] testimony
2. We would like 1 more copy of the Jury Instructions
3. We would like 4 more copies of the counts.

Again, Judge Huck called the attorneys into the courtroom to discuss a response. The following note was sent back to the jury room:

1. A transcript of Defendant, Zarabozo's testimony (or the testimony of any other witness) is not readily available. It would take several days to prepare. Therefore, the Court requests that you rely on your collective rec-

ollection as to what the testimony in this case has been, and continue your deliberations.
2. The Court is providing four (4) more copies of the jury instructions.
3. The Court is providing four (4) more copies of the superseding indictment.

The prosecutors were mildly optimistic. Zarabozo's testimony had been so riddled with inconsistencies and outright lies that the jury probably was confused about what he had actually said and when. That should be held against him, they felt.

Another note was delivered by the court security officer who sat outside the jury room: "We would like a copy of Carlos Moulet's [sic] testimony."

Judge Huck sent back a response: "The Court requests that you rely on your collective recollections as to what the testimony in this case has been, and continue your deliberations."

Although Carlos Mulet had tried to leave some wiggle room for Guillermo Zarabozo, he had clearly testified that he had introduced Archer and Zarabozo, and that they began to develop a plan concerning stealing a boat; then, according to Archer, they went to "Plan B." Again, the prosecutors were cautiously optimistic.

The fourth jury note read: "We would like to speak with Judge Huck to clarify wording in the counts. (counts 4–7)."

The counts referred to concerned conspiracy and an "act of violence." The lawyers and Judge Huck agreed that there should be no colloquy in the courtroom with the jury.

Judge Huck sent this response to the jury: "State precisely what you would need clarified regarding counts 4–7." Again, Judge Huck adhered to procedure developed over decades of federal case law concerning exactly what the jury should be told regarding the meaning of the laws they were sworn to apply to the facts they determined in the case. To some, it might seem easier just to call them into court and discuss the matters they had questions about. But any such discussion might open the deliberations, and any resulting verdict, to question. Each and every word in the jury instructions was the result of years of rulings in federal courts, and it would be dangerous to risk even an unintentional alteration in those strict precedents.

The next jury note read:

1. In the murder counts, does the term "cause" mean "as a result of direct action," or by participation in the conspiracy?
2. On page 14 of the Jury Instructions, title 18, please define what an "act of violence" can include? Bodily injury? Intimidation?

This time, the defense team had reason for at least a glimmer of optimism. The note seemed to imply some doubt about, or at least discussion of, exactly what Guillermo Zarabozo had done while aboard the *Joe Cool*. And that was something the prosecution couldn't prove with direct evidence.

Judge Huck responded:

1. The answer to the first part of your jury note No. 5 can be found in the jury instructions, specifically from page 9 to page 28. You should reread these instructions and consider them in the context of the jury instructions as a whole. After doing so, if you have any further questions, please let the Court know.
2. Regarding the second part of your jury note No. 5, the term "action of violence" should be given its ordinary, common meaning.

Finally, on February 19, 2009, at 2:30 P.M., the jury sent the note everyone had been waiting for: "We have reached a verdict." They had deliberated for a total of eight hours over two days, and they were ready.

Everyone rapidly assembled in the courtroom. The jury was called in. "Have you reached a unanimous verdict?" Judge Huck asked. They had. The court security officer took the note from the jury foreman and handed it to Judge Huck. He read it, his face displaying no emotion. Then it was returned to the foreman to be read to the court.

This jury had found Guillermo Zarabozo, now twenty years old, guilty, right down the line, on all sixteen counts. His mother broke down in tears. The families of the victims were relieved and grateful. Amie Gamble and John Gibbons stepped outside to the atrium and hugged, kissed, and literally jumped up and down. But eventually everyone recognized that even with Guillermo Zarabozo's conviction and Kirby Archer's guilty plea now behind them, they would have to face the rest of their lives without their beloved family members and friends. Having Zarabozo and Archer in prison forever would help some, but nothing could bring their loved ones back.

JUDGE Huck thanked and dismissed the jury, ordered a presentence investigation report to be prepared by United States Probation and Pretrial Services, and set Guillermo Zarabozo's sentencing for May 6, 2009. Defense lawyers stated their intention to appeal the verdict. Finally, it was time for the lawyers to pack up their trial cases and laptops and volumes of paper, and leave the courtroom.

Outside, *Miami Herald* reporter Jay Weaver spoke with the jury foreman, Edison Farrow, who said Zarabozo's version of events was unbelievable and contradictory to the evidence from other witnesses. "His story was impossible," he told Weaver. "His testimony contradicted all of the evidence." Zarabozo had been in it from the start. "He had many opportunities to leave the whole plot," Farrow told

Weaver. Apparently the prosecution had succeeded in giving the jury a look inside Zarabozo's head, and they didn't like what they saw.

Amie Gamble also spoke with Weaver. "I believe in my heart he shot my brothers and he shot Sammy. He felt no remorse whatsoever."

Jon Branam told him, "If he wasn't part of it, well then he should have known. I think life in prison is harsher than death."

CHAPTER TWENTY-SIX

Sentencing Guillermo Zarabozo

On May 6, 2009, Guillermo Zarabozo and his lawyers appeared for his sentencing hearing, along with prosecutors, spectators, and family members on both sides of the gallery. A life in prison sentence was a foregone conclusion, but there were a few details to be determined, such as whether multiple life sentences should be served consecutively or concurrently, and whether an additional term of years should be added, as well as a monetary penalty. A presentence investigation report had been prepared, which among other things concluded that Guillermo Zarabozo and Kirby Archer were "equally culpable," a conclusion that the defense team contested at the hearing and lost. "They are equally culpable," Judge Huck ruled.

Guillermo Zarabozo's mother, Francisca Alonso, addressed the court with the assistance of a translator:

> The first thing I want to say is I feel the pain here today. There have been two families that have been destroyed. I

feel their pain. My family also has been destroyed. I know that my son was there, but he didn't do the bad things, the things that he is being accused of. And I ask you for mercy for my son. And I feel terrible about what has happened to their family. But I know that my son didn't kill anyone.

Then defendant Guillermo Zarabozo spoke on his own behalf:

I would like to say I'm sorry to the family for the loss. I want to say I have nothing to do about it. When I got on the boat I didn't know what Archer was going to do. I didn't know what he was planning. I'm sorry for the loss of the family members. I had no intention of hurting anyone. When I got on the boat I had nothing in my mind that I was going to do anything bad to anyone. I'm sorry.

In his comments at the sentencing hearing, Judge Huck's view of the case was apparent for the first time. For sixteen long months of pretrial proceedings, hearings, and rulings, and throughout two lengthy jury trials, the judge's demeanor had been impeccably neutral. He kept a tight rein on his courtroom, his schedule, and the behavior of the lawyers appearing before him, but he never betrayed the slightest hint of his personal views. The only exception was his angry outburst to the elder Guillermo Zarabozo, who had come dangerously close to witness tampering in his confrontation with Andy Pla.

The presentence investigation report did not recommend an adjustment in the sentence for "obstruction of justice." The government objected, and Judge Huck sustained their objection, finding that Guillermo Zarabozo's testimony at his two trials had indeed amounted to obstruction of justice. The judge had kept his personal notes on Zarabozo's testimony from the first trial and the second trial, and he had reviewed them carefully in reaching his conclusion.

Judge Huck said:

> In essence, [Zarabozo's] explanation every time there was an inconsistency was someone else was wrong, someone else was not telling the truth or was misinterpreting things. Everyone else forgot. Everyone else got it wrong. Which led me to believe his explanation was a total fabrication—I should not say a total fabrication, but a large portion was a fabrication in both trials. . . .
>
> The mere fact that he took the stand and testified differently than other witnesses I agree does not in and of itself justify obstruction of justice. This is not that case. This is a case that appeared to be almost a total fabrication. In the second trial, it was so clearly obvious that Mr. Zarabozo was developing a story somewhat on the run, having previously testified. He was inconsistent with his own testimony. . . .
>
> It was clear to me as I heard the testimony. I wrote my comments down contemporaneous with the testimony not based on the verdict given by the jury.

Judge Huck moved on to another comment. He had carefully read letters to him from Zarabozo's parents and friends. The judge said:

> I have read the letters. There were a number of letters filed on behalf of Mr. Zarabozo. Several of them expressing the same sentiment his mother expressed, that he had nothing to do with the deaths. . . . The jury found otherwise. In addition, several of the letters made the same comment and suggest the Court should give Mr. Zarabozo the opportunity, a further opportunity, to prove his innocence.
>
> It occurred to me the people that wrote the letters

were not here in the courtroom—certainly were not here in the courtroom during pretrial matters. And did not have the opportunity to observe the Federal Public Defender's Office defending Mr. Zarabozo in this matter.

I don't think any defendant has had a better more extensive, more thorough, more impassioned defense than Mr. Zarabozo had. The extent to which the Public Defender's Office went to do everything that it felt was appropriate to defend Mr. Zarabozo was done in this case. They did an extraordinary job. I just want to make sure those people who still carry the lingering thought that Mr. Zarabozo should have an additional opportunity to prove his innocence. They were obviously not here during the trial, obviously were not privy to what was going on outside of the trial at other hearings and matters. There was extremely extensive pretrial preparation.

Mr. Zarabozo got not only one trial, but two trials. I just want to let everyone know that and compliment the Public Defender's Office for the work they have done.

Amie Gamble spoke again for the families and friends of the victims:

Thank you for allowing me to speak. I want to speak to [Judge Huck] and then to Mr. Zarabozo. Your Honor, I would like to thank you for the search of truth and justice in this case. I believe the way you conducted the courtroom and the way you sought out and approached the rule of law was fair for both sides. As you may know, we have dealt with many judges and attorneys since this senseless murder occurred. I feel none have been more professional and just than you. I am happy that you were chosen to try this case. Now that you must make a final decision of a fair and just sentence I am sure you have searched your soul long and hard to do the right thing.

I too have searched and thought of many possible

scenarios, and I can only come up with the fact that Mr. Zarabozo took four innocent lives. He had many opportunities to not commit these horrific crimes, yet he chose to go forward with his actions. . . .

Your Honor, we're seeking justice for Jake and Kelley, Scott and Sammy and their two innocent children whose lives have totally been destroyed. Although the family will never heal from the tremendous loss we will feel the justice in knowing that this man will never harm anyone again. Thank you for your service to the people in this difficult case.

To Mr. Zarabozo. There are no winners here today, just lots of sorrow. All of the Branam, the Clow [Scott's mother, Shirley] and Gamble family and the Kairy family are deeply suffering for the loss of our sons, daughters, sisters and grandchildren. Today two very young children have been robbed of the most precious part of their lives, their loving parents. Their lives have been destroyed and their innocence shattered. All because you chose to commit a senseless crime of violence. . . .

I don't think this is what your parents had in mind when they struggled to bring you to this country. I watched you in the courtroom licking your chops and smiling at your girlfriend hoping that she could save you so that you two could be together again. . . .

You not only took Jake from us, you took Jake and his crew from the world. Jake was a hero. He saved many lives in his short years on earth. You were a coward, you chose to take innocent lives. I only hope that you can do some good where you are going so your mother might have something to be proud of.

I watched your mother suffer through the trial and my heart bled for her. She didn't deserve what you did to her. I am sure she will stand by you to the end. I hope somehow you can help her see that what you did was not her fault. . . .

I am sure she's a good person, and now she will be condemned to a life of pain, sorrow and loss due to your choices. So many lives have been destroyed, not just the crew of the *Joe Cool*, but the living of both families. . . .

You truly are a monster.

Judge Huck sentenced Guillermo Zarabozo to five consecutive life sentences without possibility of parole, plus an additional eighty-five years and a restitution obligation of $789,210. The sentence was an upward departure from the federal advisory sentencing guidelines, in consideration of the multiple victims and other factors considered by the court.

Judge Huck complimented all the lawyers "for the way they have represented their respective clients, and the very civil and professional way each and every lawyer involved had performed. I appreciate it. It made my job in a very difficult case much easier."

Finally, it was over.

Except for Guillermo Zarabozo's inevitable appeal. The Federal Public Defender's Office in Miami has a well-deserved reputation for excellence. Their appellate experts combed through everything that happened in the second trial, and all the orders and decisions that helped shape it.

It is a tribute to Judge Paul C. Huck's meticulous management of the case that the experts could find only two grounds for appeal: the admission of evidence taken from defendant Guillermo Zarabozo's home; and the admission of evidence from the defendants' luggage from the *Joe Cool*'s life raft taken aboard the Coast Guard cutter *Confidence*. The appeal brief, the government's answer brief, and the defendant's reply were filed with the United States Court of Appeal for the Eleventh Circuit. The federal public defender did not request oral argument on the case.

The Eleventh Circuit ruling was swift: AFFIRMED. The conviction would stand.

CHAPTER TWENTY-SEVEN

Family Court, Continued

Nearly three years after the murders of Jake and Kelley Branam that orphaned their two young children, after the conclusion of all proceedings in a federal capital case that included one guilty plea, two jury trials on sixteen separate counts, one conviction, and one federal appeal and ruling, the fate of the children was still unresolved.

In 2010, Miami-Dade Family Court judge Sandy Karlan continued to preside over the contentious issue of who should be awarded custody. On September 28, 2007, Judge Karlan had appointed Margaret C. F. Quinlivan, Esquire, as guardian ad litem for the children. Under Florida law, the duties of a guardian ad litem were to investigate and protect the rights of the persons she was appointed to represent and submit a report and recommendations to the court. Psychological experts had also been appointed, examinations and evaluations were conducted, but final reports and recommendations were delayed again and again. As the case dragged on, family relationships worsened, new litigation was instituted in federal court, and new issues were raised in the custody case, two of which went to the Third District Court of Appeal in Miami.

The following parties were competing for custody: Jake Branam's grandfather, Harry; his grandmother, Jeannette (Harry's former wife); Jake's uncle Jeff (son of Harry and Jeannette); Leanne Van Laar–Uttmark (Kelley Branam's mother) and her husband, Robert; and Kelley's half sister Genny Van Laar (also Leanne's daughter). During the first year of the proceedings, some progress had been made. All the parties attended a mediation conference on March 24, 2008, which continued from 9:00 A.M. until 7:00 P.M. The psychological experts and the guardian ad litem participated by telephone. The following day, March 25, all the parties except Jeff Branam and Jeannette Branam held a telephone conference call with their counsel, after which they contacted the court seeking an immediate hearing to announce a stipulation regarding the resolution of some of the pending issues. Judge Karlan set a hearing for the next day, March 26, at 8:30 A.M. At that hearing, counsel for Leanne and her husband announced that his clients and Harry Branam had reached agreement that Genny Van Laar should have primary temporary residential custody of the children in Michigan. This agreement was based upon certain conditions, most important of which was that Genny provide them with regular, scheduled visitation and frequent telephone and/or video contact with the children.

As part of the stipulation, Genny agreed to ensure visitation and family contact and stated her commitment to working with family members. She also said that she would take a one-year absence from her work as a high school math teacher in Michigan to focus solely on the children and that she had the financial means to support them. These representations satisfied Harry Branam and Leanne and Robert Uttmark. Leanne agreed to send Genny $500 per month for one year to help support the children. In exchange, Harry, Leanne, and Robert agreed not to pursue their petitions for custody. The stipulated oral agreement was dated March 26, 2008, read into the court record, and approved by Judge Sandy Karlan. Jeannette Branam withdrew her custody petition. This left only Genny Van Laar and Jeff Branam vying for custody of the children.

Jeff Branam's counsel, Barry S. Franklin, immediately objected that he had not had notice and an opportunity to prepare for the hastily called hearing on March 26 and that nothing was presented in writing—no motions, no written stipulation, not even the partial one submitted orally to Judge Karlan. Neither of the psychological experts nor the guardian ad litem had yet provided written reports and recommendations, but it was clear that the substance of their recommendations had been disclosed during the conference call. He then moved to disqualify Judge Karlan on these grounds, but she denied the motion.

Next, Mr. Franklin went to the Third District Court of Appeal with a petition seeking an order prohibiting Judge Sandy Karlan from exercising further jurisdiction in the case. The basis for the petition was Judge Karlan's "improper denial" of the motion to disqualify her. The Third District Court of Appeal denied the petition on April 11, 2008, one day after it was filed.

Jeff Branam then hired his own psychological experts to support his petition for custody, but in the end, Judge Karlan awarded primary temporary custody to Genny. The court's corrected final judgment awarding temporary custody, dated June 17, 2008, incorporated the mediated settlement agreement of the parties entered into on March 26, awarded temporary custody to Genny Van Laar, and permitted her to take the children to Michigan to live. The judgment stated that this award was based upon the recommendations of the court-appointed psychologists and the guardian ad litem as well as the mediated settlement agreement of the parties. The judgment also recited that the guardian ad litem's recommendations included a transition process for the children beginning with "Genny spending at least two weeks in Florida with Jeff Branam and allowing the children to see [Harry] and Maria, but not overnight"; holding family farewell events for the children before they left Florida; and then Jeff Branam traveling to Michigan "to assist in the transitioning process" for Genny and the children. The guardian ad litem also recommended that no litigation be initiated against Jeff Branam, his companies, or the family interests as this would be too disruptive to tenuous family relationships.

These recommendations were undoubtedly made with the best intentions, but everyone who really knew the parties predicted that the "transition" would never happen as prescribed and that further litigation against Jeff and his affiliated companies was a certainty. Everyone hoped for the best concerning family contact with the children and visitations, which was for them the most important recommendation, but doubts and worries lingered.

On the day that Genny arrived in Miami for the transition with the children, she was refused admission to Star Island, according to a document her attorney filed with the court seeking emergency consent for Genny and the children to stay in "a condo." As happened frequently in this fractured family, Harry and Maria were the ones who got the call for assistance. Genny had stayed with Harry and Maria on previous occasions when her visits to Star caused trouble. Once again, they welcomed Genny back to their condo, this time with the children, where they remained for several days. But then, according to Maria, Genny suddenly decided to take the children to Michigan prior to the planned family party.

Jeff declined to go to Michigan, citing business reasons. Genny asked her mother, Leanne, to accompany her and the children and to help get them settled in. Leanne agreed, but she was unhappy that her granddaughter didn't get to attend the family farewell party she had been looking forward to. Leanne and Genny traveled with the children to Genny's home in Michigan in the summer of 2008. Once again, everyone hoped for the best.

Although Genny had been awarded only temporary custody of the children, not permanent custody or adoption, it was clear that the tide had turned in her favor. Unfortunately, however, the battle in family court would continue for another two years.

DURING the evaluations of the parties before the temporary custody order was entered, Genny Van Laar had told the guardian ad litem and psychologist Dr. Firpi that when Genny was a child, her mother had virtually abandoned her and the other children while Leanne was working as a flight attendant for TWA.

When Leanne learned what Genny had said, she was heartbroken. Part of what Genny said was true, according to Leanne, but she had never "abandoned" her children. Leanne did begin work in January 1990, as a flight attendant, and she was often away from home on work trips. But she had hired a succession of live-in nannies, with the help of Michigan social services, to care for her children in her absence. Genny had been a difficult teenager, according to her mother, and by the time Leanne went to work for TWA, Genny was fifteen and living with her uncle, Leanne's brother, David Van Laar, who tried to provide a structured home for her. After less than a year, though, David found that he couldn't control his niece, and he sent her back home. During one of Leanne's work absences, Genny then moved to her grandparents' home in Kalamazoo, and her maternal grandmother, posing as Genny's mother, enrolled her in high school there for her senior year.

When she returned home and found Genny gone, Leanne was furious with both her daughter and her mother. She went to court in an effort to get Genny sent back home. But by the time the case was heard, Genny was almost seventeen, the age of majority in Michigan, and her high school graduation only weeks away. According to Leanne, the judge decided the case was moot as a practical matter, and recommended that Genny stay with her grandparents and graduate with her class. Leanne reluctantly agreed.

Leanne had kept some records from Michigan that would support her side of the story, but she could no longer afford an attorney to represent her. She sent copies of her few records to the guardian ad litem and the court, but it was too little and too late.

DURING a September 2009 hearing before Judge Karlan, there was a complaint that someone had been using so-called social media to conduct a plea for a "memorial" to Kelley and Jake Branam. The "memorial" utilized the children's names and ages and contained a summary of the tragedy of the *Joe Cool* murders that had left them orphans.

Judge Karlan was appalled at what she considered an attempt to exploit the children who were still under her jurisdiction, even though they were now living in Michigan with Genny Van Laar. She ordered that the children's names and personal information be removed from the site within twenty-four hours. It was not clear who had created the memorial, but Genny, participating in the hearing by telephone, suggested that it might have been "a friend of Kelley's." Genny agreed to see that the site was removed.

During this hearing, the issue of a proposed book concerning the tragedy of the *Joe Cool* murders came up. Maria Gagliardo, Harry Branam's companion and a frequent caretaker of the children, was in the courtroom, and she stated that she was writing a memoir about her experiences over the past several years with the Branam family. Maria Gagliardo was not a party to the custody case. She was not a family member and she was not seeking custody of the young children, although she had frequently cared for them and loved them dearly.

During the hearing, Judge Karlan decided to enter an order preventing "any family member" from publicizing the names or photographs or whereabouts of the children or discussing them or their family or what happened to their family members with "any third party." The order specifically included memorials and social media, since a memorial had already appeared on one of the social media sites. The order also restrained Maria Gagliardo by name from disclosing any information concerning the children or their family or what happened to their family to a third party, even though she wasn't a party to the case.

Miami attorney Robert Rosenblatt was in the courtroom representing Harry Branam when the judge stated the substance of her order on the record. Although he was not representing Maria Gagliardo, Mr. Rosenblatt attempted to warn the judge away from error in entering such a broad prior restraint on speech naming a person who wasn't even a party to the case. He recognized that if such an order were entered, it would constitute a "gag" order, a classic prior restraint on speech that would violate the First Amendment's guarantee of free speech. Rosenblatt raised the matter with Judge Karlan on four separate occasions during the hearing, first as an officer of the court and then, by agreement, as a representative of Maria Gagliardo for this sole issue.

But Judge Karlan rejected Rosenblatt's warnings and stated: "I can put in whatever restrictions I like that would be as broad as possible."

When Rosenblatt again objected, Judge Karlan answered: "You know what, Mr. Rosenblatt, you're free to take it up to the Third District Court of Appeal. It is fine with me."

Judge Karlan followed up with a written order, which stated in part: "No party shall distribute any photographs of the children, of their home or their school to any third person or to a social networking site, or for a tribute (for example) or information about the children or *what has happened to them or to their family*.[1] This order precludes the parties, and Ms. Gagliardi [*sic*], who is specifically included in this Order because she considers herself a relative, a grandmother and should abide by the same restrictions that are on the family members of which she believes she is a part."

Maria Gagliardo had no intention of distributing photographs of the children, and she had no objection to that part of the order. However, at the time of the *Joe Cool* murders, she was in the midst of writing a book about her ten-year personal experience with the Branam family. She envisioned a multigenerational saga about the foibles, successes, and follies of the Branam clan, who had gone from humble beginnings to luxury on Star Island only to be torn apart by their own dysfunctional personalities. Gagliardo had enlisted a friend, English author Valerie Austin, to assist her in writing and producing a book/movie project, which Austin was then promoting at the Cannes film festival. The book/movie about Gagliardo's experiences with the Branam family would necessarily include the *Joe Cool* murders in 2007 and the fate of the young orphans as a result of their parents' death. This, she believed, was "information about the children and what has happened to their family," which was forbidden by Judge Karlan's order. Maria felt that she could not go forward with her book/movie project without violating that order, which she refused to do. According to Maria, because of the order, she lost her opportunity to have her book published and made into a movie with her coauthor.

Maria Gagliardo immediately contacted the American

---

1. Emphasis added.

Civil Liberties Union for advice as to whether Judge Karlan's order constituted a prior restraint on free speech in
violation of her constitutional rights under the First Amendment. The ACLU was a group Maria said she didn't really
understand and certainly never imagined she would have
any need for, since she was "a law-abiding citizen." The
ACLU's assistant legal director, Maria Kayanan, reviewed
Judge Karlan's order and agreed that it was an impermis-
sible "gag" order against Maria, a classic prior restraint that
violated the free speech guarantee of the First Amendment.
Kayanan promptly agreed to represent Maria Gagliardo and
filed an appeal notice to the Third District Court of Appeal.

The Third District Court of Appeal heard oral argument
in the case on January 26, 2010. By that time, Maria Gagliardo had been "gagged" by Judge Sandy Karlan's order
for four months. The book/movie deal was long gone.
ACLU attorney Maria Kayanan argued for Maria Gagliardo
on the unconstitutionality of the prior restraint on speech
contained in that order. For purposes of the appeal, Judge
Sandy Karlan appointed Miami attorney Lauri Ross as
guardian at law to defend the constitutionality of the order
"on behalf of the Branam children." No other party or attorney came forward in support of the order.

The panel of judges who heard the appeal comprised
Chief Judge David M. Gersten, Judge Barbara Lagoa, and
Judge Angel A. Cortiñas. Maria Kayanan's argument to the
court was simple. On its face, the order was an impermissi-
ble, unconstitutional prior restraint on free speech in violation of the First Amendment of the United States Constitution
and must be vacated as to her client, Maria Gagliardo. There
simply was no case law under which Judge Karlan's order
could be sustained.

Lauri Ross, an effective and well-respected appellate
attorney, had an extremely difficult—which is to say,
impossible—position to defend in the case, and she readily
conceded almost all of the points on appeal. What she

hoped to achieve in her argument, she told the court, was acknowledgment of the trial court's right to enter a proper order protecting the privacy rights of the children.

But Judge Angel Cortiñas had a different view of the message for the trial court. "What the trial courts have to know is that they can't enter the kind of order they just entered [in this case]. It's unconstitutional on its face. It's outrageous," he said.

On March 24, 2010, Florida's Third District Court of Appeal ruled in Gagliardo's favor. Their order stated in part: "Prior restraints on speech and publication are the most serious and least tolerable infringement on First Amendment rights. . . . Accordingly, we reverse and remand for the trial court to vacate the portion of the order that restricts the writer's ability to distribute 'information about the children or about what has happened to them or to their family.'"

But by then it was too late to revive Gagliardo's book/movie project.

MORE legal proceedings ensued, this time in federal court in Miami. Despite the recommendations of the guardian ad litem in the custody case, three separate lawsuits were filed against Jeff Branam and his affiliated corporate entities: by Scott Gamble's parents, Shirley Clow and Albert Gamble; by Sammy Kairy's parents; and by Leanne Van Laar–Uttmark, as personal representative of the Estate of Kelley Van Laar Branam. As personal representative of her daughter's estate, Leanne was the only one who had legal standing to bring this case on behalf of her daughter and grandchildren. Leanne cooperated with Genny and her attorneys in order to obtain funds to help support the children.

The suits were brought in federal court for the wrongful deaths of the deceased, Scott Gamble, Samuel Kairy, and Kelley Van Laar Branam, respectively, and sought damages against Jeff Branam and the various corporate entities that owned and/or operated the *Joe Cool*. The cases alleged that Jeff Branam was negligent in not taking proper security precautions before sending the *Joe Cool* out with two armed men, Kirby Archer and Guillermo Zarabozo, resulting in the deaths of the captain, his wife, and the others aboard.

The cases were consolidated and then settled out of court for an undisclosed amount that included a structured settlement for the young orphans and a separate award for Genny Van Laar. All three cases have now been dismissed with prejudice.

Jeff Branam was bitter about the suit brought against him to benefit Genny Van Laar and to help her care for the children. During the custody case, he had tried in vain to demonstrate to the guardian ad litem and Judge Sandy Karlan that Genny Van Laar did not have the financial means to care for and raise the children, despite her representations to the contrary.

Next, Genny Van Laar instituted conservatorship litigation in a Michigan probate court, seeking more access to funds held in trust for the minor children as she was unable to provide for them without more financial assistance. According to Leanne, Genny told the Michigan judge that she was "struggling financially." Each month, she received the children's Social Security checks, as well as payments from the structured settlement for the children from the litigation against Jeff Branam, but she contended that it wasn't enough to cover the children's health care and day care expenses. Genny took one semester off from her teaching job and then went back to work, according to her mother, earning approximately $43,000 per year. During the summer breaks from school, the children had no health insurance coverage from Genny and they received health insurance benefits from Medicaid. A substantial bank account supposedly set aside for the children by Genny's grandmother, Donna Van

Laar, did not exist, according to Leanne. Donna Van Laar died on January 18, 2010, leaving nothing in her will for Kelley's children.

Virtually all the family members complained that they had been denied visitation and the weekly telephone/video contact that had been promised, or even photographs of the children and updates on their progress. When they tried to visit in Michigan, they said, their visits were refused. When they called on the phone, Genny either told them that the children didn't want to talk or simply hung up. They pointed out that visitation and family contact were advocated by the court-appointed psychologist, Dr. Firpi, recommended by the guardian ad litem, and ordered by Judge Sandy Karlan. Family members said that they had spent hundreds of thousands of dollars on the case and were still unable to have court-ordered visitation with the children. Leanne and Robert Uttmark claimed to have spent over $250,000, and even though they consented to an award of temporary custody to Genny, they were still denied visits. According to Leanne, "None of the things we were promised for the children have happened."

On May 18, 2010, Judge Sandy Karlan held a hearing on Genny Van Laar's motion to proceed with adoption. During the hearing, Leanne Van Laar–Uttmark's attorney, Mauricio Padilla, citing allegations of drug and alcohol abuse, presented a motion to randomly test Genny's hair follicles and administer other tests for drugs and alcohol.

Judge Karlan denied the motion, saying the issue "hadn't been properly noticed." This was the first time that Padilla had ever seen a family court judge refuse a request for drug and alcohol testing. In his experience, family court judges tended to err on the side of caution for the best interests of the children and order immediate testing. He was baffled by Judge Karlan's refusal to do so. Advance notice of testing defeated the purpose, since it allowed a period of time for drug and alcohol evidence to be dispersed from the body in preparation for the test.

Judge Karlan also refused to hear the concerns of family members present in the courtroom, stating, "Anything that deals with what is in the best interest of the children will come out at the adoption proceedings." But Leanne Van Laar–Uttmark and Harry Branam feared that they would not receive notice of the adoption proceedings, much less be allowed to attend or to address the court on fundamental matters concerning the children's safety and well-being. The adoption, in Leanne's words, was "like a runaway train" that they were powerless to stop or even slow down. When Harry Branam insisted on addressing the court, Judge Karlan left her courtroom, telling Harry that he could speak to the attorneys in her absence.

Harry told guardian ad litem Connie Quinlivan, "You've got to address these serious issues." Reporters and attorneys in the courtroom moved closer to listen.

Harry told those in the courtroom that on his scheduled visit to the children in Genny's Michigan house, he observed ashtrays inside the house with butts that he said "smelled like marijuana." Harry was well aware of what marijuana smelled like since he had lived near the Ethiopian Zion Coptic Church on Star Island; the church's adherents used marijuana as a "sacrament" until the Florida Supreme Court ordered the group off the island. Harry had testified against them in federal court on this very issue. He said he had also smelled marijuana on the children's clothes, and he had witnessed Genny belt down three quick beers within twenty minutes at dinner with the children during his visit.

Harry had always had reservations about Genny as custodian of the children, based upon his own past observations of her and Kelley's statements to him, including, on the weekend before she was murdered, that she didn't want Genny to have custody of her children. All of this troubled Harry deeply, but on the advice of his attorney, he had agreed to support Genny based upon the representations she made to him and to the court concerning her commitment to the family, her ability to care for the children, and the liberal visitation she promised.

"After the transfer of the children to Genny, it didn't take long for me to see evidence of what Kelley had said about her sister was possibly true," Harry said. He saw Genny's "great animosity toward her mother." Harry was also concerned about "the fear she expressed when Maria told her that she was [writing] a book about my family. Maria asked Genny if she would like to be interviewed and assured her that nothing would be printed that would harm the children. Maria also told Genny that the children would get her 20% of any royalties from the book sales." According to Harry, thereafter Genny refused to allow Maria to see the children, "although Maria and I had been with the children more time than anyone else than their parents." The totality of Genny's behavior, in Harry's words, "raised more doubts about her integrity."

After Judge Karlan returned to the bench, Mauricio Padilla, Leanne's attorney, again requested that the judge inquire into the substance of Harry's concerns. Judge Karlan again refused. The judge asked the guardian ad litem, Connie Quinlivan, to deliver a brief status report. Quinlivan said: "The children are thriving, they're doing very well, and they've attached to Genny as a parental figure," noting that she had spoken to a kindergarten teacher, Genny's therapist, and others. According to an article published in the *Daily Business Review* on May 20, 2010, and reported by Jose Pagliery, this didn't satisfy Leanne's lawyers. The article quoted Padilla: "If they wanted to give testimony as to what is in the best interests of the children, I should've been able to cross-examine her and find out how she came to that conclusion."

Judge Karlan apparently changed her mind about addressing the substance of Harry's allegations. On May 26,

Connie Quinlivan sent an e-mail to Harry, the other partici-
pants in the case, and their attorneys. In her e-mail, she
advised them that Judge Karlan had instructed her to investigate Harry's allegations of alcohol and drug abuse by
Genny. She requested that anyone with verifiable information, documentation, or other evidence on the issues furnish
copies of this information to her. In closing, Quinlivan
added that fees for her work on this subject would be billed
to Harry, since he was the one who raised the allegations
requiring her investigation. Judge Karlan had entered an
order directing the guardian ad litem to bill the party raising
an issue for her expenses and fees incurred in investigating
that issue.

Harry was livid at what he perceived as punishment and a
threat to make him pay, literally, for daring to raise these issues that the judge refused to address. A simple drug test,
which Leanne Van Laar–Uttmark's lawyer had requested on
May 18, 2010, and which Judge Sandy Karlan had refused to
order, would have put the issue to rest, one way or the other,
he said.

The day after he received Connie Quinlivan's e-mail,
Harry wrote back to her: "If you had visited Genny's house,
where you and Karlan sent the children, after they moved
in, you would have seen the same things I did."

Later, Harry added:

> Please don't threaten me that your [*sic*] going to bill me
> for doing your job. I am willing to pay for Genny's Drug
> and Alcohol tests to assure me that the children are not
> in any grave danger and to protect them. . . . Not one
> thin dime to you. Is this what kind of [guardian ad litem]
> you are to suppress evidence that would suggest that
> you are or have been incompetent?

> See you in court,
> Harry

Harry and other family members had long believed that the guardian ad litem's investigation had been inadequate, although certainly expensive. Even after Judge Karlan reduced her fees, Quinlivan was paid well over $100,000 for her work in this case. Jeff Branam also couldn't understand why Quinlivan didn't see what he considered to be an obvious misstatement of Genny's financial resources. Why, he asked, didn't Quinlivan obtain and review official bank records to determine whether the supposed account from Donna Van Laar existed?

Some family members, including Harry Branam and Leanne Van Laar–Uttmark, suspected that the guardian ad litem's conclusions and recommendations were not entirely the result of incompetence or negligence but rather some kind of bias toward Genny Van Laar from the very beginning.

On May 26, 2010, Padilla filed an emergency motion to perform hair follicle drug and alcohol testing on Genny Van Laar and requested a hearing. In support of his motion, Padilla repeated Harry Branam's observations and added Leanne Van Laar–Uttmark's "personal knowledge that Genny Van Laar has a history of alcohol abuse and is a habitual marijuana smoker." Padilla requested an emergency hearing and an order for immediate drug testing, but there was no hearing and the motion became moot. On June 11, 2010, the guardian ad litem released her postjudgment report addressing these allegations and stating that "Genny Van Laar voluntarily subjected herself to a hair follicle test on June 2, 2010, at LabCorp in Michigan. . . . The test results for all drugs were negative."

Later that month, Leanne Van Laar–Uttmark discovered more photographs of her grandchildren posted on social media sites, including a nude picture of her granddaughter. She immediately contacted Mauricio Padilla and he began preparation of an emergency motion to remove the photographs from the sites. Before the motion could be filed,

however, word was received that the children had been
adopted by Genny Van Laar in a closed proceeding. Leanne
promptly wrote a letter to Judge Karlan, the guardian ad
litem, and the chief judge of the Miami-Dade Circuit Court
advising them of her discovery of the photographs and ob-
jecting, especially to the nude photo of her young granddaughter. She received no reply.

Leanne continues to pursue visitation with her grandchildren in Michigan under a state statute that permits courts to
order that grandparent visitation be allowed.

CHAPTER TWENTY-EIGHT

———

In Memoriam

Family members and friends of the victims aboard the *Joe Cool* participated in several memorial observances for them. Some were as simple as tossing their handmade flower wreaths off the seawall on Star Island outside the cottage where Jake and Kelley Branam, their children, and Scott Gamble had lived. Maria Gagliardo and Harry Branam hosted a gathering in their memory at their Belle Isle condo, and other Branam family members gathered at the Star Island compound. There was the flotilla of boats that traveled the waters near the Miami Beach Marina where those aboard the *Joe Cool* had spent some of their happiest hours. The boats circled in quiet water, prayers were spoken, and flowers were scattered in their memory. The ocean, after all, was their only memorial place.

AMIE Gamble still surrounds herself with mementos of her lost family and Sammy Kairy. Hobie, Scott's shaggy black dog, lives with her. She drives Jake's old truck, a silver 2001 Nissan. Behind the steering wheel, she has posted pictures of her two lost brothers, her sister-in-law, and her friend Sammy. In the passenger's side door pocket are various receipts left over from when Jake and Kelley used the truck, and the Book of Mormon, bookmarked with a nightclub receipt. Amie leaves the notes, receipts, and the book exactly where she found them. The sun visor on the passenger's side flips down to reveal a dusty vanity mirror, on which fingerprints are clearly visible. Amie refuses to allow anyone to clean the mirror as she is convinced that the fingerprints are those of Jake or Kelley.

In the truck's rear window, she had an artist paint a tribute in script to her lost brothers, Scott and Jake, and the crew of the *Joe Cool*, with the date September 22, 2007. Beneath the script is the artist's depiction of the *Joe Cool*. Amie says that many people have stopped to ask her about the inscription on her truck. One young man told her that he had been aboard the Coast Guard helicopter that rescued the killers, Kirby Archer and Guillermo Zarabozo, from the ocean near the *Joe Cool*'s life raft. He told her that the experience had had a profound emotional effect upon all those who came into contact with them.

Amie still cannot come to terms with the loss of her brothers, whom she describes as "my protectors," her adored sister-in-law, and her friend Sammy. Sometimes she regrets begging her brother Scott to come back home to Florida from Arizona. He had been back less than a year when the tragedy on the *Joe Cool* took place. Amie loves and misses the two young children who were also a big part of her life. Her young son often played with them. Her boyfriend, John Gibbons, who also helped care for them, says, "You look at [their son], and you see Jake. Same curly hair, same facial expressions. [Their daughter] was the love of my life."

According to Amie Gamble, her mother—Scott and

Jake's mother—has fallen into a deep depression. She rarely leaves her home in Illinois and she hasn't been able to visit her grandchildren.

THE *Sissy Baby* sportfisher, which Jon Branam operated as a charter fishing vessel, caught fire near Key Biscayne, burned to the water line, and sank. The crew and passengers were picked up by other boats in the area. Jon Branam has moved to Orlando, Florida.

Head west on the MacArthur Causeway from Miami Beach, look to your right at the first island, and you can see the enormous white house on Star Island Drive and the *Joe Cool* at the dock behind it, an abandoned, derelict hulk. Harry Branam estimates that the boat has only salvage value now, since, according to him, it has been stripped of its electronics and sustained transmission damage during towing. No prospective buyers have come forward.

SAMMY Kairy's family wishes him to be remembered "like a dolphin," because of his intelligence, his wit, his ready smile, and his love of the ocean. They recognize that he wanted to be a part of the ocean—literally—but this cannot ease their grief. After the Coast Guard released the *Joe Cool* back to Jeff Branam, Albert and Marian Kairy went to Star Island to look at the boat, to see where their son died. They were shocked at how small the spaces were on the fly bridge, the aft deck, and the salon.

The Coast Guard found a camera on the abandoned *Joe Cool* when they recovered it. Inside the camera were photos, which they had printed out. One was of Sammy with a huge hammerhead shark on the aft deck of the boat, hauling the giant fish through the stern gate. They gave the photo to his parents.

*　*　*

IN August 2010, Judge Paul Huck announced his decision
to become a senior U.S. district judge, which would permit
him to remain on the bench and handle a reduced workload.
But he made clear that he intended to maintain a full schedule of cases and teach at the law schools of the University
of Miami and the University of Florida, his alma mater, and
high school civics classes. During his distinguished ten-
year career on the federal bench, Judge Huck had presided
over many important high-profile cases, including sentencing disgraced former lobbyist Jack Abramoff and approving
the extradition of former Panamanian dictator Manuel
Noriega to France. An article published by the *Daily Business Review* on August 17, 2010, stated: "[Judge Huck]
cites the murders of the crew of four on the Joe Cool charter
fishing boat at sea, which went to trial twice, as one of his
most interesting cases."

By the time Judge Huck took senior status, the Ferguson
Courthouse finally had an operating cafeteria called the
Constitution Café.

CHAPTER TWENTY-NINE

Kirby Logan Archer

All of the family members and friends of the lost captain and crew of the *Joe Cool* have the same question: why? There would be no answer from Guillermo Zarabozo, who continued to deny any culpability in the crimes.

The only other living witness to the murders is Kirby Logan Archer, the admitted killer of Jake and Kelley, now serving his five consecutive life sentences, plus eighty-five years, at USP Pollock (the U.S. maximum security penitentiary in Pollock), near Alexandria, Louisiana. Would he—could he—provide any answers?

The city of Alexandria is located in the geographical center of Louisiana on the banks of the Red River, a wide, sluggish stream of brown water that meanders through the region. The city's population is listed as 147,000, which includes several small towns in the surrounding area. People who live and work in the area refer to Alexandria as "a real high school town," where everyone takes a keen interest in the goings-on in the local high school, especially the football team. It's also a highly religious town, mostly Southern Baptist, where a main highway boasts a single large billboard: PRAY. And although the land looks dry and barren, with occasional clumps of scruffy pine, residents claim that the economy of the area has actually grown. The housing market hasn't deteriorated here as it has in most of the country. There is a large Procter & Gamble plant and substantial logging and forestry operations. England Air Base, a onetime United States Air Force base, was closed in 1992 during one of the government's periodic cutbacks, but the airfield is now the site of a modern, attractive airport, one of only two international airports in the entire state. The surrounding road is still called Airbase Road, and the former officers' club has been converted to a quaint "boutique hotel," the Parc England, and the Bistro on the Bayou restaurant, the nicest available in this area of inexpensive fast-food restaurants and chain motels. And then there is the federal correctional compound in Pollock (FCC Pollock), just north of Alexandria, which employs about six hundred people.

The local population and economy got a boost in 2001 when the federal Bureau of Prisons opened FCC Pollock, just fifteen miles north of Alexandria in the Kisatchie National Forest. The compound includes a satellite prison camp for minimum-security males and USP Pollock, a maximum-security penitentiary housing male offenders, up to fifteen hundred at a time. The penitentiary is home for inmates serving long sentences, sometimes consecutive life sentences, who have no hope of release or downgrading to a less secure facility. The prison, known locally as "the Big House on the Bayou," has a national reputation as a very dangerous place for corrections officers and inmates alike. Pollock is what's known as "a very active prison" among the correctional officers. According to one, working at Pollock is "95% sheer boredom and 5% sheer terror." Every year, numerous assaults occur, usually between inmates, but sometimes an officer is assaulted. Homicides among the prison population are common, with seven reported in 2007 alone, which made Pollock first in the nation that year. By June 2010, two homicides had already occurred. When violence erupts, the institution goes into lockdown mode, sometimes for weeks, depending on the severity of the crimes. As punishment, offenders are sent to "the hole" or "the SHU" (special housing unit) for solitary confinement. USP Pollock is always short-staffed, always posting "urgently needed" job openings for corrections officers willing to work there.

Driving north from Alexandria on U.S. 167, the left turn to the FCC is marked by Motel Max, a cheap motel catering to prison visitors. The left turn leads to another Airbase Road, and a few miles farther, visitors see a small, discreet sign directing a right turn down another lengthy, well-maintained two-lane road, past the Pollock Satellite Prison Camp, and straight to the main gate of USP Pollock. Huge modern guard towers dominate the four corners of the prison block, which is surrounded by coiled bales of concertina wire inside massive chain-link fences. Buildings in the compound are made of poured concrete outer walls and painted concrete blocks on interior walls. In the central entrance building, two heavy doors open into a large reception area, where visitor "processing" begins. Visitors wait patiently in line before a desk manned by staff who check credentials, collect forms filled out by visitors confirming they are not carrying weapons or drugs, and attach the visitor's driver's license to the form. Visitors are only permitted to carry in clear plastic bags with up to $20 in coins and small bills for use in the vending machines in the common area. Snacks and drinks may be purchased by visitors only, and inmates may never touch the money or use the vending machines. Visitors are sent to a waiting room while inmates are located and, if they are eligible to receive visitors, issued fresh teal jumpsuits and moved into a large common room with groups of metal chairs and small tables secured to the floor. Visitors are not allowed to wear khaki or beige, because unless they are in the visitation room, the inmates wear khaki clothes at all times. If a corrections officer patrolling the visitation area sees someone in khaki, he will assume that an inmate somehow has gotten out into the visiting population, which will create a big problem for everyone.

During processing, small groups of visitors are assembled in the reception area by a corrections officer and then moved together through a heavy, automatic sliding glass door into another holding area. There, all visitors have their right hands stamped with invisible ink. Visitors must then place their right hands inside a small scanning device that is visually monitored by a corrections officer behind a one-way mirror in an adjoining room. At a signal, another heavy glass door opens on the opposite wall, and an officer leads visitors single file down a narrow sidewalk through an open, grassy area to stand together in a small yellow-painted semi-circle of cement. A barred gate opens into another small space, and visitors are escorted inside where they can see into the visiting area through heavy glass windows. Finally, another heavy, automatic door opens, and visitors join the inmates.

There are three levels of visit at Pollock: the visitation room, remote visits by computer and audio, and face-to-face visits by telephone in an enclosed room partitioned by bulletproof glass and under guard. In the common area, inmates mingle freely with their visitors. A separate children's playroom is in the common area, filled with bright plastic toys and board games, with colorful cartoon characters painted on the walls. Only children are allowed inside, and they seem happy enough at play, but it is by far the saddest place in the prison.

In the third level, a separate room, the "attorney room," sits directly across from the officer's elevated desk, in full view at all times through large, heavy windows that form one wall of the room. There is a small table, a worn desk chair with faded, stained fabric padding, and a molded green plastic chair on the other side of the desk. It is this room, in March 2010, to which Kirby Archer is brought for an interview.

IN March 2010, Kirby Archer looks much better than he did at his sentencing hearing in Miami in October 2008. His face has lost some of the puffiness, he's obviously slimmed down, and his skin looks as if he's been outdoors in the sun recently. In his teal jumpsuit, he looks clean and groomed. A neatly trimmed reddish beard is growing out along his jaw, and his dark hair looks thick and healthy. "Mousse," he says. He is now thirty-eight years old.

Archer speaks fluently and fast, but he has what amounts to a strange, twitchy, persistent verbal tic. Regardless of the subject, he speaks several very fast sentences, and then, for no apparent reason, he looks down and chuckles to himself nervously before continuing. This makes him look shifty and deceptive, even though his demeanor is calm and quiet. Without apparent irony, he describes himself as "a peaceful person" who abhors violence. This is just the beginning of a strange dichotomy, a cognitive dissonance between what Archer says about himself and the brutal murders to which he freely admits. He refers to the murders as "the situation," and in fact now claims "responsibility" for all four murders aboard the *Joe Cool,* though he admits to killing only Captain Jake Branam and his wife, Kelley. But he can't bring himself to say he's sorry about any of it or admit if he ever even thinks about it. All of this probably enhances his bad reputation among the inmates, who mostly avoid him.

The basic facts of his background seem ordinary, commonplace, and give no hint of the chaos, crimes, and violence that were to come. Archer claims to have a good relationship with his family, parents Betty and Sam, two brothers, and a sister, but they don't come to visit. He spent most of his life

in Arkansas, where his parents still live. He didn't graduate
from high school but joined the army and completed a GED.

"I liked the structure of the army. I loved my job [as an
MP and investigator]. I loved teaching investigation," he
says.

Nevertheless, he went AWOL after several years "because of family problems." Family problems, trouble with
women—he has three ex-wives—and allegations of child
sexual abuse are a constant thread in his life. His first marriage was "a marriage of convenience" and lasted only eleven
months. The second time around, he married Michelle Stein,
a half-Filipino and half-German woman with whom he had
two sons while he was stationed in Germany. Michelle "had
problems of her own," he says, and she accused him of sexually abusing their two young sons. He vehemently denies
ever sexually abusing a child, but the allegations came from
many sources and followed him all his adult life. Nevertheless, after Kirby and Michelle divorced, he got custody of the
kids. He married a third time, to a woman named Michaela,
who already had three children. "It was a blended family," he
says. Soon, there were allegations of what Archer calls "kids
playing sex tag in the pool." He shrugs. Kids will be kids.
Nothing to do with him.

Archer portrays himself as almost saintly in his toler-
ance of others, his nonviolence, and his inability even to
dislike anyone. He doesn't hate anyone, he says, and reluctantly admits that the only person in the world he "doesn't
really like" is second wife, Michelle. That's mainly because
of her accusations of child sexual abuse against him. Although he initially had custody of the boys, they were eventually returned to her in a court proceeding. Archer feels
Michelle's false accusations "cost him his boys." His sons
are the only subject over which he displays any emotion.

In 1995, Archer was still in the army, working in Guantánamo, Cuba, for eight months on a joint task force called
Sea Signal, an operation to intercept fleeing Cuban refugees

and hold them in a detention tent camp until they could legally immigrate to the United States. He loved the work ("helping families") and he loved Cuba. "I just fell in love with those people," he says. Archer worked shifts of twelve hours on, twelve hours off, and in his free time, he learned to dive and snorkel. He bought a book and taught himself Spanish, practicing with the refugees in the camps. Despite many published reports, Archer never met Guillermo Zarabozo or the Zarabozo family in Guantánamo. But he did meet the Perez family, with whom he remained friendly. Years later, he looked them up in Hialeah, Florida, and stayed with them for several months.

Before he went on the lam in Arkansas, Archer was living with his parents, Betty and Sam. He wanted to work for a large corporate employer that could provide the structure he sought, so he got a job at Wal-Mart, getting regular promotions and fast-tracking his way up the ladder. So why did he steal $92,000 from Wal-Mart and take off in January 2007?

Archer finds it difficult to explain this decision, as he does many others. He realized, he says, that because of all the false allegations of child sexual abuse against him, he was likely "to lose my boys." He feared that any day, someone from the child protection agency would show up and take them away. So he decided to go back to court and turn over custody of the children to their mother. Once he did that, Archer had to leave. "It tore me up bad," he says. His face trembles in sections, the left half beginning to crumble first, and he begins to cry. Teardrops fall on his jumpsuit. He takes a break, composes himself, and continues. Everything reminded him of his boys: their toys and clothes at his parents' house, just hearing someone call "Daddy" on the street. He knew he had to go.

So he made a plan, and then he implemented it. "Once I was in that mode, it was almost like I was working [an investigation]," he says.

He would keep it all inside, suck it up, act normal, and

continue to work at Wal-Mart as usual. In the meantime, he bought a police radio scanner and hoarded his savings. He made appointments for interviews with child abuse investigators on days when he knew he would already be gone. That way, they were unlikely just to show up at his parents' house or Wal-Mart. Archer arranged to borrow his uncle's van. When the time came, he packed up a few things, including his laptop, but he didn't let on to anyone that he was leaving. Going to work that day, he wore jeans and a pullover under his slacks, shirt, tie, and Wal-Mart vest, and he went to work as usual. Archer faked a problem with the "money cart" by removing some screws from it. He made his rounds at Wal-Mart as usual and collected cash from the registers. In the back room, he stashed everything he had collected inside a new microwave he had taken off a shelf. He told his co-workers he was going on break, purchased the cash-stuffed microwave using his employee discount, and left the store. Once outside, he put the microwave in his truck and drove to the place where he had left his uncle's van. Then he took off his work clothes, transferred the microwave and his bag to the van, and headed off toward Nashville. Archer had nearly $100,000 in cash with him. He felt an overwhelming sense of relief.

He expected to have a ten- to twelve-hour head start, since no one would even be looking for him in the store for a couple of hours, and they probably wouldn't figure out what really happened until the following morning. By the time police sent out a BOLO—"be on the lookout"— for him, he would have disappeared in Nashville. Plus, he had his police scanner on and heard nothing about Wal-Mart or himself.

But suddenly there was a patrol car behind him, flashing lights. Archer pulled over. The van he was driving had one headlight out, a detail Archer says he should have checked out before he took the van. He apologized, chatted politely with the cop, and promised to get it fixed promptly. The cop gave him a ticket and let him go. "I can usually talk my way out of things," Archer says. When the officer later learned what Kirby Archer had done aboard the *Joe Cool*, he immediately made the connection with the van he had stopped that night in January. He was shocked and chagrined. If only I had taken him in that night, maybe none of this would have happened, he thought. It haunted him.

But Archer was on his way again and, as he puts it, "The whole world is out there waiting to be taken." He ditched the van in Nashville and took a cab across town. Then he took another cab to another part of town and found a motel, checked in under an alias, and paid cash. He stayed several days. He lightened his hair. He spent his time sorting through all the clothes he had brought with him, dumping some and keeping others, and listening to his police scanner. Nothing turned up. He knew he would be safer in a big city than in a small town, and he considered going to New York, where he knew some people. But he didn't want to look up any old friends because that might cause trouble for them—and him. He decided on Miami. He liked Miami and thought he "could live pretty good in Miami" on the money he had left. He bought a pay-as-you-go untraceable cell phone, packed up his stuff, and took a cab out of town.

Cabs were the best, completely anonymous, strictly a cash transaction. Archer cabbed south from one city to another, sometimes backtracking to conceal his real destination, sometimes paying $300 or more for a ride. What did it matter? He had plenty of cash and no one asked for ID on his trip, except a few times when he checked into a motel. On those occasions, he either talked his way around it or slipped the desk clerk some cash. He never bothered to get fake ID until he reached Florida.

Finally, Archer cabbed to Fort Lauderdale and bought an ID in the name of Michael David, using a Nashville address that was actually the Opryland mall. He stayed a week, looking at pictures of his kids on his laptop and lounging around.

He got bored. He never called home and found out later that his parents feared he had committed suicide. He decided to check up on the folks by playing online Yahoo games of dominoes and poker anonymously with his mother, who was a regular player. He knew her screen name, so it was easy to set up games with her. He never revealed his true identity. He invented a screen name, got up some games, and hoped he and his mother would develop an online relationship so that she would write about him, how much she missed him, what she was thinking. But she eventually broke contact and the games stopped.

Archer was lonely. He decided to look up the Perez family, and he found their Hialeah address. He went to visit and stayed several months. Of course, he used his real name with them, since they remembered him from Guantánamo, but he never told them anything about being on the run from Arkansas. He told them he was "relocating," and he began to settle in. He bought a car, a 2000 Firebird. He occasionally worked as a club bouncer or other low-level security jobs to make a little money—all cash, no ID required. He sometimes bought furniture or food for the Perez family. He set up a MySpace page and put their photos on it. He hung around in Hialeah, especially in a chop-shop where he got his car fixed. He became known as "the Gringo." The guy who owned the chop-shop was Carlos Mulet.

After a while, Kirby Archer got bored—again. He started thinking about "the Cuba Idea." What was that? Again, Archer has trouble explaining his ideas, his thoughts and plans. He says he met families in Hialeah, all of whom had sad stories about relatives left behind in Cuba, and he wanted to help them. "I just fell in love with those people," he says. So, was he going to smuggle people out of Cuba? Reunite deserving families? No, not exactly. He knew some people who smuggled, but that's not what he had in mind. What, then? An incursion, an infiltration into Cuba "to help families," he says. So, the Cuba Idea was some sort of humanitarian endeavor? Archer can't really explain it. He wanted to go to Cuba "for redemption." But redemption for what? He can't really say. Maybe "a little bit of guilt about the way [he] left Arkansas." He just wanted to go and "feel around" in Cuba, check it out, see if he could do something. "It's all there for the taking," he says. But he didn't want to live in Cuba long term. Too expensive, he says. And bad food and bad hotels.

Whatever the reason, once the Cuba Idea took hold, Archer concentrated all his efforts on research and planning for the "incursion" into Cuba. In North Miami, he upgraded his ID in the name of Kevin Porter and got a driver's license, a MasterCard and a debit card through Bank of America, and put some money on the card. He says he sent money, clothes, cameras, his nasal spray, and half a case of cigarettes to "a contact in Cuba," so he would have these things available as soon as he arrived. He had "people to meet in Cuba, to check it out, to see if I could do something." His plan to leave the United States had nothing to do with the Arkansas warrant out for his arrest, Archer says, or the child abuse investigation. There was "no active pursuit," as he puts it, and so he wasn't really worried. He says, "I wasn't fleeing the country. I didn't feel I had to. I consider myself smart enough to make a life in Miami. I talked to the Hialeah cops all the time. I gave them a flyer to sell my car."

During his research and planning phase, Archer decided he needed a gun, so he asked Carlos Mulet where he could get one. Carlos suggested Guillermo Zarabozo, one of the kids who hung around his shop and worked occasional private security jobs. Carlos made the introduction and Zarabozo came up with an untraceable Sig Sauer, which he sold to Archer for $400. Archer did some research and decided a boat was the best way to get from Miami to Cuba. He would need a fairly large boat, one that could take heavy seas—maybe sixty or seventy feet. He bought some charts of the area and a handheld marine radio. He started looking around at boats and thinking about personnel for the Cuba

Idea. If he took a large boat out, he might need another body, someone to help him manage the boat trip and watch his back. But first, he decided to do more research, on an actual charter fishing boat, to see how hard it would be to drive and how many people would be required.

Archer invited the Perez family, the men, on a charter fishing trip as a gift. The boat they took had a captain and one first mate, which he concluded was usual, and it seemed big enough to get to Cuba. They had a great time on the water, although Archer discovered he had a tendency to get seasick if the boat wallowed in the waves.

He would definitely need backup, Archer decided, so he turned again to Carlos Mulet. Plus, Carlos was a mechanic with some experience working on diesel engines, the kind that a large boat would have. He told Carlos that he needed someone for a big job. Again, Carlos suggested Guillermo Zarabozo. He was tall and strong, kept himself in good shape, and would be able to handle "a big job," as Archer described it. And he had experience with weapons.

Archer focused his attention on Guillermo Zarabozo. Did he have what it takes? Would he do whatever was necessary for the Cuba Idea, the incursion, the infiltration, to succeed? Archer decided to vet Guillermo with a fabricated scenario, just to test his reactions. He pretended to confide in Guillermo. He told Guillermo that he had once done a contract hit, a murder for hire. The kid was interested, not appalled. He wanted to hear more. Archer explained that it was a business thing that went bad, and he had been hired to kill a man in his office at his desk. Archer got inside the office and strangled the man, hauled his body out on a furniture dolly, and dumped him. According to Archer, Guillermo had only one question: How much do you get to charge for something like that? Archer knew he'd found his assistant for the Cuba Idea. Just to add a little more sizzle, Archer "smoke-screened" Guillermo with plans about smuggling and working as a spy for the CIA. Guillermo

Zarabozo was on board with that, no question. During their planning and preparation phase, Zarabozo tried to get Archer to buy some AK-47s, but he declined. We don't need that kind of firepower, Archer said. "Just get a handgun."

Next, Archer and Guillermo considered whether Carlos Mulet could be useful to them. He knew about diesel engines and he knew something about boats. He knew who left their keys on unattended boats. He was obviously unscrupulous, since he ran a notorious chop-shop. How could they vet Carlos for their job? They decided to smoke him with a story about Archer's high-level government contacts and his ability to get things done on the other side of the law. For instance, Archer told Carlos, "I can get your [driver's] record cleaned." They knew this would get to Carlos since his driving record was so bad he couldn't even get insurance. Zarabozo knew it was a farce, but Archer told him, "Just don't say too much." Carlos fell for it.

Carlos Mulet sent Archer and Zarabozo to someone he knew who does charters, but that didn't work out. Archer and Zarabozo researched marinas and boats around South Florida. Once, while they were driving around, Guillermo's mother called his cell to tell him that a letter had arrived accepting him into the October training class for the Miami-Dade Police. But it was too late. By then, he only wanted to make money. He was after the quick buck.

Archer believes that Guillermo Zarabozo lacked supervision at home. He seemed to be the boss of the household, and Archer thought that was a bad idea.

On a visit to Haulover Beach Park Marina, they discussed how they would take control of a charter boat and what level of force would be necessary. Archer recalls that he lectured Zarabozo about protective force as a minimum and deadly force only as a last resort. "The last thing we need," he recalls telling Zarabozo, "is to hurt anybody on that boat. We don't want to be sought after for any unnecessary killing." But Zarabozo replied that if anyone were allowed to live, "they might recognize me later." After discussing their options, they agreed that "if need be, we have to protect ourselves and what we're doing." Archer says that they understood that to mean shooting people on the boat if they had to, in order for the mission to succeed.

Archer says he schooled Zarabozo in the preparations they would have to make for their trip. He taught Zarabozo "the rule of three"—that meant traveling from one place to another at least three times before you go where you are really headed. That's why they stayed in so many different motels in different places in the days before their actual departure.

That was another part of the plan. Never let anyone know when you are really leaving. Archer says he told Zarabozo to start cutting his ties with his friends and family but not to let anyone know when they were actually leaving. Zarabozo was supposed to pretend to leave at least three days before September 22—the actual day of departure aboard the *Joe Cool*. He was supposed to tell his friends and family that he was leaving earlier that week. That way, when the hijacking came out on the news, everyone would be diverted. They would all think that it couldn't be Guillermo Zarabozo and his friend, because they had left much earlier. They were already gone. For Archer, everything was about misdirection, diversion.

Archer told Zarabozo that he should start winding things up for their trip. He should sell his car, for one thing, and he had to come up with a story to let his friends and his family know that he was going away. He should also tell them that they might see "something about him" on the news, but not to worry, that he would be safe.

On another scouting trip, they came across Sammy Kairy cleaning up the *Joe Cool* after a fishing charter at the Miami Beach Marina. Archer struck up a conversation, telling Sammy that they were looking for a ride to Bimini. According to Archer, Sammy said they were booked for the next week, but if nothing else turned up, they should come back on the weekend.

Archer and Zarabozo started moving around from motel to motel, using cash or Zarabozo's bank card to pay. "I never wanted to be the face man," Archer says. "I tried to stay in the background" at the motels and stores where there might be surveillance video running.

The following Friday night, September 21, 2007, Archer and Zarabozo had dinner at Monty's, just beside the Miami Beach Marina. After dinner, they walked down to the dock. There, under a big SISSY BABY SPORT FISHING CHARTERS sign was the same boat and the same guy, Sammy Kairy, with whom Archer had spoken a week or so earlier.

Archer said, "You remember me?"

Sammy replied, "Oh, yeah, you wanted to go to Bimini." They talked. Archer told Kairy that nothing else had turned up and they were still interested in chartering the boat for a one-way trip to Bimini. According to Archer, Sammy got Jake on his cell, explained what they wanted, and handed the phone to Archer. Jake told Archer that the boat already had a charter the next morning, Saturday, September 22, but they could make the trip to Bimini at 3:00 or 4:00 P.M. They discussed the price, $2,000–3,000, as Archer recalls, and he told Jake outright that he didn't have a passport.

Archer recalls that he said, "If we don't meet our girlfriends [in Bimini Bay], we may need to go to the big island and we might have to look for them. Make sure there's plenty of fuel." Jake agreed, very courteously, as Archer recalls, and said, "Don't mention any passport problems tomorrow at the marina or on the boat. When we get to Bimini, we'll put out the quarantine flag, and after dark, we can move around until we find your friends."

Later on that Friday night, Archer recalls that he and Zarabozo took a cab to a hotel. The next morning, Jake called Archer's cell phone to say that because of fuel prices, the trip would cost $4,000. Archer agreed. He and Zarabozo cabbed to Miami Beach Marina in the afternoon. The minute they walked down the dock, carrying all their luggage, Kirby Archer says he was shocked to see so many people on and around the boat. He had been certain there would be only the captain and first mate. Instead, he saw seven or eight people milling around, including a young woman. How many people would actually be going along on the trip? Guillermo Zarabozo got nervous. "I almost called it off," Archer says. "I should have, in hindsight." But he didn't. He remembers that Zarabozo made a hand signal to him. *You take two and I take two?* Archer nodded.

Archer met Jeff Branam, a man he described as having "a lot of gray hair." Jeff was very curious and questioned Archer—where are you from, what do you do for a living, that kind of thing. Archer told him they were surveyors who had finished a job early. "I think I had read about something Donald Trump was doing, so I said we were working on that job," Archer recalls. Guillermo Zarabozo gave his real name, but Archer called himself Kevin Porter. "People will believe anything," Archer says, with that unnerving chuckle. Jeff seemed to accept their explanations, but Archer says, "He was still suspicious." Archer was carrying a long, black duffel bag with a rifle scope in it and quills—metal spikes sharp on both ends, like porcupine quills. His duffel was large enough to carry a rifle, but no one asked about it. No one asked him to open it or tell them what was inside. He paid Jeff $4,000 in cash in hundred-dollar bills. Archer recalls that Jeff handed a little money, "maybe $1,000 of it," to Jake for the trip.

Archer says that Jake was also apprehensive about the trip. "I could tell," he says. But whatever hesitation there might have been, Archer says, "They weren't going to give up the $4,000." The kid, Jon Branam, was especially suspicious of Archer. "He didn't like me from the get-go," Archer recalls. "I've interviewed hundreds of people. I could see it." Archer saw Jon take Jake aside and tell him, be careful out there. Either Jon decided not to go on the trip, or his father, Jeff, wouldn't let him. Archer's not sure which way it went. Either way, Kelley, Jake, Sammy, and Scott climbed aboard and Jon stayed behind. Zarabozo climbed up to the fly bridge and Archer stayed below with Scott. They talked about family stuff, and Archer recalls that Scott "was a very nice guy." Scott told him that Kelley was on board only because she didn't want Jake to go to Bimini alone, no way. She didn't trust him around other women. Archer liked Scott, and indeed all the crew, especially Sammy. "They didn't do anything wrong," he says. "They didn't deserve that end. For them, it was just wrong place, wrong time. For me?" Archer shrugs.

What about Jake and Kelley's two young children? They lost their parents on the *Joe Cool*. They are orphans now. "They were really little," Archer says with another shrug. "They don't even remember their parents." Their daughter was almost three years old. She definitely remembers her parents and she misses them very much. Archer says, "They'll get over it."

Archer was slightly seasick most of the way, so he stayed below. Looking out the cabin windows, he thought he recognized the skyline of Bimini on the horizon. He and Zarabozo held a hasty conference in the salon. "It's time," Archer said. Scott was on the fly bridge with Kelley and Jake. Sammy was on the lower deck. Archer told Zarabozo that he would "take care of" Scott, Kelley, and Jake on the fly bridge, and Zarabozo should handle Sammy. "Just take him down," Archer recalls telling Zarabozo. He says he meant that Zarabozo should overpower Sammy and confine him physically, so he wouldn't be a problem. Is that what the handcuffs were for? "Yes," Archer says. "I wanted to drop them off on a rock or an island somewhere. There's much less heat over a missing boat than four dead people."

Archer reached inside his bag, took out the Sig Sauer, and stuck it in the front of his waistband. He recalls beginning to climb the ladder to the fly bridge when a gust of wind came up and flattened his shirt against his body. He was afraid that Kelley or Scott might have seen the outline of his gun, so he slowed down on the ladder and took his time. Apparently no one noticed, because when he reached the top of the ladder, Scott was just beginning to descend past him. Now what? Could Zarabozo "confine and control" both Sammy and Scott? Archer says he continued up to the fly bridge and placed himself between Jake at the controls and the emergency position-indicating radio beacon nearby. Immediately thereafter, he recalls, he heard the first shot— or maybe two—from below. Archer shot Jake instantly, and Jake fell off the fly bridge, landing on the deck below. As Archer turned to look, he saw Scott jump down from the ladder and rush over to Jake, bending over him.

Archer turned back to Kelley beside him. "I'll never forget the look on her face," he says. "She froze. She completely froze. She left. She just wasn't there anymore. Her eyes didn't leave me, but she wasn't looking at me, she was looking through me."

Archer shot Kelley and she fell off the fly bridge, landing on the lower deck next to her husband. "Once I heard that first shot, it was maybe five seconds tops, the decision [to shoot] was instantaneous. These people are not going to be able to make it." In his retelling, Archer makes this deliberate slaughter, these cold-blooded murders sound inevitable and completely beyond his control. "These people are not going to be able to make it." Simple as that.

What about the trial testimony about Kelley or Jake being thrown overboard alive? Completely false, Archer says. When he said something on the helicopter, and later to FBI special agent David Nuñez, about the girl being wounded but maybe still alive, it was an attempt at misdirection. He was trying to divert attention away from himself, hoping there would be a big search for a wounded survivor. Kelley and Jake were killed instantly, as were Scott and Sammy, Archer says.

Why did Zarabozo tell Nuñez that maybe Jake was still alive when he was thrown overboard? Same concept. Misdirection. It wasn't true. While they were on the raft together all those hours, Archer told Zarabozo that they should each give a story that reversed their positions on the boat. That is, Zarabozo should say he was on the fly bridge and Archer would say he was below. That way, neither could inadvertently slip and admit to anything, because Zarabozo didn't know what really happened on the fly bridge and Archer didn't know what really had happened in the cabin below. This seems perfectly logical and reasonable to Archer. He suspects that Zarabozo had been trying to contain Sammy physically, but then saw Scott coming down the ladder and panicked, killing both men.

After the killings, Archer says he was worried about Zarabozo, who had apparently vomited over the side of the boat. Are you okay? he asked. Can you handle throwing them overboard and washing down the deck? It was very bloody, Archer recalls. Lots of blood. Zarabozo said he could handle it, but his leg was shaking and he couldn't make it stop. Archer needed a clean shirt, so he went into the cabin and took one of Jake's. He recalls that it had a logo on it: SISSY BABY SPORT FISHING CHARTERS, just like the sign on the dock above the boat.

Archer recalls that he was able to relax as he drove the boat south. It was peaceful. A cruise ship appeared nearby and the crew contacted him on the radio. He invented a call sign—a name—for the boat: *The Lazy Day*. It was just late-night chatter: Hey, what are you doing, that type of thing. The cruise ship gradually disappeared over the horizon.

Once the boat ran out of fuel, he and Zarabozo threw out

the anchor and climbed into the life raft. He told Zarabozo
to retrieve all his belongings from the salon, but obviously
he didn't.

Archer says he wanted to put as much distance between
the life raft and the boat as possible to make their pirate
story more believable. He pulled up the drogue, the sea anchor, so the life raft would move faster on the northbound
current of the Gulf Stream, away from the boat. But soon it
was very choppy, so he lowered the drogue again to stabi-
lize the raft. He says he was listening on the handheld marine radio when the Coast Guard found the boat. He knew
then that it was only a matter of time before they would be
picked up.

When they were aboard the cutter *Pea Island*, Archer
says, he overheard Zarabozo tell Agent Nuñez that he didn't
recognize the *Joe Cool* being towed behind them, that he
had never seen that boat before, that he had never been on
a boat called *Joe Cool*. The FBI agents believed he was
lying, but finally Archer put it all together for himself, he
says. *Joe Cool* must be the name of the boat they had traveled on, not *Sissy Baby*. He had assumed the boat was
named *Sissy Baby* because of the sign on the dock and the
logo on Jake's borrowed shirt. Neither he nor Zarabozo had
ever seen the name *Joe Cool* painted on the stern of the
boat, because the stern was close to the dock when they
climbed aboard. When they opened the gate on the stern to
get aboard the raft, they didn't see the name. It was dark.
On the trip back to Miami, the cutter *Pea Island* was towing
the boat bow first behind them, so they couldn't see the
name on the stern. Archer says he and Zarabozo just assumed all along that they were on a boat called the *Sissy
Baby*. The name *Joe Cool* meant nothing to them. But Archer didn't say anything at the time.

Archer has read many of the news accounts of the murders. He is amused by the many references to his being "a
spy for the CIA" and planning a life of espionage. It wasn't

like that, he says. The only time he tried to smoke anyone with the "high government contacts" thing was when he and Zarabozo pulled that on Carlos Mulet. No way Zarabozo really believed the CIA thing, Archer says. Maybe he was living in his own fantasy. "If I had known," Archer says thoughtfully, "I might have used that to my advantage." What Zarabozo did know was how carefully Archer was researching and preparing for the Cuba Idea. Archer says he always carried three cell phones, one as an emergency backup only. Archer was doing what he calls "under the table work" for money, and he was also using the Internet for research on places to land in Cuba. He says he never intended to go to Hemingway Marina. Too big. Archer was looking at a marina in Matanzas as a landing point. His plan was to slide into a smaller marina and disappear into the local population.

What did Zarabozo think was going to happen once they landed in Cuba? Archer says that Guillermo Zarabozo believed the infiltration was all about money. "Zarabozo was all about the money," Archer says. "That's all he wanted." When the boat ran out of fuel, Archer says, at that point, he only needed Zarabozo for one more hour. If they could have gotten to Cuba, he would have ditched Zarabozo. Would he have killed Zarabozo? Archer had thought about it. In fact, several people had asked him the same thing. Kill him? Probably not. Maybe just give him some money and tell him to go away. So, you weren't partners in some spy adventure? Of course not; Archer laughs outright at that suggestion. "What would someone like me want with someone like him? He's the kind you just send to pick up a package or something." But, Archer says, he's glad he didn't kill Zarabozo.

"If I had gotten to Cuba and done what I wanted to do, I would feel better about it," Archer says. "It"—the situation on the *Joe Cool*—was a very bad thing. If he could take it all back, he would. But if he had gotten to Cuba, it might have been worth it. How could some grand humanitarian mission begin with the murder of four innocent people? Archer can't explain it. He was really only planning on two people being on the boat. What if there had been six? Eight? Ten? Was there any number at which Archer might have aborted the whole thing? Was there any number of murders where he would have drawn the line? Any number at which the Cuba Idea wouldn't have been worth that waste of life? Archer can't say. "The Cuba Idea was an act of redemption." He was looking for purpose. He had screwed up his life. "My mother has nothing to be proud of," he says, without emotion. The monetary part was only supportive, not the main goal. Archer is not religious and does not believe in God, although he used to go to a Baptist church with his family as a child. When he gets to listen to music, though, he always chooses gospel, and sings along loudly. Nothing religious, he just likes the sound.

If Archer had been able to land the boat anywhere— Cuba, the Bahamas, the Florida Keys—he would have simply disappeared, he says.

At his sentencing in Miami, he recalls the victims' family members speaking to him. A young woman he believes was Kelley's sister—actually Amie Gamble—tried to make eye contact with him as she spoke, but she couldn't do it. She'd meet his eyes and then her glance would slide away. She brought two pictures of Kelley and Jake's children to show Archer, but he didn't want to touch them. "I knew the family didn't even want me to speak their names or touch those pictures," he says. When Harry Branam spoke, he reminded Archer of his own uncle. He wondered what his uncle would say about him.

PRISON life is not so bad for Archer. According to other visitors, the inmates all know who he is and are afraid to turn their backs on him. After all, he claims responsibility for four cold-blooded murders, even though he admitted that he shot "only" two, Jake and Kelley, and that Zarabozo shot Scott and Sammy. "Responsibility" for four murders instead of two enhances his reputation for violence. Other inmates stay out of his way.

Archer says there's lots of structure in prison, "like the army," and he has plenty to do. He says he has been teaching GED classes with a staff member. In the evenings, he teaches creative writing, although he doesn't actually write anything himself. He works out six days a week and rests and reads on Sundays. His favorite book is *The Count of Monte Cristo*, by Alexandre Dumas, which he has read several times. The only thing he misses is being able to take off on the weekends, like he used to. Archer says he is resigned to his situation and he deserves it. All this is said without apparent emotion. "With the exception of my children, I'm not very emotional," Archer says. He believes he has "grown a thick skin" because of all the things he saw as a military investigator. He says he's very adaptable.

"In the military, in combat, people see such violence. They come home and they suffer PTSD, they have bad dreams, have to take Valium or sleeping pills," Archer says.

"But some of them don't have nightmares or suffer or have to take sleeping pills," he explains. "And those are the ones you have to watch out for.

"Unfortunately," he says, "I'm one of those people."

ACKNOWLEDGMENTS

I have always loved water: streams, pools, rivers, lakes, and especially the ocean. As long as I can remember, I've wanted to write a book about the ocean. But not this book.

When the *Joe Cool* went missing in September 2007, I was mesmerized by the mystery as was everyone who read or heard about it. I followed the story through news reports, and somewhere along the way, I decided to write a book about it. But when I began this task, I couldn't have imagined the scope of the tragedy that befell the young captain, his wife, his brother, and his best friend aboard their beautiful boat. At first, they were only names and faces on the news, but during my research, I came to know and mourn them through their families and the many friends whose lives they touched. This book can never do justice to the young lives lost, but I hope it will serve as a modest memorial to their ambitions and dreams, their love of life and each other, and especially their devotion to their families and friends.

I am especially grateful for the kindness and assistance of Harry Branam, Maria Gagliardo, Leanne Van Laar–Uttmark, Amie Gamble and John Givens, and Marian, Albert, Ilan, and Kassin Kairy, who were always willing to answer my questions, even when their memories were unbearably painful. Many others who contributed greatly to this book have asked to remain anonymous. I respect their wishes and offer my gratitude for their invaluable assistance. You know who you are, and I thank you.

In my research, I met some fine journalists who were covering this story. During the federal trials, they generally sat together in the back of the courtroom and often generously shared information with me. Thanks to Jay Weaver, Vanessa Blum, Curt Anderson, Annette Lopez, Ileana Varela, Peter D'Oench, and Hank Tester.

I am most grateful to the lawyers who participated in this case, the Assistant United States Attorneys and the Assistant Federal Public Defenders, and to United States District Judge Paul C. Huck and his talented, hardworking staff (especially court reporter Patricia Sanders). Our justice system depends upon the intelligence, diligence, and fairness of the judges, the lawyers, the FBI, the United States Coast Guard, and other law enforcement officers and investigators who work hard every day, and often on nights and weekends, with little compensation and almost no recognition for the excellent service they provide to keep the rest of us safe.

Thanks to my excellent literary agent, Jill Marsal, I had the opportunity to work with Berkley editor Shannon Jamieson Vazquez, a terrific storyteller, a much better writer than I am, and infinitely patient.

As always, my daughter, Caroline, and my husband, Jerry, cheerfully shouldered the burden of keeping me on track and at my desk. I appreciate their love and support more than I can say.